Adaptive

THE FIRST AND ONLY **ADAPTIVE READING EXPERIENCE** DESIGNED TO TRANSFORM THE WAY STUDENTS READ

> More students earn **A's** and **B's** when they use McGraw-Hill Education **Adaptive** products.

SmartBook®

Proven to help students improve grades and study more efficiently, SmartBook contains the same content within the print book, but actively tailors that content to the needs of the individual. SmartBook's adaptive technology provides precise, personalized instruction on what the student should do next, guiding the student to master and remember key concepts, targeting gaps in knowledge and offering customized feedback, driving the student toward comprehension and retention of the subject matter. Available on smartphones and tablets, SmartBook puts learning at the student's fingertips—anywhere, anytime.

> Over **4 billion questions** have been answered, making McGraw-Hill Education products more intelligent, reliable, and precise.

STUDENTS WANT

SMARTBOOK®

95% of students reported **SmartBook** to be a more effective way of reading material

100% of students want to use the Practice Quiz feature available within **SmartBook** to help them study

100% of students reported having reliable access to off-campus wifi

90% of students say they would purchase **SmartBook** over print alone

95% reported that **SmartBook** would impact their study skills in a positive way

Mc Graw Hill Education

*Findings based on a 2015 focus group survey at Pellissippi State Community College administered by McGraw-Hill Education

P O W E R

Learning

Online
Success

Robert S. Feldman
University of Massachusetts Amherst

P.O.W.E.R LEARNING: ONLINE SUCCESS

1 2 3 4 5 6 7 8 9 RMN 21 20 19 18 17 16

ISBN 978-1-259-82022-9 (student edition)
MHID 1-259-82022-x (student edition)
ISBN 978-1-259-96072-7 (annotated instructor's edition)
MHID 1-259-96072-2 (annotated instructor's edition)

Chief Product Officer, SVP Products & Markets: *G. Scott Virkler*
Vice President, General Manager, Products & Markets: *Michael Ryan*
Director: *Scott Davidson*
Director, Product Development: *Meghan Campbell*
Executive Marketing Manager: *Keari Green*
Product Developer: *David Ploskonka*
Senior Digital Product Developer: *Kevin White*
Digital Product Analyst: *Thuan Vinh*
Senior Director, Content Design & Delivery: *Terri Schiesl*
Executive Program Manager: *Mary Conzachi*
Senior Content Project Manager: *Danielle Clement*
Content Project Manager: *Karen Jozefowicz*
Senior Buyer: *Sandy Ludovissy*
Design Manager: *Debra Kubiak*
Senior Content Licensing Specialist (Image): *Shawntel Schmitt*
Content Licensing Specialist (Text): *Lori Slattery*
Cover Image: © *JGI/Tom Grill/Blend Images LLC*
Typeface: *11/13 STIX Mathjax Main*
Compositor: *SPi Global*
Printer: *R. R. Donnelley*

All credits appearing on page or at the end of the book are considered to be an extension of the copyright page.

Library of Congress Cataloging-in-Publication Data
Names: Feldman, Robert S. (Robert Stephen), 1947- author.
Title: P.O.W.E.R. learning : online success / Robert S. Feldman, University
    of Massachusetts Amherst.
Other titles: POWER learning
Description: New York, NY : McGraw-Hill Education, [2017]
Identifiers: LCCN 2016021266 | ISBN 9781259820229 (alk. paper)
Subjects: LCSH: College student orientation. | Internet in education. |
    Distance education. | Study skills. | Life skills. | Success.
Classification: LCC LB2343.3 .F4396 2017 | DDC 378.1/98—dc23
LC record available at https://lccn.loc.gov/2016021266

Dedication

To my students, who make teaching a joy.

About the Author

ROBERT S. FELDMAN

Courtesy of Juliana Sohn

Bob Feldman still remembers those moments of being overwhelmed when he started college at Wesleyan University. "I wondered whether I was up to the challenges that faced me," he recalls, "and—although I never would have admitted it at the time—I really had no idea what it took to be successful at college."

That experience, along with his encounters with many students during his own teaching career, led to a life-long interest in helping students navigate the critical transition that they face at the start of their own college careers. Professor Feldman, who went on to receive a doctorate in psychology from the University of Wisconsin–Madison, is now Deputy Chancellor and Professor of Psychological and Brain Sciences at the University of Massachusetts Amherst. He is founding director of *POWER Up for Student Success*, the first-year experience course for incoming students.

Professor Feldman's proudest professional accomplishment is winning the College Outstanding Teaching Award at UMass. He also has been named a Hewlett Teaching Fellow and was Senior Online Instruction Fellow. He has taught courses at Mount Holyoke College, Wesleyan University, and Virginia Commonwealth University.

Professor Feldman is a Fellow of the American Psychological Association, the Association for Psychological Science, and the American Association for the Advancement of Science. He is the winner of a Fulbright Senior Research Scholar and Lecturer award and has written over 200 scientific articles, book chapters, and books. His books, some of which have been translated into Spanish, French, Portuguese, Dutch, Japanese, and Chinese, include *Improving the First Year of College: Research and Practice*; *Understanding Psychology*, 12/e; and *Development Across the Life Span*, 7/e. His research interests encompass the study of honesty and truthfulness in everyday life, the development of nonverbal behavior in children, and the social psychology of education. His research has been supported by grants from the National Institute of Mental Health and the National Institute on Disabilities and Rehabilitation Research.

With the last of his three children completing college, Professor Feldman occupies his spare time with pretty decent cooking and earnest, but admittedly unpolished, piano playing. He also loves to travel. He lives with his wife, who is an educational psychologist, in a home overlooking the Holyoke mountain range in western Massachusetts.

Brief Table of Contents

Table of Contents

3 Taking Notes

4 Taking Tests

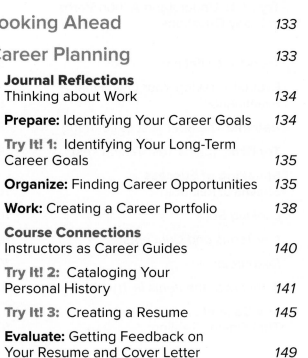

© Mark Andersen/Getty Images RF

7 Technology and Information Competency   162

© Rubberball Productions/Getty Images RF

8 Making Decisions and Problem Solving

9 Diversity and Relationships

© Design Pics Inc/Alamy Stock Photo RF

Images that appear in the front matter: *Robert S. Feldman (author photo): Courtesy of Juliana Sohn; Adult female student wearing backpack: © Mark Andersen/Getty Images RF; Male student in black coat: © Rubberball Productions/Getty Images RF; Pharmacist: © Design Pics Inc/Alamy Stock Photo RF.*

Preface

In the first edition of *P.O.W.E.R. Learning*—the book on which this text is based—I wrote about Mark Johnson, a student whom I encountered early in my teaching career. Smart, articulate, and likable, he certainly wanted to succeed in college, and he seemed every bit as capable as those students who were doing quite well. Yet Mark was a marginal student, someone who allowed multiple opportunities to succeed to pass him by. Although he clearly had the talent necessary to be successful in college—and ultimately in life—he lacked the skills to make use of his talents.

Over the years, I encountered other students like Mark. I began to wonder: Was there a way to teach *every* student how to succeed, both academically and beyond the classroom? *P.O.W.E.R. Learning: Online Success* embodies the answer to this question.

Targeted toward students with a strong career orientation, *P.O.W.E.R. Learning: Online Success* is based on the conviction that *good students are made, not born.* The central message is that students can be successful in college and later in their careers if they follow the basic principles and strategies presented in this book.

This text is designed to be used by students in courses that promote student success. For many students, the first-year experience course is a literal lifeline. It provides the means to learn what it takes to achieve academic success and to make a positive social adjustment to the campus community. If students learn how to do well in their first term of college, they are building a foundation that will last a lifetime.

I wrote *P.O.W.E.R. Learning: Online Success* because no existing text provided a systematic framework that could be applied in a variety of topical areas and that would help students to develop learning and problem-solving strategies that would work effectively both in and out of the classroom. The book is an outgrowth of my experience as a college instructor, most of it involving first-year students, combined with my research on the factors that influence learning.

Judging from the response to the earlier versions of this book—now in use at hundreds of colleges and universities around the world, and translated into languages ranging from Chinese to Spanish—the approach embodied in the book resonates with the philosophy and experience of many educators. Specifically, the text provides a framework that students can begin to use immediately to become more effective students. That framework is designed to be

▶ Clear, easy to grasp, logical, and compelling, so that students can readily see its merits.

▶ Effective for a variety of student learning styles—as well as a variety of teaching styles.

▶ Workable for both online courses and in-person classes.

▶ Valuable for use in learning communities.

▶ Transferable to settings ranging from the classroom to the residence hall room to the board room.

▶ Effective in addressing both the mind *and* the spirit, presenting cognitive strategies and skills, while engaging the natural enthusiasm, motivation, and inclination to succeed that students carry within them.

Based on comprehensive, detailed feedback obtained from both instructors and students, *P.O.W.E.R. Learning: Online Success* meets these aims. The book will help students confront and master the numerous challenges of the college experience through use of the P.O.W.E.R. Learning approach, embodied in the five steps of the acronym *P.O.W.E.R.* (*P*repare, *O*rganize, *W*ork, *E*valuate, and *R*ethink). Using simple—yet effective—principles, *P.O.W.E.R. Learning: Online Success,* **1/e** teaches the skills needed to succeed in college and careers beyond.

The Goals of *P.O.W.E.R. Learning: Online Success*

P.O.W.E.R Learning: Online Success addresses five major goals for students enrolled in online classes:

▶ **To provide a systematic framework for organizing the strategies that lead to success in college and careers:** First and foremost, the book provides a systematic, balanced presentation of the skills required to achieve student and career success. Using the *P.O.W.E.R.* framework and relying on proven strategies, *P.O.W.E.R. Learning: Online Success* provides specific, hands-on techniques for achieving success as a student.

▶ **To offer a wide range of skill-building opportunities:** *P.O.W.E.R. Learning: Online Success* provides a wealth of specific exercises, diagnostic questionnaires, case studies, and journal writing activities to help students to develop and master the skills and techniques they need to become effective learners and problem solvers. *Readers learn by doing.*

▶ **To demonstrate the connection between academic success and career success:** Stressing the importance of *self-reliance* and *self-accountability,* the book demonstrates that the skills required to be a successful student are tied to career and personal success as well.

▶ **To develop critical thinking skills:** Whether to evaluate the quality of information found on the Internet or in other types of media, or to judge the merits of a position taken by a friend, colleague, or politician, the ability to think critically is more important than ever in this age of information. Through frequent questionnaires, exercises, journal activities, and guided group work, *P.O.W.E.R. Learning: Online Success* helps students to develop their capacity to think critically.

▶ **To provide an engaging, accessible, and meaningful presentation:** The fifth goal of this book underlies the first four: to write a student-friendly book that is relevant to the needs and interests of its readers and that will promote enthusiasm and interest in the process of becoming a successful student. Learning the strategies needed to become a more effective student should be a stimulating and fulfilling experience. Realizing that these strategies are valuable outside the classroom as well will provide students with an added incentive to master them.

In short, *P.O.W.E.R. Learning: Online Success* gives students a sense of mastery and success as they read the book and work through its exercises. It is meant to engage and nurture students' minds and spirits, stimulating their intellectual curiosity about the world and planting a seed that will grow throughout their lifetime.

The P.O.W.E.R. to Evolve

More than ever before, the concept of "student" is changing. The idea that a student encompasses a cross-section of 18-year-olds attending a four-year university no longer applies as universally as it once did.

Students are also

Employees
Employers
Co-workers
Parents
Friends
Siblings
Little League coaches
Taxi drivers
Overworked
Overcommitted
Overwhelmed

The list can probably go on from there. What else are you?

The purpose of this text is to take the P.O.W.E.R. framework, which has been proven effective, and apply it to a different type of student. While understanding your own study habits is important, how to study in a dorm is not information that every student needs. Just as our ideas of students are evolving, so can be the texts that serve them.

We want all students to understand what it takes to be successful in school, life, and career. By providing a context that applies to students in a variety of educational models, we can better foster connections between the classroom and the professional arena. The educational conversation this text facilitates should speak to students who are more than just . . . students.

Succeed Now

School + Career + Life

Text Features: Achieving the Goals of P O W E R Learning

P.O.W.E.R. Learning provides a systematic framework for organizing the strategies that lead to success

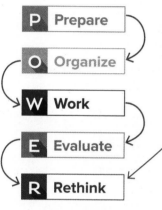

P Prepare
O Organize
W Work
E Evaluate
R Rethink

P.O.W.E.R. Plan

Each chapter utilizes the principles of the **P.O.W.E.R. system (Prepare, Organize, Work, Evaluate, and Rethink),** so students can clearly see how easy it is to incorporate this effective process into their everyday routine. The P.O.W.E.R. plan illustration highlights the key steps for the corresponding chapter material.

Handy, updated **reference charts** appear throughout the text for quickly accessing and organizing important material.

figure 2.3
Weekly Timetable

Week of:_____	Mon	Tues	Wed	Thurs	Fri	Sat	Sun	Week #____
6–7 a.m.								
7–8 a.m.								
8–9 a.m.								
9–10 a.m.								
10–11 a.m.								
11–12 (noon)								
12 (noon)–1 p.m.								
1–2 p.m.								
2–3 p.m.								
3–4 p.m.								
4–5 p.m.								
5–6 p.m.								
6–7 p.m.								
7–8 p.m.								
8–9 p.m.								
9–10 p.m.								
10–11 p.m.								
11 p.m.–12 (midnight)								
12 (midnight)–1 a.m.								
1–2 a.m.								
2–3 a.m.								
3–4 a.m.								
4–5 a.m.								
5–6 a.m.								

daily to-do list
A schedule showing the tasks, activities, and appointments due to occur during the day.

Daily To Do Lists

Finally, you'll need a **daily to-do list**. The daily to-do list can be written on a small, portable calendar that includes a separate page for each day of the week. Or you can keep it virtually on a smartphone or tablet to-do list. Whatever form your daily to-do list takes, make sure you can keep it with you all the time.

The basic organizational task you face is filling in these three schedules. You'll need at least an hour to do this, so set the time aside. In addition, there will be some repetition across the three schedules, and the task may seem a bit tedious. *But every minute you invest now in organizing your time will pay off in hours that you will save in the future.*

table 4.3	**Action Words for Essays**
These words are commonly used in essay questions. Learning the distinctions among them will help you answer essay questions effectively.	
Analyze: Examine and break into component parts.	
Clarify: Explain with significant detail.	
Compare: Describe and explain similarities.	
Compare and contrast: Describe and explain similarities and differences.	
Contrast: Describe and explain differences.	
Critique: Judge and analyze, explaining what is wrong—and right—about a concept.	
Define: Provide the meaning.	
Discuss: Explain, review, and consider.	
Enumerate: Provide a listing of ideas, concepts, reasons, items, etc.	
Evaluate: Provide pros and cons of something; provide an opinion and justify it.	
Explain: Give reasons why or how; clarify, justify, and illustrate.	
Illustrate: Provide examples; show instances.	
Interpret: Explain the meaning of something.	
Justify: Explain why a concept can be supported, typically by using examples and other types of support.	
Outline: Provide an overarching framework or explanation—usually in narrative form—of a concept, idea, event, or phenomenon.	
Prove: Using evidence and arguments, convince the reader of a particular point.	
Relate: Show how things fit together; provide analogies.	
Review: Describe or summarize, often with an evaluation.	
State: Assert or explain.	
Summarize: Provide a condensed, precise list or narrative.	
Trace: Track or sketch out how events or circumstances have evolved; provide a history or timeline.	

Essays are improved when they include examples and point out differences. Your response should follow a logical sequence, moving from major points to minor ones, or following a time sequence. Above all, your answer should address every aspect of the question posed on the test. Because essays often contain several different, embedded questions, you have to be certain that you have answered every part to receive full credit. (After reviewing Table 4.3, complete **Try It!** 4.)

P.O.W.E.R. Learning offers a wide range of skill-building opportunities

Every chapter offers numerous **Try It!** activities for gaining hands-on experience with the material covered in the chapter. These include questionnaires, self-assessments, and group exercises to do with classmates.

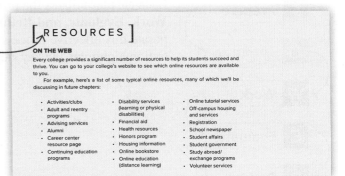

1 | **Try It!** P O W E R

Determine the Diversity of Your Community

Try to assess the degree of diversity that exists in your community. *Community* can be a loosely defined term, but for this Try It! think of it as the group of people you encounter and interact with on a regular basis. When thinking of diversity, remember to include the many different ways in which people can be different from one another, including race, ethnicity, culture, sexual orientation, physical challenges, and so on.

Overall, how diverse would you say your community is?

Are there organizations in your community that promote diversity? Are there organizations that work to raise the visibility and understanding of particular groups within your community?

Is your online college community more or less diverse than your community at large? Why do you think this might be?

How does the diversity in your community compare to the following statistics on diversity in the United States as of the 2010 census: white, 72 percent; Hispanic or Latino, 16 percent; Black or African American, 13 percent; Asian, 5 percent; two or more races, 3 percent; American Indian and Alaska Native, .9 percent; Native Hawaiian and other Pacific Islander, .2 percent; other race, 6 percent? (Note: Percentages add up to more than 100 percent because Hispanics may be of any race and are therefore counted under more than one category.)

Every chapter includes an updated list of the three types of **resources** that are useful in finding and utilizing information relevant to the chapter: websites, books, and (for schools that have them) on-campus resources. This material helps students study and retain important concepts presented in the chapter, as well as guiding future inquiry.

[RESOURCES]

ON THE WEB

Every college provides a significant number of resources to help its students succeed and thrive. You can go to your college's website to see which online resources are available to you.

For example, here's a list of some typical online resources, many of which we'll be discussing in future chapters:

- Activities/clubs
- Adult and reentry programs
- Advising services
- Alumni
- Career center resource page
- Continuing education programs
- Disability services (learning or physical disabilities)
- Financial aid
- Health resources
- Honors program
- Housing information
- Online bookstore
- Online education (distance learning)
- Online tutorial services
- Off-campus housing and services
- Registration
- School newspaper
- Student affairs
- Student government
- Study abroad/exchange programs
- Volunteer services

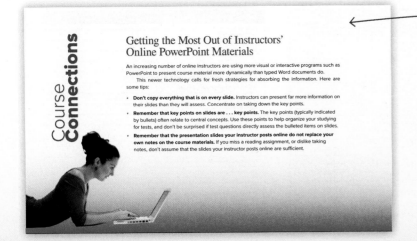

Course Connections

Getting the Most Out of Instructors' Online PowerPoint Materials

An increasing number of online instructors are using more visual or interactive programs such as PowerPoint to present course material more dynamically than typed Word documents do.

This newer technology calls for fresh strategies for absorbing the information. Here are some tips:

- **Don't copy everything that is on every slide.** Instructors can present far more information on their slides than they will assess. Concentrate on taking down the key points.
- **Remember that key points on slides are . . . key points.** The key points (typically indicated by bullets) often relate to central concepts. Use these points to help organize your studying for tests, and don't be surprised if test questions directly assess the bulleted items on slides.
- **Remember that the presentation slides your instructor posts online do not replace your own notes on the course materials.** If you miss a reading assignment, or dislike taking notes, don't assume that the slides your instructor posts online are sufficient.

Most chapters include a **Course Connections** box that shows students how to use the chapter's content to maximize their success in particular classes.

The goals of *P.O.W.E.R. Learning: Online Success* are achieved through a consistent, carefully devised set of features common to every chapter. Students and faculty endorsed each of these elements.

P.O.W.E.R. Learning demonstrates the connection between academic success and success beyond the classroom

Career Connections

The Job of Reading

Memos. Annual reports. Instructions. Continuing education assignments. Professional journals.

Each of these items illustrates the importance of developing critical reading skills for on-the-job success. Virtually every job requires good reading expertise, and for some professions, reading is a central component. Polishing your reading skills now will pay big dividends when you enter the world of work. The better you are at absorbing and remembering written information, the better you'll be at carrying out your job.

For instance, in many corporations, vital information is transmitted through the written word, via e-mails, hard-copy memos, technical reports, or web-based material. The job of repairing broken appliances or automobiles requires reading numerous service manuals to master the complex computer diagnostic systems that are now standard equipment. Nurses and others in the healthcare field must read journals and reports to keep up with the newest medical technologies.

Furthermore, because not all supervisors are effective writers, you'll sometimes need to read between the lines and draw inferences and conclusions about what you need to do. You should also keep in mind that there are significant cultural differences in the ways in which people write and the type of language they use. Being sensitive to the cultural background of colleagues will permit you to more accurately interpret and understand what you are reading.

In short, reading is a skill that's required in virtually every profession. Developing the habit of reading critically while you are in college will pave the road for future career success.

The **Career Connections** feature links the material in the chapter to the world of work, demonstrating how the strategies discussed in the chapter are related to career choices and success in the workplace.

Speaking *of* Success

Courtesy of Javier Olivarez

NAME: Javier Olivarez

SCHOOL: Southern New Hampshire University, Manchester, NH

MAJOR: Communications with concentration in Public Relations

Imagine a world where your classroom is anywhere you happen to be at any given moment. For Javier Olivarez, a senior at Southern New Hampshire University, it is a reality he embraces.

"Being a full-time employee and a member of several committees at SNHU, it was important that I have the flexibility of attending classes on my time," he noted. "Now there are no excuses because college is wherever I want to be."

But there are special challenges that make online learning different from being in a traditional classroom.

"One of the challenges I encountered in pursuing my degree online was communicating electronically versus face-to-face in a campus environment," said Olivarez. "Electronic communication can be misinterpreted or be unclear especially when it comes to understanding an assignment or professor's expectations. As a student pursuing a communications degree, I took this as a challenge upon myself to understand my professor's communication style and bridge the gaps of communication.

"Usually a week before the new term starts, I e-mail my professors, introduce myself, and then ask a few standard questions to help me get a feel for the expectations.

This leads to a successful first week and sets the pace for the term," he added.

As an SNHU peer leader, Olivarez works closely with College of Online and Continuing Education (COCE) students guiding them through the initial processes of pursing a degree online.

"I share my tips for having a successful term, the most important being organization. For example, I have a picture of the binders I create for each course and the reminders that I have set up for important due dates," Olivarez said. "Life is busy and it helps to have these reminders to ensure success throughout the term. Taking online courses has enhanced my time management skills and helped me become more accountable."

While the idea of taking a course anywhere at any time is appealing, Olivarez stresses that it requires a strong commitment to the courses, and most importantly to oneself.

"My goal was to be a top student. In order to achieve success, you have to make it a priority," Olivarez added. "After a few terms, I became skilled at time management and now I am reaching my goal by graduating Summa Cum Laude this year."

[RETHINK]
- Why is it important for a student pursing an online degree to have especially solid skills in time management?
- Do you think that communication is more difficult in online classes than in face-to-face classes? Why, and how can you avoid such difficulties?

Speaking of Success articles profile real-life success stories. Some of these people are well-known individuals, whereas others are current students or recent graduates who have overcome academic difficulties to achieve success. In addition, **critical thinking questions** end each **Speaking of Success** profile.

From the Perspective of . . . This feature highlights how the lessons learned in this course impact you both now and in your future career. Created to show the correlation between academic and professional life, these features answer the question of why this course matters and how it will impact student growth long after graduation.

- *Recite.* Describe and explain to yourself the material you have just read and answer the questions you have posed earlier.
- *Record.* Write in your textbook, make notes, or create flash cards.
- *Review.* Review the material, looking it over, reading end-of-chapter summaries, and answering the in-text review questions.

In addition to *SQ4R,* you can also make up your own system. The truth is that it doesn't matter what system you use, as long as you use a system. What does matter is that you're systematic in the work of reading.

From the perspective of . . .

A STUDENT To truly retain what you are reading, you must give your reading your undivided attention. Make a list of your biggest distractions and consider strategies for avoiding those distractions when you read.

© CMCD/Getty Images RF

P.O.W.E.R. Learning helps you develop critical thinking skills

Most chapters feature a **P.O.W.E.R. Profile Assessment tool** that gives students a sense of where they stand—both numerically and graphically—in relation to the key topics addressed in the book. The **"P.O.W.E.R. Profile"** helps students identify their strengths and weaknesses and determine how they want to improve. Students can return to the **P.O.W.E.R. Profile** at the end of the course to assess and chart their progress.

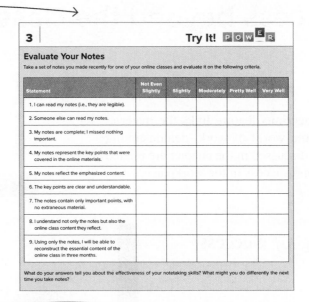

The **Journal Reflections** feature provides students with the opportunity to keep an ongoing journal, making entries relevant to the chapter content. Students are asked to reflect and think critically about related prior experiences. These conclude with questions designed to elicit critical thinking and exploration.

Journal Reflections

How I Feel about Tests

1. How do you feel about tests in general?

2. What are your first memories of being in a testing situation? What were your feelings, and why?

3. What makes a test "good" and "bad" from your perspective?

4. What factors contribute to your success or failure on a particular exam? Which of these factors are under your control?

5. What strategies do you use when taking tests to maximize your performance? Which have been particularly effective, and why?

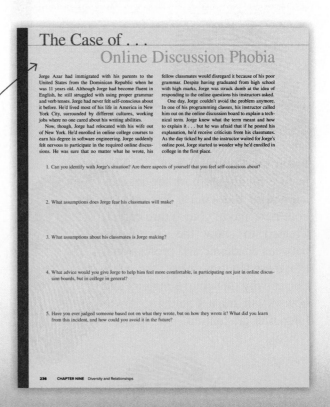

Each chapter ends with a **case study (The Case of . . .)** to which the principles described in the chapter can be applied. Case studies are based on situations that students might themselves encounter. Each case provides a series of questions that encourage students to consider what they've learned and to use critical thinking skills in responding to these questions.

P.O.W.E.R. *Learning* provides an engaging, accessible, and meaningful presentation

An appealing design and visual presentation highlight large, clear photos carefully selected to show the diversity of students as well as the latest in technological aids and devices.

Chapter-opening scenarios describe an individual grappling with a situation that is relevant to the subject matter of the chapter. Readers will be able to relate to these vignettes, which feature students running behind schedule, figuring out a way to keep up with reading assignments, or facing a long list of vocabulary words to memorize.

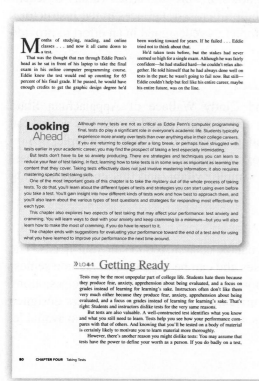

Learning Outcomes
By the time you finish this chapter, you will be able to

» LO4-1   Identify the kinds of tests you will encounter in college.

» LO4-2   Explain the best ways to prepare for and take various kinds of tests.

» LO4-3   Analyze the best strategies for answering specific kinds of test questions.

CHAPTER **4**

Taking Tests

Key terms appear in boldface in the text and are linked to definitions in the end-of-book glossary. In addition, they are listed in a *Key Terms and Concepts* section at the end of the chapter.

[KEY TERMS AND CONCEPTS]

Acronym (p. 121)	Frontmatter (p. 109)	Rehearsal (p. 120)
Acrostic (p. 121)	Learning disabilities (p. 125)	Visualization (p. 123)
Advance organizers (p. 108)	Mnemonics (p. 121)	
Attention span (p. 111)	Overlearning (p. 123)	

All of these reviewed and tested features are designed not only to help students understand, practice, and master the core concepts presented in this text, but also to collectively support the main goals and vision of this text, as demonstrated on the following pages.

The P.O.W.E.R. Resources

The same philosophy and goals that guided the writing of *P.O.W.E.R. Learning: Online Success* led to the development of a comprehensive teaching package. Through a series of focus groups, questionnaires, and surveys, we asked instructors what they needed to optimize their courses. We also analyzed what other publishers provided to make sure that the ancillary materials accompanying *P.O.W.E.R. Learning: Online Success* would surpass the level of support to which instructors are accustomed. As a result of the extensive research that went into devising the teaching resources, we are confident that whether you are an instructor with years of experience or are teaching the course for the first time, this book's instructional package will enhance classroom instruction and provide guidance as you prepare for and teach the course.

Print Resources

ANNOTATED INSTRUCTOR'S EDITION

The Annotated Instructor's Edition (AIE), prepared by Joni Webb Petschauer and Cindy Wallace of Appalachian State University, contains the full text of the student edition of the book with the addition of notes that provide a rich variety of teaching strategies, discussion prompts, and helpful cross-references to the Instructor's Resource Manual. The AIE has been completely redesigned in an effort to provide more frontline teaching assistance.

INSTRUCTOR'S RESOURCE MANUAL

Written by Joni Webb Petschauer and Cindy Wallace of Appalachian State University with additional contributions from experienced instructors across the country, this manual provides specific suggestions for teaching each topic, tips on implementing a first-year experience program, handouts to generate creative classroom activities, audiovisual resources, sample syllabi, and tips on incorporating the Internet into the course.

CUSTOMIZE YOUR TEXT

P.O.W.E.R. Learning: Online Success can be customized to suit your needs. The text can be abbreviated for shorter courses and can be expanded to include semester schedules, campus maps, and additional essays, activities, or exercises, along with other materials specific to your curriculum or situation. Chapters designed for student athletes, transferring students, and career preparation are also available.

Human Resources

WORKSHOPS WITH AUTHOR AND AUTHOR TEAM

Are you faced with the challenge of launching a first-year experience course on your campus? Would you like to invigorate your college success program, incorporating the most recent pedagogical and technological innovations? Is faculty recruitment an obstacle to the success of your program? Are you interested in learning more about the P.O.W.E.R. system?

Workshops are available on these and many other subjects for anyone conducting or even just considering a first-year experience program. Led by author Robert Feldman, *P.O.W.E.R. Learning: Online Success* Instructor's Resource

Manual authors Joni Webb Petschauer and Cindy Wallace, or one of the McGraw-Hill P.O.W.E.R. Learning consultants, each workshop is tailored to the needs of individual campuses or programs. For more information, contact your local representative, or e-mail us at **student.success@mheducation.com**.

Digital Resources

LASSI: LEARNING AND STUDY STRATEGIES INVENTORY

The LASSI is a 10-scale, 80-item assessment of students' awareness about and use of learning and study strategies related to skill, will, and self-regulation components of strategic learning. The focus is on both covert and overt thoughts, behaviors, attitudes, and beliefs that relate to successful learning and that can be altered through educational interventions. Research has repeatedly demonstrated that these factors contribute significantly to success in college and that they can be learned or enhanced through educational interventions.

The LASSI is available in print or online at **www.hhpublishing.com**. Ask your McGraw-Hill sales representative for more details.

IMPLEMENTING A STUDENT SUCCESS COURSE

This innovative web content (available on the OLC) assists you in developing and sustaining your Student Success course. Features include a "how to" guide for designing and proposing a new course, with easy-to-use templates for determining budget needs and resources.

MCGRAW-HILL *CONNECT*®

Connect® offers a number of powerful tools and features to make managing assignments easier, so faculty can spend more time teaching. With *Connect,* students can engage with their coursework anytime and anywhere, making the learning process more accessible and efficient.

LEARNSMART

LearnSmart is an adaptive study tool proven to strengthen memory recall, increase class retention, and boost grades. Students are able to study more efficiently because they are made aware of what they know and don't know. Real-time reports quickly identify the concepts that require more attention from individual students—or the entire class.

SMARTBOOK

SmartBook is the first and only adaptive reading experience designed to change the way students read and learn. It creates a personalized reading experience by highlighting the most impactful concepts a student needs to learn at that moment in time. As a student engages with SmartBook, the reading experience continuously adapts by highlighting content based on what the student knows and doesn't know. This ensures that the focus is on the content he or she needs to learn, while simultaneously promoting long-term retention of material. Use SmartBook's real-time reports to quickly identify the concepts that require more attention from individual students—or the entire class. The end result? Students are more engaged with course content, can better prioritize their time, and can be prepared to participate.

MCGRAW-HILL CAMPUS™

McGraw-Hill Campus™ is a new one-stop teaching and learning experience available to users of any learning management system. This institutional service allows faculty and students to enjoy single-sign-on (SSO) access to all McGraw-Hill Higher Education materials, including the award-winning McGraw-Hill *Connect* platform, from directly within the institution's website. McGraw-Hill Campus provides faculty with instant access to teaching materials (e.g., eTextbooks, test banks, PowerPoint slides, animations, and learning objectives), allowing them to browse, search, and use any ancillary content in our vast library. Students enjoy SSO access to a variety of free products (e.g., quizzes, flash cards, narrated presentations), and subscription-based products (e.g., McGraw-Hill *Connect*). With McGraw-Hill Campus, faculty and students will never need to create another account to access McGraw-Hill products.

The POWER to Succeed!

The POWER of Support!

Let the McGraw-Hill Student Success Team support your course with our workshop program.

- ▶ Planning to develop a first-year experience course from scratch?
- ▶ Reenergizing your first-year experience course?
- ▶ Trying to integrate technology in your class?
- ▶ Exploring the concept of learning communities?

We offer a range of author- and consultant-led workshops that can be tailored to meet the needs of your institution.

Our team of experts, led by *P.O.W.E.R. Learning: Online Success* author Robert Feldman, can address issues of course management, assessment, organization, and implementation. How do you get students to commit to your program? How do you achieve support from your institution? How can you evaluate and demonstrate the effectiveness of your first-year experience course? These are questions that every program faces. Let us help you to find an answer that works for you.

Other workshop topics may include

- ▶ Classroom Strategies for Enhancing Cultural Competence: The P.O.W.E.R. of Diversity
- ▶ Using Learning Styles in the Classroom
- ▶ Creating Student Success Courses Online
- ▶ Motivating Your Students

To schedule a workshop, please contact your local McGraw-Hill representative. Alternately, contact us directly at **student.success@mheducation.com** to begin the process of bringing a P.O.W.E.R. Learning workshop to you.

The POWER to Create Your Own Text!

Do you want to

- ▶ Cover only select chapters?
- ▶ Personalize your book with campus information (maps, schedules, registration materials, etc.)?
- ▶ Add your own materials, including exercises or assignments?
- ▶ Address specific student populations, such as student athletes and transferring students?

P.O.W.E.R. Learning: Online Success can be customized to suit your needs.*

*Orders must meet our minimum sales unit requirements.

WHY CUSTOMIZE?

Perhaps your course focuses on study skills and you prefer that your text not cover life issues such as money matters, health and wellness, or information on choosing a major. Whatever the reason, we can make it happen, easily. McGraw-Hill Custom Publishing can deliver a book that perfectly meets your needs.

WHAT WILL MY CUSTOM BOOK LOOK LIKE?

Any chapters from the *P.O.W.E.R. Learning: Online Success* book that you include will be in full color. Additional materials can be added between chapters or at the beginning or end of the book in black and white. Binding (paperback, three-hole punch, you name it) is up to you. You can even add your own custom cover to reflect your school image.

WHAT CAN I ADD?

Anything! Here are some ideas to get you started:

- ▶ **Campus map** or anything specific to your school: academic regulations or requirements, syllabi, important phone numbers or dates, library hours.
- ▶ **Calendars** for the school year, for local theater groups, for a concert series.
- ▶ **Interviews** with local businesspeople or your school's graduates in which they describe their own challenges and successes.
- ▶ **Your course syllabus or homework assignments** so your students have everything they need for your course under one cover and you don't have to make copies to hand out.

SPECIAL CHAPTERS DESIGNED FOR THE UNIQUE NEEDS OF YOUR STUDENTS!

Several additional chapters are available for your customized text and have been designed to address the needs of specific student populations.

- ▶ *Strategies for Success for Student Athletes.* This chapter discusses the unique challenges of student athletes, such as managing school and team pressures, using resources and understanding eligibility, and knowing when and how to ask for help. It also addresses special concerns such as burnout, dealing with injury, and hazing.
- ▶ *Taking Charge of Your Career.* This chapter helps students determine the best career choices that fit personal goals. It provides important tips on how to develop a career portfolio, prepare a resume and cover letters, and have a successful interview, including follow-up strategies.
- ▶ *Transfer Strategies: Making the Leap from Community College to a Four-Year School.* Designed for the potential transfer student, this chapter looks at the pros and cons of moving beyond a two-year degree and what personal decisions to make. It guides students through the transfer process, including applications, credit transfer, financial assistance, and transfer shock.

HOW DO I CREATE A CUSTOM BOOK?

The secret to custom publishing is this: Custom Publishing Is Simple!

Here are the basic steps:

▶ You select the chapters you would like to use from *P.O.W.E.R. Learning: Online Success* with your McGraw-Hill sales representative.

▶ Together, we discuss your preferences for the binding, the cover, etc., and provide you with information on costs.

▶ We assign your customized text an ISBN and your project goes into production. A custom text will typically publish within 6–8 weeks of the order.

▶ Your book is manufactured and it is put into inventory in the McGraw-Hill distribution center.

▶ You are sent a free desk copy of your custom publication.

▶ Your bookstore calls McGraw-Hill's customer service department and orders the text.

You select what you want—we handle the details!

Contact us:

Canada: 1-905-430-5034

United States: 1-800-446-8979

E-mail: **student.success@mheducation.com**

Acknowledgments

I am indebted to the many reviewers of *P.O.W.E.R. Learning: Online Success* who provided input at every step of development of the book and the ancillary package. These dedicated instructors and administrators provided thoughtful, detailed advice, and I am very grateful for their help and insight. They include the following:

Judith Lynch, Kansas State University; Dr. G. Warlock Vance, Randolph Community College; Leah Graham, Broward College; Sara Henson, Central Oregon Community College; Jamie Jensen, Boise State University; Barbara West, Central Georgia Technical College; Pauline Nugent, Missouri State University; Rob Bertram, Bradley University; Anne Knop, Manor College; Ashley Stark, Dickinson State University; Christie Carr, Austin Community College; Andrea Smith, Florida Gateway College; Dale S. Haralson, Hinds Community College; Donna Burton, NC State University; Norman Smith, Eckerd College; Sam Mulberry, Bethel University; Diane Fox, Saint Mary's College; Amy Hassenpflug, Liberty University; Mary Beth Willett, University of Maine; Jennifer Clevenger, Virginia Tech; Heidi Zenie, Three Rivers Community College; Jeffrey Hall, Ashford University; Jennifer Scalzi-Pesola, American River College, Sierra; Jarlene DeCay, Cedar Valley College; Beverly Dile, Elizabethtown Community and Technical College; Linda Girouard, Brescia University; Malinda Mansfield, Ivy Tech Community College; Karline Prophete, Palm Beach State College; Kelley Butler Heartfield, Ivy Tech Community College; Stephen Coates-White, South Seattle College; Erin Wood, Catawba College; Cari Kenner, St. Cloud State University; Amanda Bond, Georgia Military College–Columbus; Alex E. Collins, Miami Dade College; Erik Christensen, South Florida State College; J. Andrew Monahan, Suffolk County Community College; Chad Brooks, Austin Peay State University; Cindy Stewart, Blue Ridge CTC; Sherri Stepp, Marshall University; Amy Colon, SUNY Sullivan; Darla Rocha, San Jacinto College; Suzanne F. Pearl, Miami Dade College, Wolfson Campus; Kalpana Swamy, Santa Fe College; Rebecca Samberg, Housatonic Community College; Jeannette McClendon, Napa Valley College; Jeri O'Bryan-Losee, Morrisville State College; Donna Ragauckas, Santa Fe College; Professor Terry Rae Gamble, Palm Beach State College; Barbara Putman, Southwestern Community College; Nikita Anderson, University of Baltimore; Maria Christian, Oklahoma State University Institute of Technology; Alexandra Lis, Miami Dade College, Kendall Campus; Kim Cobb, West Virginia State University; Kim Thomas, Polk State College; Michael Turner, Northern Virginia Community College; Candace Weddle, The South Carolina School of the Arts at Anderson University; Elizabeth Kennedy, Florida Atlantic University; Ronda Jacobs, College of Southern Maryland; Kim Crockett, West Georgia Technical College; Melissa Woods, Hinds Community College; Joe French, Columbia Southern University and Waldorf College; Faye Hamrac, Reid State Technical College; Jyrece McClendon, Palm Beach State College; Aubrey Moncrieffe Jr., Housatonic Community College; Karen Jones, Zane State College; Peggy Whaley, Murray State University; Marilyn Olson, Chicago State University; Joyce McMahon, Kansas City, Kansas Community College; Kaye Young, Jamestown Community College; Diana Ivankovic, Anderson University; Matt Kelly, Murray State University; Ronda Dively, Southern Illinois University–Carbondale; Dr. Julia Cote, Houston Community

College; Beverly Russell, College of Southern Maryland; Donna Hanley, Kentucky Wesleyan College; Shane Williamson, Lindenwood University; Cheyanne Lewis, Blue Ridge Community and Technical College; Linda Randall, Georgia Southwestern State University; Linda Gannon, College of Southern Nevada (CSN); Ronnie Peacock, Edgecombe Community College; Deborah Vance, Ivy Tech Community College; Melinda Berry, Trinity Valley Community College; Sandy Lory-Snyder, Farmingdale State College; Melody Hays, South College–Asheville; Dwedor Ford, Central State University; Kim Smokowski, Bergen Community College; Dr. Brenda Tuberville, Rogers State University; Professor Jeannie Gonzalez, Miami Dade College, Kendall Campus; Joyce Kevetos, Palm Beach State College; Kelly S. Moor, Idaho State University; Brad Broschinsky, Idaho State University; Debbie Gilmore, Temple College; Miriam Chiza, North Hennepin Community College; Paul Hibbitts Jr., Central Georgia Technical College; Mark Hendrix, Palm Beach State College; Laurie Sherman, Community College of Rhode Island; Pamela Moss, Midwestern State University; Alison Collman, Palm Beach State College; Julie Hernandez, Rock Valley College; Nina M. Scaringello, Suffolk County Community College–Grant Campus; Dr. J. Brown, Temple College, Temple, Texas; Stephen Phelps, Temple College; Yvonne Mitkos, Southern Illinois University Edwardsville; Annette Fields, University of Arkansas at Pine Bluff; Christopher L. Lau, Hutchinson Community College; Mary Davis, Angelina College; Pat Wall, Isothermal Community College; Winifred Ferguson Adams, Angelina College; Barbara A. Sherry, Northeastern Illinois University; Jose L. Saldivar, The University of Texas–Pan American; Dr. Michael J. Alicea, Miami Dade College; Karen Nelson, Craven Community College; Jennifer Boyle, Davidson County Community College; Dianna Stankiewicz, Anderson University; Brent Via, Virginia Western Community College; Brent Jackson, Central Carolina Technical College; Professor Lottie T. McMillan, Miami Dade College, North Campus; John Pigg, Tennessee Technical University; Andrea Serna, National American University; Mirjana M. Brockett, Georgia Institute of Technology; Linda McCuen, Anderson University; Charlene Latimer, Daytona State College; Eleanor Paterson, Erie Community College; Keri Keckley, Crowder College; June DeBoer, Calvin College; Chareane Wimbley-Gouveia, Linn-Benton Community College; Ross Bandics, Northampton Community College; Gloria Alexander, Bowie State University; Bickerstaff, Holmes; Scott H. O'Daniel, Ivy Tech Community College; Lourdes Delgado, Miami Dade College; Julie Bennett, Central Methodist University; Miriam McMullen-Pastrick, Penn State Erie; Kay Flowers, Idaho State University; Joseph Kornoski, Montgomery County Community College; Jacqui Slinger, Bluffton University; Mark A. Dowell, Randolph Community College; Eva Menefee, Lansing Community College; Shari Waldrop, Navarro College; Liese A. Hull, University of Michigan; Jenny Beaver, Rowan-Cabarrus Community College; Kenneth Christensen, University of Southern Mississippi; Susan Bossa, Quincy College; Daniel Thompson, CSU Long Beach; Betty Stack, Rowan Cabarrus Community College; Kristin Asinger, University of Pittsburgh–Bradford; Carmalita M. Kemayo, EdD, University of Illinois Springfield; MaryJo Slater, Community College of Beaver County; Jeannette Sullivan, Palm Beach State College; Michael Corriston, Southeast Kentucky Community and Technical College.

I am also very grateful to Heather Fullerton of Berkeley City College, who provided significant assistance in the development of the online student version of this title.

P.O.W.E.R. Learning: Online Success author Bob Feldman and some of his first-year experience program participants.

Courtesy of Robert S. Feldman

The students in my own first-year experience courses (some of whom are shown here) provided thoughtful and wise advice. I thank them for their enthusiasm and eager willingness to provide constructive feedback.

Professors Cindy Wallace and Joni Webb Petschauer of Appalachian State University wrote the Instructor's Resource Manual and provided notes and tips for the Annotated Instructor's Edition. I thank both of them for their enthusiasm, good ideas, dedication, and friendship.

Edward Murphy, Ed.D, an educational testing expert, helped develop the exercises in the book, and I'm grateful for his excellent work.

John Graiff was a great help on every level in putting this book together, and I thank him for his willingness to go the extra mile. I could not have written this book without his unflagging support.

I am proud to be part of an extraordinary McGraw-Hill editorial, marketing, and sales team. My publisher, Scott Davidson, has brought enthusiasm and intelligence to the project, and I welcome his good work, support, and friendship. I am also grateful to David Ploskonka, product developer who worked on the project, whose keen editorial eye, creativity, and wealth of good ideas have improved this book significantly. I would also like to thank team members Danielle Clement, senior content project manager; Debra Kubiak, senior designer; and Kevin White, digital product developer, who helped modify and create the P.O.W.E.R. series digital content.

There are several folks who, while no longer officially working on the project, still patiently answer my queries and offer their advice, for which I am extremely grateful. Andy Watts made superb contributions in extending the reach of *P.O.W.E.R. Learning: Online Success*, and I'm very grateful for his work and even more for his friendship. Phil Butcher, Thalia Dorwick, David Patterson, Allison McNamara, and Alexis Walker were part of the team that developed the book, and I'm ever thankful for their efforts. Above all, I'm grateful to Rhona Robbin, the first development editor on the project, and sponsoring editor Sarah Touborg, who provided the impetus for the book. Certainly, the pages of *P.O.W.E.R. Learning: Online Success* continue to reflect their many contributions.

Without a doubt, there is no better publishing group in the business than the one that worked on *P.O.W.E.R. Learning: Online Success*. I count myself extremely lucky not only to have found myself a part of this world-class team, but to count each of them as friends.

In the end, I am eternally indebted to my family, both extended and immediate. Sarah, Jeff, and Lilia; Josh, Julie, and Naomi; Jon, Leigh, Alex, and Miles; and of course Kathy, thank you for everything.

Robert S. Feldman

Congratulations! You are at the beginning of an academic journey that will impact your future in ways you can only imagine. This text and the online course you are taking are designed to help make that journey as meaningful and enriching as possible. As you begin this chapter of your life, remember that you are not alone.

Every student encounters challenges. Whether it be juggling family, work, and school or preparing for a test, the challenges you face are daunting.

This is where *P.O.W.E.R. Learning: Online Success* comes in. It is designed to help you to master the challenges you'll face in your online classes as well as in life after graduation. The P.O.W.E.R. Learning system—which is based on five key steps embodied in the word P.O.W.E.R. (Prepare, Organize, Work, Evaluate, and Rethink)—teaches strategies that will help you become a more successful student and that will give you an edge in attaining what you want to accomplish in life.

But it's up to you to make use of the text. Familiarize yourself with the features (described above) and use the built-in learning aids, on the accompanying website and in *Connect*. By doing so, you'll maximize the book's usefulness and get the most out of it.

Finally, I welcome your comments and suggestions about *P.O.W.E.R. Learning: Online Success,* as well as about the website that accompanies the book. You can write me at the Chancellor's Office at the University of Massachusetts, Amherst, Massachusetts 01003. Even easier, send me an e-mail message at **feldman@chancellor.umass.edu**. I will write back!

P.O.W.E.R. Learning: Online Success presents the tools that can maximize your chances for academic and life success. But remember that they're only tools, and their effectiveness depends on the way in which they are used. Ultimately, you are the one who is in charge of your future. Make the journey a rewarding, exciting, and enlightening one!

Robert S. Feldman

Dear Online Student

CHAPTER 1

Learning Outcomes

By the time you finish this chapter, you will be able to

» LO 1-1   Explain the benefits of a college education.

» LO 1-2   Identify the basic principles of P.O.W.E.R. Learning.

» LO 1-3   Identify your learning styles and how they affect your academic success.

P.O.W.E.R. Learning: Becoming an Expert Student

© Mint Images Limited/Alamy Stock Photo RF

The day has started off with a bang. Literally. As Abbie Suarez struggles sleepily to turn off her clock radio's continual buzzing at 6:35 a.m., she knocks it off the table next to her bed. The loud bang it makes as it hits the floor not only wakes her fully but also rouses her daughters, sleeping in the next room, who grumble resentfully.

Struggling out of bed, Abbie reflects on the day ahead. It's one of her most intense days—two shifts at two different part-time jobs on different sides of town. She also must get her children ready for school and then take them to swimming lessons in the afternoon. And on top of all that, she has an exam that she must complete before 10:00 a.m. for one of her online college classes.

After a quick shower, Abbie manages to get her daughters off to school, and then drives to the nearest library to log into the class's online learning management system for her exam. She glances at her paralegal textbook and feels a wave of anxiety flood over her: Will I do well enough on my exam? How will I manage to hold down two jobs, take care of my family, and have enough time to study? Will I find a job as a paralegal after graduation? Will I make my children proud? . . . *And underlying all these questions is a single challenge: Will I be successful in college and in my career?*

Looking Ahead

Whether academic pursuits are a struggle or come easily to you . . . whether you are returning to college or attending for the first time . . . whether you are gaining new skills for your current job or are starting on a whole new career path, college is a challenge. Every one of us has concerns about our capabilities and motivation, and new situations—like starting college—make us wonder how well we'll succeed.

That's where this book comes in. It is designed to help you learn the most effective ways to approach the challenges you encounter, not just in college but in your career, too. It will teach you practical strategies, hints, and tips that can lead you to success, all centered around an approach to achieving academic and career success: P.O.W.E.R. Learning.

This book is designed to be useful in a way that is different from other college texts. It presents information in a hands-on format. It's meant to be used—not just read. Write on it, underline words and sentences, use a highlighter, circle key points, and complete the questionnaires right in the book. The more exercises you do, the more you'll get from the book. Remember, this is a book to help you throughout college and throughout your career, so it's a good idea to invest your time here and now. If the learning techniques you master here become second nature, the payoff will be enormous.

This first chapter lays out the basics of P.O.W.E.R. Learning. It will also help you determine the way in which you learn best and how you can use your personal learning style to study more effectively.

» LO 1-1 Why Go to College?

Congratulations. You're in college.

But why? Although it seems as if it should be easy to answer why you're continuing your education, for most people it's not so simple. The reasons that people go to college vary from the practical ("I need new skills for my job"), to the lofty ("I want to build a better life for my family"), to the vague ("Why not?—I don't have anything better to do"). Consider your own reasons for attending college as you complete **Try It! 1**.

Surveys of first-year college students at all types of institutions show that the vast majority say they want to learn about things that interest them, get training for a specific career, land a better job, and make more money (see **Figure 1.1**). Statistics clearly demonstrate that a college education helps people find better jobs. On average, college graduates earn about 75 percent more than high school graduates over their working lifetime. That difference adds up: Over the course of their working

Why Am I Going to College?

Place 1, 2, and 3 by the three most important reasons that you have for attending college:

_____ I want to get a good job when I graduate.

_____ I want to make my family proud.

_____ I couldn't find a decent job.

_____ I want to try something different.

_____ I want to get ahead at my current job.

_____ I want to pursue my dream job.

_____ I want to improve my reading and thinking skills.

_____ I want to become a more cultured person.

_____ I want to meet new people from different backgrounds.

_____ I want to make more money.

_____ I want to learn more about things that interest me.

_____ A mentor or role model encouraged me to go.

_____ I want to prove to others that I can succeed.

Now consider the following:

- What do your answers tell you about yourself?
- What reasons besides these did you think about when you were applying to college?
- How do you think your reasons compare with those of other students who are starting college with you?

lifetimes, college graduates earn close to a million dollars more than those with only a high school degree. Furthermore, as jobs become increasingly complex and technologically sophisticated, college will become more and more of a necessity.

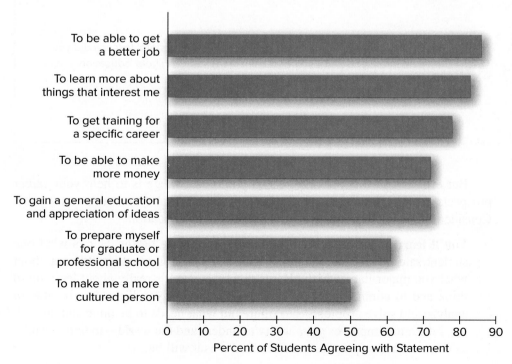

Percent of Students Agreeing with Statement

figure 1.1

Choosing College

These are the most frequently cited reasons that first-year college students gave for why they enrolled in college when asked in a national survey.

Source: © 2008 The Regents of the University of California.

Journal Reflections

My School Experiences

Throughout this book, you will be given opportunities to document your thoughts. These opportunities—called Journal Reflections—offer a chance to think critically about the chapter topics and record your personal reactions to them. As you create your reflections, be honest.

Completing these Journal Reflections provides a variety of benefits. Not only will you be able to mull over your past and present academic experiences, you'll also begin to see patterns in the kind of difficulties—and successes!—you encounter. You'll be able to apply solutions that worked in one situation to others. And one added benefit: You'll get practice in writing.

If you save these entries and return to them later, you may be surprised at the changes they record over the course of the term. You can either write them out or keep an actual journal.

1. Think of one of the successful experiences you've had during your previous years in school or on the job. What was it?

2. What made the experience successful? What did you learn from your success?

3. Think of an experience you had in school that did not go as you had hoped, and briefly describe it. Why did it occur?

4. What could you have done differently to make it successful? What did you learn from it?

5. Based on these experiences of success and failure, what general lessons did you learn that could help you be more successful in the future, in your education and in your career?

But even if you feel the only reason you're in college is to help your career prospects, remember that the value of college extends far beyond dollars and cents. Consider these added reasons for pursuing a college education:

▶ **You'll learn to think critically and communicate better.** Here's what one student said about his college experience after he graduated: "It's not about what you major in or which classes you take. . . . It's really about learning to think and to communicate. Wherever you end up, you'll need to be able to analyze and solve problems—to figure out what needs to be done and do it."[1]

Education improves your ability to understand the world—to understand it as it is now and to prepare to understand it as it will be.

- ▶ **You'll be able to better deal with advances in knowledge and technology that are changing the world.** Genetic engineering . . . drugs to reduce forgetfulness . . . computers that respond to our thoughts. No one knows what the future will hold, but you can prepare for it through a college education. Education can provide you with the intellectual tools that you can apply regardless of the specific situation in which you find yourself.

- ▶ **You'll acquire skills and perspectives that will shape how you deal with new situations and challenges.** The only certainty about how your life will unfold is that you will be surprised at what is in store for you. College prepares you to deal with the unexpected that characterizes all our lives.

- ▶ **You'll be better prepared to live in a world of diversity.** The racial and ethnic composition of the United States is changing rapidly. Whatever your ethnicity, chances are you'll be working and living with people whose backgrounds, lifestyles, and ways of thinking may be entirely different from your own.

    You won't be prepared for the future unless you understand others and their cultural backgrounds—as well as how your own cultural background affects you.

- ▶ **You'll make learning a lifelong habit.** College isn't the end of your education. There's no job you'll have that won't change over time, and you'll be required to learn new skills. College starts you down the path to lifelong learning.

To help you attain these benefits, it's time to introduce you to a process that will help you achieve success, both in college and in life beyond: P.O.W.E.R. Learning.

≫LO 1-2 P.O.W.E.R. Learning: The Five Key Steps to Achieving Success

P.O.W.E.R. Learning itself is merely an acronym—a word formed from the first letters of a series of steps—that will help you take in, process, and make use of the information you'll acquire in college. It will help you achieve your goals, both while you are in college and after you graduate.

Prepare, **O**rganize, **W**ork, **E**valuate, and **R**ethink. That's it. It's a simple framework, but an effective one. Using the systematic framework that P.O.W.E.R. Learning provides (and that is illustrated in the P.O.W.E.R. Plan diagram) will increase your chances of success at any task, from writing a college paper to buying your weekly groceries to filling out a purchase order.

Keep this in mind: P.O.W.E.R. Learning isn't a product that you can simply pull down off the bookshelf and use without thinking. P.O.W.E.R. Learning is a process, and you are the only one who can make it succeed. Without your personal investment in the process, P.O.W.E.R. Learning consists of just words on paper.

Relax, though. You already know each of the elements of P.O.W.E.R. Learning, and you may discover that you are already putting this process, or parts of it, to work for you. You've applied and been accepted into college. You may also have held down a job, started a family, and paid your monthly bills. Each of these accomplishments required that you use P.O.W.E.R. Learning. What you'll be doing throughout this book is becoming more aware of these methods and how they can be used to help you in situations you will encounter in college and your career.

P.O.W.E.R. Learning
A system designed to help people achieve their goals, based on five steps: *Prepare, Organize, Work, Evaluate,* and *Rethink.*

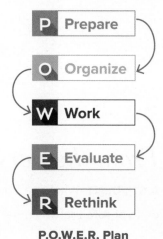

P.O.W.E.R. Plan

Everyone goes to school for his or her own reason. Gwen recently visited a friend in the hospital and was struck by how much she wanted to be a part of the health-care community. John has survived several rounds of layoffs at his job and wants to make himself more marketable.
(L) © Mint Images Limited/Alamy Stock Photo RF, (R) © Daniel Thistlethwai /Image Source, all rights reserved. RF

 **Prepare**

Chinese philosopher Lao Tzu said that travelers taking a long journey must begin with a single step.

But before they even take that first step, travelers need to know several things: what their destination is, how they're going to get there, how they'll know when they reach the destination, and what they'll do if they have trouble along the way. In the same way, you need to know where you're headed as you embark on the academic journeys involved in college. Whether it be a major, long-term task, such as landing a new and better job, or a more limited activity, such as getting ready to complete a paper due in the near future, you'll need to prepare for the journey.

Setting Goals

Before we seek to accomplish any task, all of us do some form of planning. The trouble is that most of the time such planning is done without conscious thinking, as if we are on autopilot. However, the key to success is to make sure that planning is systematic.

The best way to plan systematically is to use goal-setting strategies. In many cases, goals are clear and direct. It's obvious that our goal in washing dishes is to have the dishes end up clean. We know that our goal at the gas station is to fill the car's tank with gas. We go to the post office to buy stamps and mail letters.

Other goals are not so clear-cut. In fact, the more important the task—such as going to college—the more complicated our goals may be.

From the perspective of . . .

A STUDENT What goals did you set when you decided to go to school? What can you do to ensure that you meet these goals?

What's the best way to set appropriate goals? Here are some guidelines:

▶ **Set both long-term and short-term goals. Long-term goals** are aims relating to major accomplishments that take some time to achieve. **Short-term goals** are relatively limited steps you would take on the road to accomplishing your long-term goals. For example, one of the primary reasons you're in college is to achieve the long-term goal of helping your career. But to reach that goal, you have to accomplish a series of short-term goals, such as completing a set of required courses and earning your degree. Even these short-term goals can be broken down into shorter-term goals.

long-term goals
Aims relating to major accomplishments that take some time to achieve.

short-term goals
Relatively limited steps toward the accomplishment of long-term goals.

In order to complete a required course, for instance, you have to accomplish short-term goals, such as completing a paper, taking several tests, and so on. For practice in setting long- and short-term goals, complete **Try It! 2**, "What Are Your Goals?"

▶ **Make goals realistic and attainable.** Someone once said, "A goal without a plan is but a dream." We'd all like to win gold medals at the Olympics or be the CEO of Nike or write best-selling novels. Few of us are likely to achieve such goals.

Be honest with yourself. There is nothing wrong with having big dreams. But it is important to be realistically aware of all that it takes to achieve them. If our long-term goals are unrealistic and we don't achieve them, the big danger is that we may wrongly reason that we are inept and lack ability, then use this as an excuse for giving up. If goals are realistic, we can develop a plan to attain them, spurring us on to attain more.

▶ **State goals in terms of behavior that can be measured against current accomplishments.** Goals should represent some measurable change from a current set of circumstances. We want our behavior to change in some way that can usually be expressed in terms of numbers—to show an increase ("raise my grade point average 10 percent") or a decrease ("reduce wasted time by two hours each week") or to be maintained ("keep in touch with my out-of-town friends by sending four e-mail messages each month"), developed ("participate in one workshop on job interview skills"), or restricted ("reduce my cellphone expenses 10 percent by texting less").

▶ **Choose goals that involve behavior over which you have control.** We all want world peace and an end to poverty. Few of us have the resources or capabilities to bring either about. In contrast, it is realistic to want to work in small ways to help others, such as by volunteering at a local food bank.

▶ **Identify how your short-term goals fit with your long-term goals.** Your goals should not be independent of one another. Instead, they should fit together into a larger dream of who you want to be. Every once in a while, step back and consider how what you're doing today relates to the kind of career that you ultimately want to have.

◯ Organize

By determining where you want to go and expressing your goals in terms that can be measured, you have already made a lot of progress. But there's another step you must take on the road to success.

What Are Your Goals?

Before you begin any journey, you need to know where you are going. To plan your academic journey—and your later career—you first need to set goals. *Short-term goals* are relatively limited objectives that bring you closer to your ultimate goal. *Long-term goals* are aims relating to major accomplishments that take more time to achieve.

In this Try It!, think about your short- and long-term academic and career goals for a few minutes, and then list them. Because short-term goals are based on what you want to accomplish in the long term, first identify your long-term goals. Then list the short-term goals that will help you reach your long-term goals. An example is provided for the first goal:

Long-Term Goal #1 Get a college degree

   Related Short-Term Goals:

- Complete four courses with a grade of B or above each term
- _____
- _____
- _____
- _____

Long-Term Goal #2: _____

   Related Short-Term Goals:

- _____
- _____
- _____
- _____
- _____

Long-Term Goal #3: _____

   Related Short-Term Goals:

- _____
- _____
- _____
- _____
- _____

Long-Term Goal #4: _____

   Related Short-Term Goals:

- _____
- _____
- _____
- _____
- _____

Long-Term Goal #5: _____

   Related Short-Term Goals:

- _____
- _____
- _____
- _____
- _____

After you complete the chart, consider how easy or difficult it was to identify your long-term goals. How many of your long-term goals relate to college, and how many to your future career? Do any of your short-term goals relate to more than one long-term goal?

The second step in P.O.W.E.R. Learning is to organize the tools you'll need to accomplish your goals. Building on the goal-setting work you've undertaken in the preparation stage, it's time to determine the best way to accomplish the goals you've identified.

How do you do this? Suppose you've decided to paint a room in your house. Let's say that you've already determined the color you want and the kind of paint you need (the preparation step in P.O.W.E.R. Learning). The next stage involves buying the paint and brushes and preparing the room for being painted—all aspects of organizing for the task.

Similarly, your academic success will hinge to a large degree on the thoroughness of your organization for each academic task that you face. In fact, one of the biggest mistakes that students make in college is plunging into an academic project—studying for a test, writing a paper, or completing an online assignment—without being organized.

The Two Kinds of Organization: Physical and Mental

On a basic level is *physical organization,* involving the mechanical aspects of task completion. For instance, you need to ask yourself if you have the appropriate tools, such as a computer, Internet access, or a printer. Do you have a way to back up your files? Do you have the books and other materials you'll need to complete the assignment? Is there a library near your home that will be open when you need it? Do you have a comfortable place to work?

Mental organization is even more critical. Mental organization is accomplished by considering and reviewing the academic skills that you'll need to successfully complete the task at hand. You are an academic general in command of considerable forces; you will need to make sure your forces—the basic skills you have at your command—are at their peak of readiness.

For example, if you're working on a math assignment, you'll want to consider the basic math skills that you'll need and brush up on them. Just actively thinking about this will help you organize mentally. Similarly, you'd want to mentally review your knowledge of engine parts before beginning repair work. Why does producing mental organization matter? The answer is that it provides a context for when you actually begin to work. Organizing paves the way for better subsequent performance.

Too often students or workers on the job are in a hurry to meet a deadline and figure they had better just dive in and get it done. Organizing can actually *save* you time because you're less likely to be anxious and end up losing your way as you work to complete your task.

Much of this book is devoted to strategies for determining—*before* you begin work on a task—how to develop the mental tools for completing an assignment. However, as you'll see, all of these strategies share a common theme: Success comes not from a trial-and-error approach but from following a systematic plan for achievement. Of course, this does not mean that there will be no surprises along the way, nor that simple luck is never a factor in great accomplishments. But it does mean that we often can make our own luck through careful preparation and organization.

You're ready. The preliminaries are out of the way. You've prepared and you've organized. Now it's time to get started actually doing the work.

Looking at the Big Picture

It's natural to view college as a series of small tasks—classes to take, a certain number of pages to read each week, a few papers due during the term, quizzes and final exams to study for, and so on.

But such a perspective may lead you to miss what college, as a whole, is all about. Using the P.O.W.E.R. Learning framework can help you take the long view of your education, considering how it helps you achieve your long- and short-term goals for your professional and personal life (the *Prepare* step) and what you'll need to do to maximize your success (the *Organize* step). By preparing and organizing even before you take your first online class, you'll be able to consider what it is that you want to get out of college and how it fits into your life as a whole.

In some ways, work is the easy part because—if you conscientiously carried out the preparation and organization stage—you should know exactly where you're headed and what you need to do to get there.

It's not quite so easy, of course. How effectively you'll get down to the business at hand depends on many factors. Some may be out of your control. There may be a power outage that closes down the library or a massive traffic jam that delays your getting to work. But most factors are—or should be—under your control. Instead of getting down to work, you may find yourself thinking up "useful" things to do—like finally cleaning underneath the couch—or simply sitting captive in front of the TV. This kind of obstacle to work relates to motivation.

Developing a Growth Mindset

Do you think some people are born smart and are destined to be high achievers, while others—maybe even yourself—don't have enough intelligence to ever do really well in school?

If you believe this, you need to think again. Intelligence is something that is not fixed. Instead, it is fluid and flexible, and through hard work and effort, people can do better than they ever thought possible. In fact, the brain is like any muscle: The more you use it, the stronger it becomes.

growth mindset
A belief that people can increase their abilities and do better through hard work.

Students who hold a **growth mindset** believe that people can increase their abilities and do better through hard work. They challenge themselves to try to increase their success, even if at first they fail. They are more persistent in the face of obstacles, and they try harder.

Can you develop a growth mindset? The answer is yes. By telling yourself that success is the result of effort, not how smart you are, you are more likely to do better on tasks in the future. Remember, success is about analyzing the causes of your performance and thinking about how you might do things differently to bring about a better outcome. It's a matter of motivation.

Finding the Motivation to Work

"If only I could get more motivated, I'd do so much better with my _____" (insert *schoolwork, job, diet, exercising,* or the like—you fill in the blank).

All of us have said something like this at one time or another. We use the concept of **motivation**—or its lack—to explain why we just don't work hard at a task. But when we do that, we're fooling ourselves. We all have some motivation, that inner power and psychological energy that directs and fuels our behavior. Without any motivation, we'd never get out of bed in the morning.

motivation
The inner power and psychological energy that directs and fuels behavior.

We've also seen evidence of how strong our motivation can be. Perhaps you love to work out at the gym. Or maybe your love of music helped you learn to play the guitar, making practicing for hours a pleasure rather than a chore. Or perhaps you're a single parent, juggling work, school, and family, and you get up early every morning to make breakfast for your kids before they go off to school.

All of us are motivated. The key to success in the classroom and on the job is to tap into, harness, and direct that motivation.

If we assume that we already have all the motivation we need, P.O.W.E.R. Learning becomes a matter of turning the skills we already possess into a habit. It becomes a matter of redirecting our psychological energies toward the work we wish to accomplish.

In a sense, everything you'll encounter in this book can help you improve your use of the motivation that you already have. But there's a key concept that underlies the control of motivation—viewing success as a consequence of effort:

Effort ⟶ Success

Suppose, for example, you've gotten a good performance review from your new supervisor. The boss beams at you as she discusses your results. How do you feel?

You will undoubtedly be pleased, of course. But at the same time you might think to yourself, "Don't get cocky. It was just luck." Or perhaps you explain your success by thinking, "The new boss just doesn't know me very well."

If you often think this way, you're cheating yourself. Using this kind of reasoning when you succeed, instead of patting yourself on the back and thinking with satisfaction, "All my hard work really paid off," is sure to undermine your future success.

A great deal of psychological research has shown that thinking you have no control over what happens to you sends a powerful and damaging message to your self-esteem—that you are powerless to change things. Just think of how different it feels to say to yourself, "Wow, I worked at it and did it," as compared with "I lucked out" or "It was so easy that anybody could have done it."

"The function of the university is not simply to teach bread-winning, or to furnish teachers for the public schools or to be a center of polite society: it is, above all, to be the organ of that fine adjustment between real life and the growing knowledge of life, an adjustment which forms the secret of civilization."

W. E. B. DuBois, author, *The Souls of Black Folk*, 1903.

In the same way, we can delude ourselves when we try to explain our failures. People who see themselves as the victims of circumstance may tell themselves, "I'm just not smart enough," when they don't do well on an academic task. Or they might say, "My co-workers don't have children to take care of."

The way in which we view the causes of success and failure is, in fact, directly related to our success. Students who generally see effort and hard work as the reason behind their performance usually do better in college. Workers who see their job performance in this way usually do better in their careers. It's not hard to see why: When such individuals are working on a task, they feel that the greater the effort they put forth, the greater their chances of success. So they work harder. They believe that they have control over their success, and if they fail, they believe they can do better in the future.

There are always things we can use as excuses for our own failures. Can you think of a time when you shifted blame away from yourself for a failure? Was it a reasonable course of action? Why or why not?

© Radius Images/Alamy Stock Photo RF

Here are some tips for keeping your motivation alive, so you can work with your full energy behind you:

▶ **Take responsibility for your failures—and successes.** When you do poorly on a test, don't blame the teacher, the textbook, or a job that kept you from studying. When you miss a work deadline, don't blame your boss or your incompetent co-workers. Analyze the situation, and see how you could have changed what you did to be more successful in the future. At the same time, when you're successful, think of the things you did to bring about that success.

▶ **Think positively.** Assume that the strengths that you have will allow you to succeed and that, if you have difficulty, you can figure out what to do, or get the help you need to eventually succeed.

▶ **Accept that you can't control everything.** Seek to understand which things can be changed and which cannot. You might be able to get an extension on a paper due date, but you are probably not going to be excused from a college-wide requirement.

To further explore the causes of academic success, consider the questions in **Try It! 3**.

E Evaluate

"Great, I'm done with the work. Now I can move on."

It's natural to feel relief when you've finished the work necessary to fulfill the basic requirements of a task. After all, if you've written the five double-spaced pages required for an assignment or completed a difficult task at work, why shouldn't you heave a sigh of relief and just hand in your work?

The answer is that if you stop at this point, you'll almost be guaranteed a mediocre result. Do you think Shakespeare dashed off the first draft of *Hamlet* and, without another glance, sent it to the Globe Theater for production? Do professional athletes just put in the bare minimum of practice to get ready for a big game? Think of one of your favorite songs. Do you think the composer wrote it in one sitting and then performed it in a concert?

In every case, the answer is no. Even the greatest creation does not emerge in perfect form, immediately meeting all the goals of its producer. Consequently, the fourth step in the P.O.W.E.R. process is **evaluation**, which consists of determining how well the product or activity we have created matches our goals for it. Let's consider some steps to follow in evaluating what you've accomplished:

▶ **Take a moment to congratulate yourself and feel some satisfaction.** Whether it's been studying for a test, writing a paper, completing a report, or completing a hard task at work, you've done something important. You've moved from ground zero to a spot that's closer to your goal.

▶ **Compare what you've accomplished with the goals you're seeking to achieve.** Think back to the goals, both short-term and long-term, that you're seeking to achieve. How closely does what you've done match what you're

evaluation

An assessment of the match between a product or activity and the goals it was intended to meet.

Examining the Causes of Success and Failure

Consider the following situations:

1. Although he made a few more sales calls than normal, Jack is told by his boss that he has failed to bring in any new business. Jack is disgusted with himself and says, "I'll never be good at attracting new clients. I'd better just give up and concentrate on the clients I already have."

2. Anne goes on a sales call and lands a major piece of new business. She is happy, but when her boss tells her the company as a whole has brought in lots of new business that month, she decides she only succeeded because the task was so easy.

3. Sales in Chen's division are slow. Because he isn't doing as well as he expected, he vows to perform better. He spends extra time researching and talking with potential clients, but sales increase only slightly. Distressed, he considers quitting his job because he thinks that he'll never be successful in sales.

Now consider the following questions about each of the situations:

1. What did each salesperson conclude was the main cause of his or her performance?
2. What effect does this conclusion seem to have on the salesperson?
3. Taking an outsider's point of view, what would *you* think was probably the main cause of the salespeople's performance?
4. What advice would you give each salesperson?

Now consider these broader questions:

1. What are the most important reasons that some people are more professionally successful than others?
2. How much does ability determine success? How much does luck determine success? How much do circumstances determine success?
3. If someone performs poorly at a job, what are the possible reasons for his or her performance? If someone performs well, what are the possible reasons for his or her performance? Is it harder to find reasons for good performance than for poor performance? Why?

aiming to do? For instance, if your short-term goal is to complete a math problem set with no errors, you'll need to check over the work carefully to make sure you've made no mistakes.

▶ **Have an out-of-body experience: Evaluate your accomplishments as if you were a respected mentor from your past.** If you've written a paper, reread it from the perspective of a favorite teacher. If you've prepared a report, imagine you're presenting it to a boss who taught you a lot. Think about the comments you'd give if you were this person.

▶ **Evaluate what you've done as if you were your current instructor or supervisor.** Now exchange bodies and minds again. This time, consider what you're doing from the perspective of the person who gave you the assignment. How would he or she react to what you've done? Have you followed the assignment to the letter? Is there anything you've missed?

▶ **Based on your evaluation, revise your work.** If you're honest with yourself, it's unlikely that your first work will satisfy you. So go back to *Work* and revise what you've done. But don't think of it as a step back: Revisions you make as a consequence of your evaluation bring you closer to your final goal. This is a case where going back moves you forward.

They thought they had it perfect. But they were wrong.

In fact, it was a $1.5 billion mistake—a blunder on a grand scale. The finely ground mirror of the Hubble space telescope, designed to provide an unprecedented glimpse into the vast reaches of the universe, was not so finely ground after all.

Despite an elaborate system of evaluation designed to catch any flaws, there was a tiny blemish in the mirror that was not detected until the telescope had been launched into space and started to send back blurry photographs. By then, it seemed too late to fix the mirror.

Or was it? NASA engineers rethought the problem for months, devising, and then discarding, one potential fix after another. Finally, after bringing a fresh eye to the situation, they formulated a daring solution that involved sending a team of astronauts into space. Once there, a space-walking Mr. Goodwrench would install several new mirrors in the telescope, which could refocus the light and compensate for the original flawed mirror.

Although the engineers could not be certain that the $629 million plan would work, it seemed like a good solution, at least on paper. It was not until the first photos were beamed back to Earth, though, that NASA knew their solution was A-OK. These photos were spectacular.

It took months of reconsideration before NASA scientists could figure out what went wrong and devise a solution to the problem they faced. Their approach exemplifies—on a grand scale—the final step in P.O.W.E.R. Learning: rethinking.

To *rethink* what you've accomplished earlier means bringing a fresh—and clear—eye to what you've done. It involves using **critical thinking**, thinking that involves reanalyzing, questioning, and challenging our underlying assumptions. Whereas evaluation means considering how well what we have done matches our initial goals, rethinking means reconsidering not only the outcome of our efforts but also our goals and the ideas and the process we've used to reach them. Critically rethinking what you've done involves analyzing and synthesizing ideas, and seeing the connections between different concepts.

Rethinking involves considering whether our initial goals are practical and realistic or if they require modification. It also entails asking yourself what you would do differently if you could do it over again.

We'll be considering critical thinking throughout this book, examining specific strategies in every chapter. For the moment, the following steps provide a general framework for using critical thinking to rethink what you've accomplished:

▶ **Review how you've accomplished the task.** Consider the approach and strategies you've used. What seemed to work best? Do they suggest any alternatives that might work better the next time?

▶ **Question the outcome.** Take a "big picture" look at what you have accomplished. Are you pleased and satisfied? Is there something you've somehow missed?

▶ **Identify your underlying assumptions; then challenge them.** Consider the assumptions you made in initially approaching the task. Are these underlying

critical thinking
A process involving reanalysis, questioning, and challenge of underlying assumptions.

P.O.W.E.R. Learning and the World of Work

As we've discussed, the P.O.W.E.R. Learning process has applications in your education and on the job. In Career Connections boxes, we'll highlight ways in which the principles we're discussing can help you excel in the workplace. Take a look at these "help wanted" advertisements and online postings. They illustrate the importance of the components of P.O.W.E.R. Learning in a wide variety of fields.

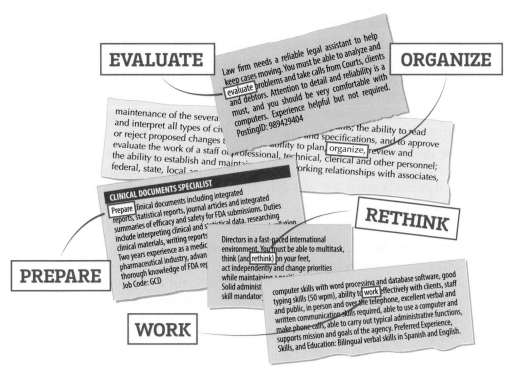

EVALUATE

Law firm needs a reliable legal assistant to help keep cases moving. You must be able to analyze and [evaluate] problems and take calls from Courts, clients and debtors. Attention to detail and reliability is a must, and you should be very comfortable with computers. Experience helpful but not required. PostingID: 989429404

ORGANIZE

maintenance of the severa... and interpret all types of civ... or reject proposed changes t... evaluate the work of a staff o... the ability to establish and mainta... federal, state, local a...

...rns; the ability to read ...and specifications, and to approve ...ability to plan, [organize,] review and ...professional, technical, clerical and other personnel; ...orking relationships with associates,

CLINICAL DOCUMENTS SPECIALIST

[Prepare] clinical documents including integrated reports, statistical reports, journal articles and integrated summaries of efficacy and safety for FDA submissions. Duties include interpreting clinical and s... clinical materials, writing reports... Two years experience as a medic... pharmaceutical industry, advan... thorough knowledge of FDA re... Job Code: GCD

RETHINK

Directors in a fast-paced international environment. You must be able to multitask, think (and [rethink]) on your feet, act independently and change priorities while maintaining a... Solid administ... skill mandator...

PREPARE

WORK

computer skills with word processing and database software, good typing skills (50 wpm), ability to [work] effectively with clients, staff and public, in person and over the telephone, excellent verbal and written communication skills required, able to use a computer and make phone calls, able to carry out typical administrative functions, supports mission and goals of the agency. Preferred Experience, Skills, and Education: Bilingual verbal skills in Spanish and English.

assumptions reasonable? If you had used different assumptions, would the result have been similar or different?

▶ **Consider alternatives rejected earlier.** You've likely discarded possible strategies and approaches prior to completing your task. Now's the time to think about those approaches once more and determine if they might have been more appropriate than the road you've followed.

▶ **Ask yourself: What would I do differently if I had the opportunity to try things again?** It's not too late to change course.

▶ **Finally, reconsider your initial goals.** Are they achievable and realistic? Do your goals, and the strategies you used to attain them, need to be modified? Critically rethinking the objectives and goals that underlie your efforts is often the most effective route to success.

Completing the P.O.W.E.R. Process

The rethinking step of P.O.W.E.R. Learning is meant to help you understand your process of work and improve the final product if necessary. But mostly it is meant to help you grow, to become better at whatever it is you've been doing. Like a painter looking at his or her finished work, you may see a spot here or there to touch up, but don't destroy the canvas. Perfectionism can be as paralyzing as laziness. Keep in mind these key points:

▶ **Know that there's always another day.** Your future success does not depend on any single assignment, paper, or test. Don't fall victim to self-defeating thoughts such as "If I don't do well on this test, I'll never graduate" or "Everything is riding on this one project." Nonsense. In school, on the job, and in life, there is almost always an opportunity to recover from a failure.

▶ **Realize that deciding when to stop work is often as hard as getting started.** Knowing when you have put in enough time studying for a test or have revised a paper sufficiently or have reviewed your figures adequately on a math problem set is as much a key to success as properly preparing. If you've carefully evaluated what you've done and seen that there's a close fit between your goals and your work, it's time to stop work and move on.

▶ **Use the strategies that already work for you.** Although the P.O.W.E.R. Learning framework provides a proven approach to attaining success, employing it does not mean that you should abandon strategies that have brought you success in the past. Using multiple approaches, and personalizing them, is the surest road to success.

As much as anything else, doing well in college and on the job depends on an awareness *of yourself*. What are your strengths? What are your weaknesses? What do you do better than most people, and what are your areas for improvement? If you can answer such questions, you'll be able to harness the best of your talents and to anticipate challenges you might face. The next section will aid you in understanding yourself better by helping you identify your personal learning styles.

≫ LO 1-3 Discovering Your Learning Styles

Members of the Trukese people, a small group of islanders in the South Pacific, often sail hundreds of miles on the open sea. They manage this feat with none of the navigational equipment used by Western sailors. No compass. No chronometer. No sextant. They don't even sail in a straight line. Instead, they zigzag back and forth. Yet they almost always reach their destination with precision.

Trukese sailors can't really explain how they learned to navigate or explain the processes that they use, but clearly they are successful sailors.

The case of Trukese sailors vividly illustrates how there are different ways to learn and to achieve our goals.

Each of us has preferred ways of learning, approaches that work best for us. Our success is dependent not just on how well we learn, but on *how* we learn.

A **learning style** reflects a person's preferred manner of acquiring, using, and thinking about knowledge. We don't have just one learning style but a variety of styles. Some involve our preferences regarding the way information is presented to us, some relate to how we think and learn most readily, and some relate to how our personality traits affect our performance. An awareness of your learning styles will help you in college by allowing you to study and learn course materials more effectively. On the job, knowing your learning styles will help you master new skills and techniques, ensuring you can keep up with changing office practices or an evolving industry.

learning style
One's preferred manner of acquiring, using, and thinking about knowledge.

We'll start by considering the preferences we have for how we initially perceive information.

What Is Your Preferred Receptive Learning Style?

One of the most basic aspects of learning styles concerns the way in which we initially receive information from our sense organs—our **receptive learning style**. People have different strengths in terms of how they most effectively process information and which of their senses they prefer to use in learning. Specifically, there are four different types of receptive learning styles:

▶ **Read/write learning style.** If you have a **read/write learning style**, you prefer information that is presented visually in a written format. You feel most comfortable reading, and you may recall the spelling of a word by thinking of how the word looks. You probably learn best when you have the opportunity to read about a concept.

▶ **Visual/graphic learning style.** Those with a **visual/graphic learning style** learn most effectively when material is presented visually in a diagram or picture. You might recall the structure of an engine or a part of the human body by reviewing a picture in your mind. Students with visual learning styles find it easier to see things in their mind's eye—to visualize a task or concept.

▶ **Auditory/verbal learning style.** Have you ever asked a friend to help you put something together by having her read the directions to you while you worked? If you did, you may have an **auditory/verbal learning style**. People with auditory/verbal learning styles prefer listening to explanations. They love podcasts and audio guides because they can easily take in the information that is being talked about.

▶ **Tactile/kinesthetic learning style.** Those with a **tactile/kinesthetic learning style** prefer to learn by doing—touching, manipulating objects, and doing things. For instance, some people enjoy the act of writing because of the feel of a computer keyboard—the tactile equivalent of thinking out loud. Or they may find that it helps them to make a three-dimensional model to understand a new idea.

To get a sense of your own receptive learning style, complete **Try It! 4**. But remember, having a particular receptive learning style simply means that it will be easier to learn material that is presented in that style. It does not mean you cannot learn any other way!

receptive learning style
The way in which we initially receive information.

read/write learning style
A style that involves a preference for written material, favoring reading over hearing and touching.

visual/graphic learning style
A style that favors material presented visually in a diagram or picture.

auditory/verbal learning style
A style that favors listening as the best approach to learning.

tactile/kinesthetic learning style
A style that involves learning by touching, manipulating objects, and doing things.

From the perspective of . . .

A MEDICAL ASSISTANT You shouldn't see your learning style as a limitation. Repeating instructions aloud as a nursing assistant is one way for auditory learners to ensure they are comprehending instructions. How can you adapt your learning style in multiple career settings?

What's Your Receptive Learning Style?

Read each of the following statements and rank them in terms of their usefulness to you as learning approaches. Base your ratings on your personal experiences and preferences, using the following scale:

1 = Not at all useful

2 = Not very useful

3 = Neutral

4 = Somewhat useful

5 = Very useful

	1	2	3	4	5
1. Studying alone					
2. Studying pictures and diagrams to understand complex ideas					
3. Listening to class lectures					
4. Performing a process myself rather than reading or hearing about it					
5. Learning a complex procedure by reading written directions					
6. Watching and listening to film, computer, or video presentations					
7. Listening to a book or lecture on tape					
8. Doing lab work					
9. Studying teachers' handouts and lecture notes					
10. Studying in a quiet room					
11. Taking part in group discussions					
12. Taking part in hands-on demonstrations					
13. Taking notes and studying them later					
14. Creating flash cards and using them as a study and review tool					
15. Memorizing and recalling how words are spelled by spelling them "out loud" in my head					

(continued)

Receptive learning styles have implications for effective studying in college or learning new skills on the job:

If you have a read/write style, consider writing out summaries of information, highlighting and underlining written material, and using flash cards. Transform diagrams and math formulas into words.

If you have a visual/graphic style, devise diagrams and charts. Translate words into symbols and figures.

16. Writing down key facts and important points as a tool for remembering them					
17. Recalling how to spell a word by seeing it in my head					
18. Underlining or highlighting important facts or passages in my reading					
19. Saying things out loud when I'm studying					
20. Recalling how to spell a word by "writing" it invisibly in the air or on a surface					
21. Learning new information by reading about it in a book					
22. Using a map to find an unknown place					
23. Working in a study group					
24. Finding a place I've been to once by just going there without directions					

Scoring: The statements cycle through the four receptive learning styles in this order: (1) read/write; (2) visual/graphic; (3) auditory/verbal; and (4) tactile/kinesthetic.

To find your primary learning style, disregard your 1, 2, and 3 ratings. Add up your 4 and 5 ratings for each learning style (i.e., a "4" equals 4 points and a "5" equals 5 points). Use the following chart to link the statements to the learning styles and to write down your summed ratings:

Learning Style	Statements	Total (Sum) of Rating Points
Read/write	1, 5, 9, 13, 17, and 21	
Visual/graphic	2, 6, 10, 14, 18, and 22	
Auditory/verbal	3, 7, 11, 15, 19, and 23	
Tactile/kinesthetic	4, 8, 12, 16, 20, and 24	

The total of your rating points for any given style will range from a low of 0 to a high of 30. The highest total indicates your main receptive learning style. Don't be surprised if you have a mixed style, in which two or more styles receive similar ratings.

If you have an auditory/verbal style, recite material out loud when trying to learn it.

If you have a tactile/kinesthetic style, incorporate movement into your study. Trace diagrams, build models, arrange flash cards and move them around. Keep yourself active when learning, taking notes, drawing charts, and jotting down key concepts.

Multiple Intelligences: Showing Strength in Different Domains

Do you feel much more comfortable walking through the woods than navigating city streets? Are you an especially talented musician? Is reading and using a complicated map second nature to you?

If so, in each case you may be demonstrating a special and specific kind of intelligence. According to psychologist Howard Gardner, rather than asking, "How smart are you?" we should be asking a different question: "How are you smart?" To answer the latter question, Gardner has developed a *theory of multiple intelligences* that offers a unique approach to understanding learning styles and preferences.

The multiple intelligences view says that we have eight different forms of intelligence, each relatively independent of the others and linked to a specific kind of information processing in our brains:

▶ *Logical-mathematical intelligence* involves skills in problem solving and scientific thinking.

▶ *Linguistic intelligence* is linked to the production and use of language.

▶ *Spatial intelligence* relates to skills involving spatial configurations, such as those used by artists and architects.

▶ *Interpersonal intelligence* is found in learners with particularly strong skills involving interacting with others, such as sensitivity to the moods, temperaments, motivations, and intentions of others.

▶ *Intrapersonal intelligence* relates to a particularly strong understanding of the internal aspects of oneself and having access to one's own feelings and emotions.

▶ *Musical intelligence* involves skills relating to music.

▶ *Bodily kinesthetic intelligence* relates to skills in using the whole body or portions of it in the solution of problems or in the construction of products or displays, exemplified by dancers, athletes, actors, and surgeons.

▶ *Naturalist intelligence* involves exceptional abilities in identifying and classifying patterns in nature.

All of us have the same eight kinds of intelligence, although in different degrees, and they form the core of our learning styles and preferences. These separate intelligences do not operate in isolation.

Instead, any activity involves several kinds of intelligence working together. And, as Gardner points out, these eight intelligences may be only scratching the

Steven Spielberg is a self-admitted visual learner. How can you use your own learning style to influence your career decisions?
© James Devaney/WireImage/Getty Images

In any given day, graphic designers must be able to create amazing visuals and also do the requisite paperwork to accompany their projects. Which types of intelligence would be most important to succeed in this career?
© Rawpixel Ltd/iStock/Getty Images Plus/Getty Images RF

surface of what our capabilities are. He suggests there may be even more intelligences that shape how we interact with the world. For example, there may be an "existential intelligence," which involves identifying and thinking about the fundamental questions of human existence.

Personality Styles

Our learning styles are also influenced by our personality. Are you likely to perform at an open mic night at a café? Or is the idea of getting on a stage totally lacking in appeal (if not completely terrifying)? Do you relate to the world around you primarily through careful planning or by spontaneously reacting?

According to the rationale of the *Myers-Briggs Type Indicator,* a questionnaire frequently used in business and organizational settings to place people in 1 of 16 categories, personality type plays a key role in determining how we react to different situations. Specifically, we work best in situations in which others—students, instructors, or co-workers—share our preferences and in which our personality is most suited to the particular task on which we are working. Four major personality dimensions are critical. Although we'll describe the extremes of each dimension, keep in mind that most of us fall somewhere between the end points of each dimension.

▶ **Introverts versus extraverts.** A key difference between introverts and extraverts is whether they enjoy working with others. Independence is a key characteristic of introverted learners. They enjoy working alone and they are less affected by how others think and behave. In contrast, extraverts are outgoing and more affected by the behavior and thinking of others. They enjoy working with others, and they are energized by having other people around.

▶ **Intuitors versus sensors.** Intuitors enjoy solving problems and being creative. They get impatient with details, preferring to make leaps of judgment, and they enjoy the challenge of solving problems and taking a big-picture approach. People categorized as sensors, on the other hand, prefer a concrete, logical approach in which they can carefully analyze the facts of the situation. Although they are good with details, they sometimes miss the big picture.

▶ **Thinkers versus feelers.** Thinkers prefer logic over emotion. They reach decisions and solve problems by systematically analyzing a situation. In contrast, feeling types rely more on their emotional responses. They are aware of others and their feelings, and they are influenced by their personal values and attachments to others.

▶ **Perceivers and judgers.** Before drawing a conclusion, perceivers attempt to gather as much information as they can. Because they are open to multiple perspectives and appreciate all sides of an issue, they sometimes have difficulty completing a task. Judgers, in comparison, are quick and decisive. They like to set goals, accomplish them, and then move on to the next task.

The Origins of Our Learning Styles

For many of us, our learning style preferences result from the kind of processing our brain "specializes" in. **Left-brain processing** concentrates more on tasks requiring verbal competence, such as speaking, reading, thinking, and reasoning. Information is processed sequentially, one bit at a time.

On the other hand, **right-brain processing** tends to concentrate more on the processing of information in nonverbal domains, such as the understanding of spatial relationships, recognition of patterns and drawings, music, and emotional

left-brain processing
Information processing primarily performed by the left hemisphere of the brain, focusing on tasks requiring verbal competence, such as speaking, reading, thinking, and reasoning; information is processed sequentially, one bit at a time.

right-brain processing
Information processing primarily performed by the right hemisphere of the brain, focusing on information in nonverbal domains, such as the understanding of spatial relationships and recognition of patterns and drawings, music, and emotional expression.

expression. Furthermore, the right hemisphere tends to process information globally, considering it as a whole. Consequently, people who naturally tend toward right-brain processing might prefer visual/graphic learning styles.

Here are some key facts to remember about learning, personality, and processing styles:

▶ **You have a variety of styles.** As you can see in the summary of different categories of styles in **Table 1.1**, there are several types of styles. For any given task or challenge, some types of styles may be more relevant than others.

table 1.1 Learning, Personality, and Processing Styles

All of us have particular learning, personality, and processing styles that we tend to rely on. At the same time, we also have capabilities in less-preferred styles. So, for example, although you may be primarily a read/write learner, you have the capacity to use auditory/verbal and tactile/kinesthetic approaches. Note in particular that the four categories of personality styles are considered independent of one another. For instance, you may be an extravert and at the same time a sensor, a feeler, and a judger. Furthermore, although the "Using the Style" column suggests ways that those with a particular style can make the most of that style, you should also try strategies that work for styles different from your own.

Category	Type	Description	Using the Style[2]
Receptive Learning Styles	Read/write	A style that involves a preference for material in a written format, favoring reading over hearing and touching.	Read and rewrite material; take notes and rewrite them; organize material into tables; transform diagrams and math formulas into words.
	Visual/ graphic	A style that favors material presented visually in a diagram or picture.	Use figures and drawings; visualize material; translate words into symbols and figures.
	Auditory/ verbal	A style in which the learner favors listening as the best approach.	Recite material out loud; consider how words sound; study different languages; tape-record training sessions.
	Tactile/ kinesthetic	A style that involves learning by touching, manipulating objects, and doing things.	Incorporate movement into studying; trace figures and drawings with your finger; create models; make flash cards and move them around; keep active during meetings, taking notes, drawing charts, jotting down key concepts.
Multiple Intelligences	Logical- mathematical	Strengths in problem solving and scientific thinking.	Express information mathematically or in formulas.
	Linguistic	Strengths in the production and use of language.	Write out notes and summarize information in words; construct stories about material.
	Spatial	Strengths involving spatial configurations, such as those used by artists and architects.	Build charts, graphs, and flowcharts.
	Interpersonal	Found in learners with particularly strong skills involving interacting with others, such as sensitivity to the moods, temperaments, motivations, and intentions of others.	Work with others in groups.

Category	Type	Description	Using the Style[2]
	Intrapersonal	Strengths in understanding the internal aspects of oneself and having access to one's own feelings and emotions.	Build on your prior experiences and feelings about the world; use your originality.
	Musical	Strengths relating to music.	Write a song or lyrics to help remember material.
	Bodily kinesthetic	Strengths in using the whole body or portions of it in the solution of problems or in the construction of products or displays, exemplified by dancers, athletes, actors, and surgeons.	Use movement in studying; build models.
	Naturalist	Exceptional strengths in identifying and classifying patterns in nature.	Use analogies based on nature.
Personality Styles	Introvert versus extravert	Independence is a key characteristic of introverted learners, who enjoy working alone and are less affected by how others think and behave. In contrast, extraverts are outgoing and more affected by the behavior and thinking of others. They enjoy working with others.	Experiment with working in groups compared with working by yourself; consider your performance collaborating compared with working on your own.
	Intuitor versus sensor	Intuitive people enjoy solving problems and being creative, often taking a big-picture approach. Sensors, on the other hand, prefer a concrete, logical approach in which they can carefully analyze the facts of the situation.	For intuitors, reflect on the personal meaning of material and seek out tasks that involve creativity. For sensors, seek out concrete tasks that involve the application of logical principles.
	Thinker versus feeler	Thinkers prefer logic over emotion, reaching decisions through rational analysis. In contrast, feelers rely more on their emotions and are influenced by their personal values and attachments to others.	Thinkers should seek to systematically analyze situations, attempting to identify patterns. For feelers, use emotional responses to reflect on material.
	Perceiver versus judger	Before drawing a conclusion, perceivers attempt to gather as much information as they can and are open to multiple perspectives. Judgers, in comparison, are quick and decisive, enjoying setting goals and accomplishing them.	Perceivers organize material sequentially and into component parts; for judgers, goal setting facilitates learning.
Brain Processing Styles	Left-brain processing	Information is processed in a way that focuses on tasks requiring verbal competence, such as speaking, reading, thinking, and reasoning; information is processed sequentially, one bit at a time.	Organize material logically; identify patterns; make tables of key information; break material into component parts.
	Right-brain processing	Information is processed in a way that focuses on information in nonverbal domains, such as the understanding of spatial relationships, recognition of patterns and drawings, music, and emotional expression.	Identify patterns; use graphs and drawings; read aloud; create models.

Furthermore, success is possible even when there is a mismatch between what you need to accomplish and your own pattern of preferred styles. It may take more work, but learning to deal with situations that require you to use less-preferred styles is important for college and your career.

▶ **Your style reflects your preferences regarding which abilities you like to use—not the abilities themselves.** Styles are related to our preferences and the mental approaches we like to use. You may prefer to learn tactilely, but that in itself doesn't guarantee that the products that you create tactilely will be good. You still have to put in work!

▶ **Your style will change over the course of your life.** You can learn new styles and expand the range of learning experiences in which you feel perfectly comfortable. In fact, you can conceive of this book as one long lesson in learning styles because it provides you with strategies for learning more effectively in a variety of ways.

▶ **You should work on improving your less-preferred styles.** Although it may be tempting, don't always make choices that increase your exposure to preferred styles and decrease your practice with less-preferred styles. The more you use approaches for which you have less of a preference, the better you'll be at developing the skills associated with those styles.

▶ **Work cooperatively with others who have different styles.** If your supervisor asks you to work cooperatively, seek out co-workers who have styles that are different from yours. Not only will working with people with differing styles help you achieve collective success, but you can also learn from observing others' approaches to tackling tasks.

Learning about Learning: The Theories That Explain How You Learn

Learning styles reflect how each of us prefers to study and approach new information that we encounter in our online classes. But all of us are affected by some basic processes that underlie learning.

learning theory
A broad explanation about how one learns.

Researchers have developed a number of **learning theories**, which are broad explanations about how we learn. Each of these theories takes a different approach and looks at somewhat different factors that help us to learn. Understanding the theories behind learning will help you study, remember information, and ultimately be a better learner. We'll consider the three main approaches.

Operant Conditioning Approaches: The Reinforcement behind Learning

Very good . . . What a clever idea . . . Fantastic . . . I agree . . . Excellent . . . Super . . . Great point . . . This is the best paper you've ever written . . . You are really getting the hang of it . . . I'm impressed . . . A+

operant conditioning
Learning in which behavior is modified by the presence of a reinforcer.

Did you ever wonder why we love to be praised? It turns out that positive affirmations of this sort underlie a type of learning known as operant conditioning, which is the basis for many of the most important kinds of learning.

reinforcer
A thing that increases the probability that a behavior will occur again.

Operant conditioning is learning in which a behavior is made more or less likely to recur regularly because of the presence of a reinforcer. **Reinforcers** are things that increase the probability that a behavior will occur again. If you study hard for a test and are rewarded with a high grade, the high grade serves as a reinforcer. Operant conditioning theory tells us that you are more likely to study hard in the future because of the reward you received. On the other hand, if you party hard the night before a test and receive a low grade, operant conditioning theory suggests that in the future you will avoid partying before a test.

Cognitive Approaches: The Thoughts behind Learning

Some learning theorists focus on the thought processes that underlie learning. According to cognitive approaches to learning, our cognitions (or thoughts) shape the way we learn. In particular, they look at the importance of observational learning, in which we learn by watching, and imitating, the behavior of other people.

Observational learning takes place in four steps:

1. Paying attention and perceiving the most critical features of another person's behavior

2. Remembering the behavior

3. Reproducing the action

4. Being motivated to learn and carry out the behavior

Not all behavior that we witness is learned or carried out. Whether we later imitate someone else depends, in part, on what eventually happens to that person as a result of the behavior.

If we observe a friend who studies more frequently than we do and notice that she receives higher grades, we are more apt to imitate her behavior than if her studying leads to nothing more than a sharp decline in her social life and an increase in fatigue. Models who are seen receiving reinforcement for their actions are more likely to be mimicked than those who are observed receiving punishment.

Classical Conditioning Approaches: Does the Name Pavlov Ring a Bell?

Ivan Pavlov was a Russian scientist who discovered, quite accidentally, one of the basic kinds of learning, called classical conditioning. In studying salivation in dogs, he found that sometimes the mere sight of the person who normally brought the dog's food, or even the sound of that person's footsteps, was enough to produce salivation in the dogs.

Pavlov's genius lay in his ability to recognize the implications of this discovery. He saw that the dogs were responding not only on the basis of a biological need (hunger) but also as a result of learning—or, as it came to be called, classical conditioning. **Classical conditioning** is a type of learning in which a neutral stimulus (such as someone's footsteps) comes to elicit a response after being paired with a different stimulus (such as food) that naturally brings about that response.

To demonstrate classical conditioning, Pavlov (1927) attached a tube to the salivary gland of a dog, allowing him to measure precisely the dog's salivation. He then rang a bell and, just a few seconds later, presented the dog with meat.

classical conditioning
A type of learning in which a neutral stimulus elicits a response after being paired with a natural stimulus.

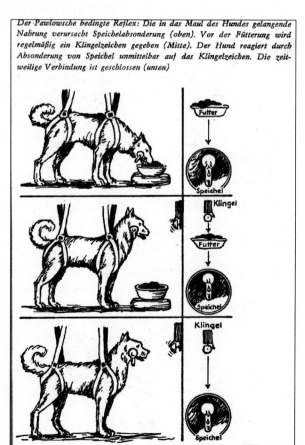

Der Pawlowsche bedingte Reflex: Die in das Maul des Hundes gelangende Nahrung verursacht Speichelabsonderung (oben). Vor der Fütterung wird regelmäßig ein Klingelzeichen gegeben (Mitte). Der Hund reagiert durch Absonderung von Speichel unmittelbar auf das Klingelzeichen. Die zeitweilige Verbindung ist geschlossen (unten)

Classical conditioning is just one of many types of learning.
© Interfoto/Personalities/Alamy Stock Photo

This pairing occurred repeatedly and was carefully planned so that each time exactly the same amount of time elapsed between the presentation of the bell and the meat. At first the dog would salivate only when the meat was presented, but soon it began to salivate at the sound of the bell. In fact, even when Pavlov stopped presenting the meat, the dog still salivated after hearing the sound. The dog had been classically conditioned to salivate to the bell.

But what about humans? In fact, Pavlov's discovery of classical conditioning has some very practical implications for how we come to associate various stimuli with responses. For example, you may not go to a dentist as often as you should because of previous associations of dentists with pain. Similarly, we may come to associate academic tests with negative emotions and anxiety, which can hinder our performance.

Why Learning Theories Matter

Although the basics of the three main learning theories are somewhat abstract, each has important practical implications for helping you to learn better. For example, operant conditioning suggests that rewarding yourself with periodic breaks while you study will make your study sessions more productive because the breaks act as a reinforcer. Similarly, using cognitive approaches to learning, you might watch the behavior of other students who have been successful and try to imitate their study habits. Finally, classical conditioning, which focuses on learning through associations, suggests that studying in the room where you'll later be taking a test will help you to perform better on the test because it will help trigger memories of the material you studied earlier—an idea that research has proven correct.

If you are wondering which of the theories is "best," you're asking the wrong question. Each of the theories takes a different approach and focuses on different aspects of learning, in much the same way that we can take multiple routes on a map to the same location. Understanding each of the learning theories, along with knowledge of your preferred learning styles, will help you develop your own personal learning system that can help you become a more successful student.

Speaking *of* Success

Courtesy of Yajaira Gijon

NAME: **Yajaira Gijon**

SCHOOL: **Columbia College Chicago, Chicago, Illinois**

As the first in her family to attend college, Yajaira Gijon faced unique challenges. The daughter of immigrants, it took her 10 years to achieve her goal of attaining a degree.

"I didn't pay much attention in high school, and my grades suffered," Gijon said. "But I pulled myself together after the death of a friend and decided to go to community college. My parents were surprised but very supportive."

Because Gijon worked full time at a graphics design company, she went to school at night. She could take only a few courses each semester.

After four years of part-time study at her community college, she decided to pursue a fine arts degree at Columbia College Chicago. It wasn't easy.

"The first semester was pretty tough," she said. "It was very competitive, and the instructors pushed you a lot. I wasn't used to that, and I had to rethink if I wanted

to stay since I found it to be a frightening experience. But I told myself I just couldn't give up," Gijon added.

Realizing she needed to put extra effort into her studies, Gijon made a commitment to being more involved.

"What I had to do was educate myself more and learn more about the design field," she explained, "and so I joined a design group. I would go to the bookstore and pick up magazines and read through them looking for ideas. I also developed a sketch book and journal, jotting down my ideas and noting what the latest trends were."

Gijon plans to eventually attend graduate school. "I have an interest in teaching, and I feel really strongly that I'd like to come back and teach in my community and be a role model for others," she said.

"The sacrifices of my parents coming to this country inspired me to keep going," she added. "If they can do that, then I can achieve my goals."

[RETHINK]

- Why do you think joining a design group was helpful to Gijon as she continued her studies?

- What advantages might Gijon receive by taking a year off before going to graduate school? Can you think of any disadvantages?

Looking Back

LO 1-1 Explain the benefits of a college education.

▶ The reason first-year college students most often cite for attending college is to get a better job, and college graduates earn more on average than nongraduates.

▶ College also provides many other benefits. These include becoming well educated, learning to think critically and communicate effectively, understanding the interconnections between different areas of knowledge and our place in history and the world, and understanding diversity.

LO 1-2 Identify the basic principles of P.O.W.E.R. Learning.

▶ P.O.W.E.R. Learning is a systematic approach people can easily learn, using abilities they already possess, to acquire successful habits for learning and achieving personal goals.

▶ P.O.W.E.R. Learning involves **P**reparation, **O**rganization, **W**ork, **E**valuation, and **R**ethinking.

▶ To *prepare,* learners set both long-term and short-term goals, making sure that their goals are realistic, measurable, and under their control—and will lead to their final destination.

▶ They *organize* the tools they will need to accomplish those goals.

▶ They get down to *work* on the task at hand. Using their goals as motivation, expert learners also understand that success depends on effort.

▶ They *evaluate* the work they've done, considering what they have accomplished in comparison with the goals they set for themselves during the preparation stage.

▶ Finally, they *rethink,* reflecting on the process they've used, taking a fresh look at what they've done, and critically rethinking their goals.

LO 1-3 Identify your learning styles and how they affect your academic success.

▶ People have patterns of diverse learning styles—characteristic ways of acquiring and using knowledge.

▶ Learning styles include read/write, visual/graphic, auditory/verbal, and tactile/kinesthetic styles (the receptive learning styles).

▶ The multiple intelligences view says that we have eight different forms of intelligence, each relatively independent of the others.

▶ Personality styles that influence learning are classified along dimensions of introversion/extraversion, intuition/sensing, thinking/feeling, and perceiving/judging.

▶ Knowing your learning styles can help you identify the specific techniques that will allow you to master material in class and on the job most effectively.

▶ Learning theories explain the ways in which we learn. The three main perspectives are operant conditioning, cognitive, and classical conditioning approaches.

[KEY TERMS AND CONCEPTS]

Auditory/verbal learning style (p. 17)

Classical conditioning (p. 25)

Critical thinking (p. 14)

Evaluation (p. 12)

Growth mindset (p. 10)

Learning style (p. 16)

Learning theory (p. 24)

Left-brain processing (p. 21)

Long-term goals (p. 7)

Motivation (p. 11)

Operant conditioning (p. 24)

P.O.W.E.R. Learning (p. 5)

Read/write learning style (p. 17)

Receptive learning style (p. 17)

Reinforcer (p. 24)

Right-brain processing (p. 21)

Short-term goals (p. 7)

Tactile/kinesthetic learning style (p. 17)

Visual/graphic learning style (p. 17)

[R E S O U R C E S]

ON THE WEB

Every college provides a significant number of resources to help its students succeed and thrive. You can go to your college's website to see which online resources are available to you.

For example, here's a list of some typical online resources, many of which we'll be discussing in future chapters:

- Activities/clubs
- Adult and reentry programs
- Advising services
- Alumni
- Career center resource page
- Continuing education programs

- Disability services (learning or physical disabilities)
- Financial aid
- Health resources
- Honors program
- Housing information
- Online bookstore
- Online education (distance learning)

- Online tutorial services
- Off-campus housing and services
- Registration
- School newspaper
- Student affairs
- Student government
- Study abroad/ exchange programs
- Volunteer services

If you are experiencing any difficulties, be certain to make use of your college's resources. College success does not come easily for anyone, particularly when it demands juggling responsibilities of work and family. You should make use of whatever support your college offers.

For additional support, the following websites provide opportunities to extend your learning about the material in this chapter.

▶ The University at Buffalo Counseling Services (**http://ub-counseling.buffalo. edu/adjusting.php**) offers a site on adjusting to campus life that includes links to relationships, health, and study skills.

▶ The Learn More Resource Center (**www.learnmoreindiana.org**), sponsored by the state of Indiana, provides information on a variety of useful topics regarding adjustment to college life, including comments by students on their experiences. It covers such topics as where to live, how to select classes, how to study and learn, and much more.

▶ EducationPlanner.org, a public service of the Pennsylvania Higher Education Assistance Agency, offers an interactive set of questions (**http://www.education planner.org/students/self-assessments/kind-of-student.shtml**) that can help you find out what kind of student you are, what your learning style is, and which study habits you can improve.

ON CAMPUS

If your college has a physical campus, additional on-ground resources may be available to you.

For example, here's a list of some typical resources that may be offered only on campus:

- Art gallery
- Bookstore
- Chaplain/religious services
- Child care center
- Cinema/theater
- Computing center/ computer labs
- Disability center (learning or physical disabilities)
- Financial aid office
- Fitness center/ gymnasium
- Health center
- Housing center
- Intramural sports
- Language lab
- Lost and found
- Math lab
- Multicultural center
- Museum
- Off-campus housing and services
- Ombudsman/conflict resolution
- Photography lab
- Police/campus security
- Post office
- Printing center
- Residential life office
- Testing center
- Work-study center
- Writing lab

If you are able to commute to your college campus, take the opportunity to meet with one of your college representatives. Remember, their job is to help you. Don't be shy about asking questions about what you may expect, how to find things, and what you should be doing.

IN PRINT

For a variety of views of what it takes to be a successful college student, read *How to Survive Your Freshman Year: By Hundreds of College Sophomores, Juniors, and Seniors Who Did,* 5th edition, published by Hundreds of Heads Books (2013).

To learn more about who your first-year classmates are across the United States, take a look at Kevin Eagan and colleagues' *The American Freshman: National Norms for Fall 2014* (Higher Education Research Institute, 2014). The book provides a comprehensive look at the attitudes and opinions of first-year college students, based on the results of a national survey.

Finally, Thomas Armstrong and Sue Teele's *Rainbows of Intelligence: Exploring How Students Learn* (2015) provides an introduction to learning styles, offering tips and suggestions for making use of the way that people learn.

ENDNOTES

1. G. Gottesman, *College Survival* (New York: Macmillan, 1994), p. 70.
2. Adapted from D. Lazear, *The Intelligent Curriculum: Using MI to Develop Your Students' Full Potential* (Tucson, AZ: Zephyr Press, 1999).

The Case of . . .
Doubting in Denver

It was during the second week of classes that the questioning started. Until then, Jesse had been fairly confident in his decision to enroll at a college in the Denver suburbs that offered online training to be a pharmacy technician. He had been excited to try something new and to start a new career, but more and more he was wondering if he'd made the right choice.

Jesse needed to keep his part-time job as an administrative assistant at a dentist's office. However, to get to work, Jesse had to take a 45-minute bus ride because his wife needed the car to get to her office in downtown Denver. And on top of that, Jesse needed to find time among work, classes, and studying to help care for his five-year-old son.

Maybe, Jesse was beginning to think, college hadn't been such a good idea. True, he could earn more money as a pharmacy technician and begin a more promising career. But was it really worth all this added time and stress? Plus, Jesse had never done very well academically. Why would college be any different? If he wanted to make more money, he could just add more shifts at his current job.

Why bother with college? Jesse thought to himself. What an expense, and what a hassle. For what?

1. What arguments could you provide Jesse as to the value of a college education?

2. Do you think that Jesse's doubts are common?

3. What might you suggest that Jesse do to help deal with his doubts about the value of college?

4. Why might a student's doubts about the value of college be especially strong during the beginning weeks of college?

5. Do you share any of Jesse's concerns about the value of a college education? Do you have additional ones?

2

Learning Outcomes

By the time you finish this chapter you will be able to

》 LO **2-1**   Discuss strategies to manage your time effectively.

》 LO **2-2**   Explain ways to balance competing priorities.

》 LO **2-3**   Identify ways to deal with surprises and distractions.

Making the Most of Your Time

© BFG Images/Getty Images RF

As Vicky Marks waits in line for her morning cup of coffee, she mentally goes over the things she needs to get done during the day: *Get to the gym at 8:00 a.m. to teach her morning exercise class . . . study for her online anatomy midterm during lunch at 12:30 . . . from 1:30 to 4:30 complete her benchmark homework assignments for her online English and medical terminology classes, which reminds her that she's almost one semester closer to earning her physical therapist's degree . . . meet her husband at 5:00 to watch her son's soccer game . . . go home, make dinner, put her son to bed by 8:00.* She has the nagging feeling that there's something else she needs to do, but she can't put her finger on it.

She finally gets to the head of the line to pay for her coffee, which she starts drinking even before she pays for it. Glancing at a clock as she leaves the coffee shop, she gives up the thought of getting in some last-minute studying for her anatomy midterm before teaching her exercise class. It will be a minor miracle if she even makes it to the gym on time.

She's been up less than an hour, and already Vicky is running behind schedule.

Looking Ahead

Are your days like Vicky's? Are you constantly trying to cram more activities into less time? Do you feel as if you never have enough time?

You're not alone: Most of us wish we had more time to accomplish the things we need to do. However, some people are a lot better at juggling their time than others. What's their secret?

There is no secret. No one has more than 24 hours a day and 168 hours a week. The key to success lies in figuring out our priorities and better using the time we do have.

Time management is like juggling a bunch of tennis balls: For most of us, juggling doesn't come naturally, but it is a skill that can be learned. Not all of us will end up perfect jugglers (whether we are juggling tennis balls or time), but, with practice, we can become a lot better at it.

This chapter will give you strategies for improving your time management skills. After first helping you learn to account for the ways you currently use—and misuse—time, it gives you strategies for planning your time, including some ways to deal with the inevitable interruptions and counterproductive personal habits that can sabotage your best intentions. It will provide you with skills that are important for success not only in college and on the job, but in your personal life as well.

We also consider techniques for dealing with competing goals. There are special challenges involved in juggling the priorities of college and work with other aspects of life, such as child rearing or hobbies.

» LO 2-1 Time for Success

Without looking up from the page, answer this question: What time is it?

Most people are pretty accurate in their answer. And if you don't know for sure, it's very likely that you can find out. Your cell phone may display the time; there may be a clock on the wall, desk, or computer screen; or maybe you're riding in a car that shows the time in the instrument panel.

Even if you don't have a timepiece of some sort nearby, your body keeps its own beat. Humans have an internal clock that regulates the beating of our heart, the pace of our breathing, the discharge of chemicals within our bloodstream, and myriad other bodily functions.

Time is something from which we can't escape. Even if we ignore it, it's still going by, ticking away, second by second, minute by minute, hour by hour. So the main issue in using your time well is, "Who's in charge?" We can allow time to slip by and let it be our enemy. Or we can take control of it and make it our ally.

Try It! P O W E R

Find Your Time Style

Rate how well each of the statements below describes you. Use this rating scale:

1 = Doesn't describe me at all   3 = Describes me fairly well

2 = Describes me only slightly   4 = Describes me very well

	1	2	3	4
1. I often wake up later than I should.				
2. I am usually late for appointments.				
3. I am always in a rush getting places.				
4. I put off big tasks and assignments until the last minute.				
5. My friends often comment on my lateness.				
6. I am easily interrupted, putting aside what I'm doing for something new.				
7. When I look at a clock, I'm often surprised at how late it is.				
8. I often forget appointments and have to reschedule them.				
9. When faced with a big task, I feel overwhelmed and turn my mind away from it until later.				
10. At the end of the day, I have no idea where the time went.				

Rate yourself by adding up the points you assigned. Use this scale to assess your time style:

10–15 = Very efficient time user

16–20 = Efficient time user

21–30 = Time use needs work

31–40 = Victim of time

P Prepare

Learn where time is going

O Organize

Use a master calender, weekly timetable, and daily to-do list

W Work

Follow the schedules you've put together

E Evaluate

Keep track of your short-term and long-term accomplishments

R Rethink

Reflect on your personal style of time management

P.O.W.E.R. Plan

By taking control of how you spend your time, you'll increase your chances of becoming more successful in college and in your career. Perhaps more important, the better you are at managing the time you devote to your studies and your job, the more time you will have to spend on your outside interests. (You can get a sense of your own personal time style by completing **Try It! 1**.)

The goal of time management is not to schedule every moment so we become pawns of a timetable that governs every waking moment of the day. Instead, the goal is to permit us to make informed choices as to how we use our time. Rather than letting the day slip by, largely without our awareness, the time management procedures we'll discuss make us better able to harness time for our own ends. In short, time management doesn't confine us. On the contrary, it frees us to do the things we want and need to do.

P Prepare

Learning Where Time Is Going and Where It Should Go

Before you get somewhere, you need to know where you're starting from and where you want to go. So the first step in improving your time management skills is figuring out how you're managing your time now.

Create a Time Log

Keep track of the way you spend your time across seven days on time logs. Insert the amount of time you spend on each activity during each one-hour period for a single day. Do the same thing for every day of the week on separate time logs. **Be sure to make copies of this log before you fill it in for the first day.**

   Analyze your log. After you complete your log for a week, analyze how you spend your time according to the major categories on the log. Add up the amount of time you spend on each category. You can also create other broad categories that eat up significant amounts of time.

   Now consider the following:

1. What do you spend most of your time on?

2. Are you satisfied with the way that you are using your time? Are there any areas that seem to use up excessive amounts of time?

3. Do you see some simple fixes that will allow you to use time more effectively?

(continued)

Create a Time Log

"Where did the day go?" If you've ever said this to yourself, one way of figuring out where you've spent your time is to create a time log. A time log is the most essential tool for improving your use of time.

   A **time log** is simply a record of how you actually have spent your time—including interruptions. It doesn't have to be a second-by-second record of every waking moment. But it should account for blocks of time in increments as short as 15 minutes.

   Look at the blank time log in **Try It! 2**. As you fill out the log, be specific, indicating not only what you were doing at a given time (for example, "studying

time log
A record of how one spends one's time.

Time Log

Day: _____   Date: _____

	personal care	food	classes	studies	work	recreation	sleep	other
6–7 a.m.								
7–8 a.m.								
8–9 a.m.								
9–10 a.m.								
10–11 a.m.								
11–12 (noon)								
12 (noon)–1 p.m.								
1–2 p.m.								
2–3 p.m.								
3–4 p.m.								
4–5 p.m.								
5–6 p.m.								
6–7 p.m.								
7–8 p.m.								
8–9 p.m.								
9–10 p.m.								
10–11 p.m.								
11 p.m.–12 (midnight)								
12 (midnight)–1 a.m.								
1–2 a.m.								
2–3 a.m.								
3–4 a.m.								
4–5 a.m.								
5–6 a.m.								

"You may delay, but time will not."
Benjamin Franklin

for economics quiz") but also the interruptions that occurred (such as "answered cell phone twice" or "switched to Internet for 10 minutes").

By looking at how much time you spend doing various activities, you now know where your time goes. How does it match with your perceptions of how you spend your time? Be prepared to be surprised because most people find that they're spending time on a lot of activities that just don't matter very much.

From the perspective of . . .

A STUDENT Time logs can be helpful tools when determining how you spend your time; they can also help you find more time for the activities you enjoy doing. What areas of your life do you wish you had more time to spend in?

» LO2-2 Set Your Priorities

By this point, you should have a good idea of what's taking up your time. But you may not know what you should be doing instead.

To figure out the best use of your time, you need to determine your priorities. **Priorities** are the tasks and activities you need and want to do, rank-ordered from most important to least important. There are no right or wrong priorities; you have to decide for yourself what you wish to accomplish. Maybe spending time on your studies is most important to you, or working to earn more money, or maybe your top priority is spending time with your family. Only you can decide. Furthermore, what's important to you at this moment may be less of a priority to you next month, next year, or five years from now.

For the purpose of effective time management in college, the best procedure is to start off by identifying priorities for an entire term. What do you need to accomplish? Don't just choose obvious, general goals, such as "passing all my classes." Instead, think about your priorities in terms of specific, measurable activities, such as "studying five hours before each exam"—*not* "studying harder," which is too vague. (Look at the example of a priority list in **Figure 2.1** and also the **Course Connections** feature.)

priorities
The tasks and activities that one needs and wants to do, rank-ordered from most important to least important.

© Photodisc/Getty Images RF

Priority	Ranking
Study for each class at least 30 minutes/day	1
Start each major paper 2 weeks in advance of due date	2
Hand in each paper on time	1
Review for test starting a week before test date	2
Be on time for job	1
Check in with Mom once a week	3
Work out 3x/week	3

figure 2.1
Sample List of Priorities

Study Time: How Much Is Enough?

What would you guess is the average number of hours instructors think you should be studying each week? In the view of instructors queried in surveys, students should spend, on average, 6 hours per week preparing for *each* class in which they're enrolled. And if they're taking courses in the sciences and engineering, instructors expect their students to put in even more hours.[1]

Keep in mind that study time does not include the actual time you need to allocate for online learning. If you add that in, someone taking four classes would need 24 hours of outside class preparation in addition to 16 hours of learning the material in the online classes—for a total of 40 hours, or the equivalent of full-time employment.

If you've underestimated the amount of time instructors believe is necessary to devote to class preparation, you may need to rethink the amount of time you'll need to allocate to studying. You might also reach out to your individual instructors to see what they believe is an appropriate amount of preparation. Although they may not be able to give exact figures, their estimates will help you to prioritize what you need to do to be a successful student.

master calendar
A schedule showing the weeks of a longer time period, such as a college term, with all assignments and important activities noted on it.

Short- and long-term priorities may not always match. What would you do if the online class you needed to graduate had a regular submission deadline that conflicted with your daughter's weekly soccer game?
© Brand X Pictures/Punchstock RF

Write your priorities on the chart in **Try It! 3**. After you've filled out the chart, organize it by giving each priority a ranking from 1 to 3. A "1" represents a priority that absolutely must be done; without it you'll suffer a major setback. For instance, showing up for work should receive a "1" for a priority ranking; carving out time to take those guitar lessons you always wanted to take might be ranked a "3" in terms of priority. The important point is to rank-order your priorities to reveal what is and is not important to accomplish during the term.

Setting priorities will help you to determine how to make the best use of your time. No one has enough time to complete everything; prioritizing will help you make informed decisions about what you can do to maximize your success.

Organize Mastering the Moment

You now know where you've lost time in the past, and your priority list is telling you where you need to head in the future.

Now for the present. You've reached the point where you can organize yourself to take control of your time. Here's what you'll need.

Master Calendars

Your first requirement is a **master calendar** that shows all the weeks of the term on one page. You don't need to buy one; you can make it easily enough yourself. It need not be great art; a rough version will do. The important point is that it must include every week of the term and seven days per week. (See the example of a master calendar in **Figure 2.2**.)

Set Priorities

Set your priorities for the term. They may include finishing papers and assignments by their due dates, completing work assignments on time, or spending time with your family. To get started, list priorities in any order. Be sure to consider priorities relating to your classes, work, family, social obligations, and health. After you list them, assign a number to each one indicating its level—giving a "1" to the highest-priority items, a "2" to medium-priority items, and a "3" to the items with the lowest priority.

List of Priorities	
Priority	**Priority Index**

    Now redo your list, putting your number 1s first, followed by as many of your number 2s and 3s as you feel you can reasonably commit yourself to.

Final List of Priorities
Priority
1.
2.
3.
4.
5.
6.
7.
8.
9.
10.
11.
12.

Now consider the following:

- What does this list tell you about your greatest priorities? Are they centered around school, your current work schedule, friends and family, or some other aspect of your life?

- Do you have so many "1" priorities that they will be difficult or impossible to accomplish successfully? How could you go back to your list and trim it down even more?

- What does this listing of priorities suggest about how successful you'll be during the upcoming term?

figure 2.2
Master Calendar Sample

				Writing		
M	**T**	**W**	**TH**	**F**	**SA**	**S**
Sept. 7	8	9 Classes Start	10	11	12 Camping →	13
14	Add/drop 15 ends	16	English 17 short paper due	18	19	20
21	Work 22	23	English 24 short paper due	Work 25	26	27
28	29	30 Math exam	OCT 1 English short paper due	Legal 2 Studies quiz	3	4
5	Legal Studies 6 paper due	7	English 8 short paper due	Work 9	10	11
12	Work 13	14	English short 15 paper due	Legal 16 Studies quiz	17	18
First-yr 19 seminar journal due	20	Math 21 exam	English 22 short paper due Dad's bd-call	Work 23	Bartending 24 job	25
Work 26	English 27 midterm exam	28	Eng-short 29 paper due	Legal Studies 30 quiz	31	NOV 1
2	3	4	English 5 short paper due	Work 6	7	8 Darcey's Wedding!
9	Work 10	Holiday- 11 Veteran's Day	Eng-short 12 paper due	Legal 13 Studies quiz Math exam	14	15
First-yr 16 seminar group project due	17	Preregistration 18 for next semester	English 19 short paper due	20	21	22
23	Work 24	25	Thanksgiving 26	No Classes! 27	28	29
30	DEC 1 Legal Studies paper due	2	English 3 short paper due	Work 4	5	6
First-yr 7 seminar final journal due	Work 8	9	Legal 10 studies quiz	Math exam 11 Last day of class!!	12	13
English 14 final exam	Legal 15 Studies final exam	16	Math 17 final exam	Legal 18 Studies exam MY birthday!	19	20
21	22	23	24	Xmas 25	26	27

Journal Reflections

Where Does My Time Go?

1. When would you prefer to wake up if you did not have the obligations and responsibilities you currently have?

2. When do you typically go to bed on a typical weekday night? When would you prefer to go to bed if you did not have the obligations and responsibilities you currently have?

3. Would you characterize yourself as a "morning person," who accomplishes the most in the early morning, or more as a "night person," who is most comfortable doing work in the evenings? What implications does this characterization have for your scheduling of work shifts?

4. Generally speaking, how would you characterize your time management skills? What would be the benefit to you personally if you could manage time more effectively? What goals might you accomplish if you had more time at your disposal?

Weekly Timetables

The **weekly timetable** is a master grid with the days of the week across the top and the hours, from 6:00 a.m. to midnight, along the side. This will permit you to write in all your regularly scheduled activities, as well as one-time appointments when they arise. (A blank weekly timetable is provided in **Figure 2.3**.)

Make a single copy of this blank timetable or use the online version. Then fill in your regular, predictable time commitments.

Next, make as many copies as you need to cover each week of the term. Then, for each week, fill in the date on the left and the number of the week in the term on the right, and add in your irregular commitments.

weekly timetable
A schedule showing all regular, prescheduled activities due to occur in the week, together with one-time events and commitments.

figure 2.3
Weekly Timetable

Weekly Timetable

Week of: _____   Week #_____

	Mon	Tues	Wed	Thurs	Fri	Sat	Sun
6–7 a.m.							
7–8 a.m.							
8–9 a.m.							
9–10 a.m.							
10–11 a.m.							
11–12 (noon)							
12 (noon)–1 p.m.							
1–2 p.m.							
2–3 p.m.							
3–4 p.m.							
4–5 p.m.							
5–6 p.m.							
6–7 p.m.							
7–8 p.m.							
8–9 p.m.							
9–10 p.m.							
10–11 p.m.							
11 p.m.–12 (midnight)							
12 (midnight)–1 a.m.							
1–2 a.m.							
2–3 a.m.							
3–4 a.m.							
4–5 a.m.							
5–6 a.m.							

daily to-do list
A schedule showing the tasks, activities, and appointments due to occur during the day.

Daily To-Do Lists

Finally, you'll need a **daily to-do list**. The daily to-do list can be written on a small, portable calendar that includes a separate page for each day of the week. Or you can keep it virtually on a smartphone or tablet to-do list. Whatever form your daily to-do list takes, make sure you can keep it with you all the time.

The basic organizational task you face is filling in these three schedules. You'll need at least an hour to do this, so set the time aside. In addition, there will be some repetition across the three schedules, and the task may seem a bit tedious. *But every minute you invest now in organizing your time will pay off in hours that you will save in the future.*

Follow these steps in completing your schedule:

▶ **Start with the master calendar, which shows all the weeks of the term on one page.** Write on the master calendar every class assignment you have for the entire term, noting it on the date that it is due. Also include major events at work, such as days when you might need to work overtime. In addition, include important activities from your personal life, drawn from your list of priorities. For instance, if your spouse or child has a performance or sporting event you want to attend, be sure to mark it down.

Finally, schedule some free time—time when you promise yourself you will do something that is just plain fun. Consider these days to be written in stone, and promise yourself that you won't use them for anything else except for something enjoyable. Just knowing that you have some downtime planned will help you to throw yourself into more demanding tasks. In addition, getting into the habit of allowing yourself time to relax and reflect on your life is as important as any other time management skill you may learn.

You now have a good idea of what the next few weeks have in store for you. You can identify just by looking at your master calendar the periods when you are going to be especially busy. You can also note the periods when you will have less to do.

Use the off-peak periods to get a head start on future assignments!

In this way, your master schedule can help you head off disaster before it occurs.

▶ **Now move to the weekly timetable provided in Figure 2.3.** Fill in the times of all your fixed, prescheduled activities—when you have to be at work, the times you have to pick up your child at day care, and any other recurring appointments.

Once you've filled in the weekly timetable, you will have a bare-bones picture of the average week. You will still need to take into account the specific activities that are required to complete the assignments on the master calendar.

To move from your "average" week to specific weeks, make photocopies of the weekly timetable that now contains your fixed appointments. Make enough copies for every week of the term. On each copy write the week number of the term and the specific dates it covers. (See a sample in **Figure 2.4**.)

Using your master calendar, add assignment due dates, tests, and any other activities on the appropriate days of the week. Then pencil in blocks of time necessary to prepare for those events.

How much time should you allocate for schoolwork? One very rough rule of thumb holds that for every hour you spend on learning the course content for your online class, it requires, on average, two hours of studying to earn a B and three hours of studying to earn an A. Do the arithmetic: If you are taking 15

Sometimes it is OK (and even necessary) to simply relax. Make sure that you make time to unwind!
© Image Source/Getty Images RF

figure 2.4
A Sample Weekly Timetable

Weekly Timetable

Week of: _10/7_   Week # _3_

	Mon	Tues	Wed	Thurs	Fri	Sat	Sun
6–7 a.m.	Drop Kids @ School						
7–8 a.m.	Library		Errands		Library	Wknd Job	Wknd Job
8–9 a.m.		Discussion Board Post		Discussion Board Post			
9–10 a.m.							
10–11 a.m.	Errands						
11–12 (noon)		Study	Study	Study	Study		
12 (noon)–1 p.m.							
1–2 p.m.		Work	Work	Work	Work		
2–3 p.m.							
3–4 p.m.							
4–5 p.m.							
5–6 p.m.							
6–7 p.m.						Study	Study
7–8 p.m.							
8–9 p.m.							
9–10 p.m.	Study	Study	Study	Study			
10–11 p.m.							
11 p.m.–12 (midnight)					Research Draft Due !!		
12 (midnight)–1 a.m.							
1–2 a.m.							
2–3 a.m.							
3–4 a.m.							
4–5 a.m.							
5–6 a.m.							

credits (with each credit equivalent to an hour of online class per week), you'll need to plan for 30 hours of studying each week to earn a B average—an intimidating amount of time. Of course, the amount of time you must allocate to a specific class will vary from week to week, depending on what is happening in the class.

For example, if you estimate that you'll need five hours of study time for a midterm exam in a certain class, pencil in those hours. Don't set up a single block of five hours. People remember best when their studying is spread out over shorter periods rather than attempted in one long block of time. Besides, it will probably be hard to find a block of five straight hours on your weekly calendar.

Keep in mind that estimates are just that: estimates. Don't think of them as set in stone. Mark them on your weekly calendar in pencil, not pen, so you can adjust them if necessary.

But remember: It's also crucial not to overschedule yourself. You'll still need time to eat, to talk with your friends, to spend time with your family, and to enjoy yourself in general. If you find that your life is completely filled with things that you feel you must do to survive and that there is no room for fun, then take a step back and cut out something to make some time for yourself in your daily schedule. Finding time for yourself is as important as carving out time for what others want you to do. Besides, if you are overworked, you're likely to "find" the time by guiltily goofing off without really setting aside the time and enjoying it.

▶ **If you've taken each of the previous steps, you're now in a position to work on the final step of organization for successful time management: completing your daily to-do list.** Unlike the master calendar and weekly timetable—both of which you develop weeks or even months in advance—complete your daily to-do list just one day ahead of time, preferably at the end of the day.

List all the things that you intend to do during the next day, and their priority. Start with the things you know you *must* do and which have fixed times, such as assignment deadlines, work schedules, and appointments. These are your first-priority items. Then add in the other things that you *should* accomplish, such as an hour of study for an upcoming test or a trip to the garage to have your oil changed. Finally, list things that are lower priority but enjoyable, setting aside time for a run or a walk, for example.

Don't schedule every single minute of the day. That would be counterproductive, and you'd end up feeling like you'd failed if you deviated from your schedule. Instead, think of your daily to-do list as a path through a forest. If you were hiking, you would allow yourself to deviate from the path, occasionally venturing onto side tracks when they looked interesting. But you'd also be keeping tabs on your direction so you ended up where you needed to be at the end and not miles away from your car or home.

Like the sample daily to-do list in **Figure 2.5**, include a column to check or cross off after you've completed an activity. There's something very satisfying in acknowledging what you have accomplished.

figure 2.5
Sample Daily To-Do List

To-Do List
for _____
(date)

Item	Priority	Completed
Call Chris to get econ notes	1	✓
Meet with Prof. Hernandez	1	✓
Finish budget reports at work	1	✓
Work on outline for legal studies paper	2	✓
Return books to library	2	
Pick up Nettie at school	1	✓
Call Deena about Saturday	2	
Do laundry	3	

A WORKING PARENT The balancing act between work and family can be a challenge. How can a weekly timetable help you ensure that all areas of your life are getting the attention they deserve?

© Stockbyte/Getty Images RF

≫ LO 2-3  **Work**

Controlling Time

You're in luck: There is no work to time management—or at least not much more than you've already done. The work of time management is to follow the schedules that you've prepared and organized. But that doesn't mean it will be easy. Our lives are filled with surprises: Things take longer than we've planned. A friend we haven't spoken to in a while calls to chat, and it seems rude to say that we don't have time to talk. A crisis occurs; buses are late; computers break down; kids get sick.

The difference between effective time management and time management that doesn't work lies in how well you deal with the inevitable surprises.

There are several ways to take control of your days and permit yourself to follow your intended schedule:

▶ **Just say no.** You don't have to agree to every request and every favor that others ask of you. You're not a bad person if you refuse to do something that will eat up your time and prevent you from accomplishing your goals. And if you do decide to do someone else a time-consuming favor, try to come up with the most efficient way of accomplishing it. Don't let all your time get taken up by the priorities of others.

▶ **Get away from it all.** Go to the library. Lock yourself into your bedroom. Find a quiet, out-of-the-way coffee shop. Any of these places can serve to isolate you from everyday distractions and thereby permit you to work on the tasks that you wish to complete. Try to adopt a particular spot as your own, such as a nook in the library or a local cafe. If you use it enough, your body and mind will automatically get into study mode as soon as you seat yourself there.

▶ **Enjoy the sounds of silence.** Although many people insist they accomplish most while a television, radio, or CD is playing, scientific studies suggest otherwise: We are able to concentrate most when our environment is silent. So even if you're sure you work best with a soundtrack playing, experiment and work in silence for a few days. You may find that you get more done in less time than you would in a more distracting environment.

▶ **Take an e-break.** Text messages, phone calls, Facebook status updates, instant messages, e-mail. Who doesn't love to hear from others?

We may not control when communications arrive, but we can make the message wait until we are ready to receive it. Take an e-break and shut down your communication sources for a period of time.

- **Expect the unexpected.** Interruptions and crises, minor and major, can't be eliminated. However, they can be prepared for.

    How is it possible to plan for surprises? Though it may still be too early in the term to get a clear picture of what sorts of unanticipated events you'll encounter, you should keep an eye out for patterns. Perhaps one instructor routinely gives surprise assignments. Maybe you're frequently asked to work extra hours on the weekends when another employee doesn't show up.

    You'll never be able to escape from unexpected interruptions and surprises that require your attention. But by trying to anticipate them in advance, and thinking about how you'll react to them, you'll be positioning yourself to react more effectively when they do occur.

- **Combat procrastination. Procrastination**, the habit of putting off and delaying tasks that need to be accomplished, is like a microscopic parasite. It is invisible to the naked eye, but it eats up your time nonetheless.

procrastination
The habit of putting off and delaying tasks that need to be accomplished.

Procrastination

You can't control interruptions and crises that are imposed on you by others. But even when no one else is throwing interruptions at us, we make up our own. Procrastination is a problem that almost all of us face. To identify whether you are a procrastinator, find your "Procrastination Quotient" (see **Try It! 4**).

If you find yourself procrastinating, several steps can help you:

- *Break large tasks into small ones.* People often procrastinate because a task they're seeking to accomplish appears overwhelming. If writing a 15-page paper seems nearly impossible, think about writing a series of five 3-page papers. If reading a 600-page book seems impossible, think of it as reading three 200-page books.

- *Start with the easiest and simplest part of a task, and then do the harder parts.* Succeeding initially on the easy parts can make the harder parts of a task less daunting—and make you less apt to procrastinate in completing the task.

- *Get the hard parts of a task out of the way first.* In contrast to the previous strategy for avoiding procrastination, it sometimes helps to tackle the hardest part of a task first. Getting the hard parts out of the way will make it a lot easier to complete the remaining parts of what you are trying to accomplish.

- *Substitute something easier for a more difficult task.* If you have to write a letter, can you write a postcard instead? Sometimes it's possible to figure out an easier way to accomplish a task that works just as well.

- *Just begin!* Sometimes the hardest part of an activity is simply getting started. So take the leap and begin the task, and the rest may follow more easily.

- *Work with others.* Just being in the same physical location with others can motivate you sufficiently to accomplish tasks that you consider unpleasant and on which you might be tempted to procrastinate. For instance, studying vocabulary words can be made easier if you plan to study them at the library, around others who are also working productively. Or you could ask your family or friends to help you study. Beware, though—if you spend too much time socializing, you lower the likelihood of success.

- *Understand that false starts are part of the learning process.* Accept that sometimes you will go in the wrong direction when working on a project.

Find Your Procrastination Quotient

Do you procrastinate?[2] To find out, circle the number that best applies for each question using the following scale:

Strongly agree	4	3	2	1	**Strongly disagree**

1. I invent reasons and look for excuses for not acting on a problem.

Strongly agree	4	3	2	1	**Strongly disagree**

2. It takes pressure to get me to work on difficult assignments.

Strongly agree	4	3	2	1	**Strongly disagree**

3. I take half measures that will avoid or delay unpleasant or difficult tasks.

Strongly agree	4	3	2	1	**Strongly disagree**

4. I face too many interruptions and crises that interfere with accomplishing my major goals.

Strongly agree	4	3	2	1	**Strongly disagree**

5. I sometimes neglect to carry out important tasks.

Strongly agree	4	3	2	1	**Strongly disagree**

6. I schedule big assignments too late to get them done as well as I know I could.

Strongly agree	4	3	2	1	**Strongly disagree**

7. I'm sometimes too tired to do the work I need to do.

Strongly agree	4	3	2	1	**Strongly disagree**

8. I start new tasks before I finish old ones.

Strongly agree	4	3	2	1	**Strongly disagree**

9. When I work in groups, I try to get other people to finish what I don't.

Strongly agree	4	3	2	1	**Strongly disagree**

10. I put off tasks that I really don't want to do but know that I must do.

Strongly agree	4	3	2	1	**Strongly disagree**

Scoring: Total the numbers you have circled. If the score is below 15, you are not a chronic procrastinator and you probably have only an occasional problem. If your score is 16–25, you have a minor problem with procrastination. If your score is above 25, you procrastinate quite often and should work on breaking the habit.

Now, consider the following:

- If you do procrastinate often, why do you think you do it?
- Are there particular kinds of assignments that you are more likely to procrastinate on?
- Is there something that you are putting off doing right now? How might you get started on it?

Don't let the fear of making mistakes hold you back. Such false starts are part of how we learn.

▶ *Keep the costs of procrastination in mind.* Procrastination doesn't just result in delay; it may also make the task harder than it would have been if you hadn't procrastinated. Not only will you ultimately have less time to complete the task, but you may have to do it so quickly that its quality may be diminished. In the worst scenario, you won't even be able to finish it at all.

Balancing School and Life

Time management is especially challenging if you are a full-time student and also have caregiver responsibilities for children or other family members such as aging parents. Not only does your family demand—and deserve—substantial amounts of time, but juggling school and family obligations is often more than a full-time job. However, there are some specific strategies that can help.

© Rubberball/Getty Images RF

Dealing with Childcare Demands

▶ *Provide activities for your children.* Kids enjoy doing things on their own for part of the day. Plan activities that will keep them happily occupied while you're doing schoolwork.

▶ *Make spending time with your children a priority.* Carve out "free play" time for your kids. Even 20 minutes of good time devoted to your children will give all of you—you and them—a lift. No matter how busy you are, you owe it to your children—and yourself—to spend time as a family.

▶ *Enlist your child's help.* Children love to play adult and, if they're old enough, to help you study. Maybe they can help you clear a space to study. Perhaps you can give them "assignments" that they can work on while you're working on your assignments.

▶ *Encourage your child to invite friends over to play.* Some children can remain occupied for hours if they have a playmate.

▶ *Use screentime appropriately.* Television viewing is not all bad, and some shows, Netflix downloads, and even video games can be not only engaging, but also educational. The trick is to pick and choose what your children watch.

▶ *Find the best child care or babysitters that are available.* The better the care your children are getting, the better you'll be able to concentrate on your schoolwork. You may still feel guilty that you're not with your children as much as you'd like, but accept that guilt. Remember, your college education builds a better future for your children.

▶ *Use your children's "downtime" effectively.* If your children are young, use their nap time as a chance to catch up on schoolwork. Or consider getting up early, before your children wake up, for a period in which you will have fewer interruptions than later in the day.

> "I had a friend who was taking online classes to become a paralegal. He always complained about how he didn't have enough time between completing his coursework and holding down his job. But he was always inviting me and his other friends out to movies, insisting we stay at the bar for one more round. It wasn't a surprise when he eventually dropped out of school. It wasn't that he didn't have enough time. It was that he spent it on all the wrong things."
>
> **Bell Hansom, restaurant manager**

▶ *Accept that studying will be harder with kids around.* It may take you longer to study, and your concentration may suffer from the noise that kids make. But remind yourself what that noise represents: the growth and development of someone that you love. One day your children will be grown, and without a doubt there will be times that you'll miss their high level of energy and activity.

Dealing with Eldercare Demands

▶ *Encourage as much independence as possible on the part of older adults for whom you are responsible.* Not only will it take some of the pressure off you, but it will be helpful to the adults.

On-the-Job Time Management

In the business world, schedules are unpredictable. Crises occur, perhaps due to manufacturing problems or client demands, which require sudden flurries of work. For employees with a demanding boss who may, without warning, give them an urgent assignment due the next morning, time is always at a premium. In some jobs, you may be forced to drop everything you normally work on and pitch in on a sudden new task. As a result, your plans to complete your everyday work may be disrupted completely.

Simply put, time management is an essential survival skill when developing your career. Learning the basic principles of time management now will help you well beyond your years in college, and throughout your later career. You'll also want to learn new time management strategies specific to the working world. For instance, if you supervise other employees, it may be possible to delegate some work to them, allowing them to help you complete assignments on time. Or sometimes it may be possible to deflect assignments brought to you by a boss to some other unit or department. Always keep in mind what it is possible for you to do alone—and what is impossible without the aid of co-workers. Don't be afraid to ask for help. In the working world, the end result is what counts above all.

▶ *Ask for support from your siblings and other family members.* Caring for an ill or aging parent should be a family affair, not a burden that falls on any one individual.

▶ *Determine what community resources are available.* Local centers for aging may provide assistance not only to the elderly but also to their caregivers.

▶ *Respect your own needs.* Remember that your own priorities are important. Elders for whom you are responsible will understand that you will sometimes need to put yourself first.

Balancing School and Work Demands

Juggling school and a job can be a real challenge. Not only must you manage your time to complete your schoolwork, but in many cases you'll also face time management demands while you are on the job. Here are some tips to help you keep everything in balance.

▶ *Make to-do lists for work, just as you would for your schoolwork.* In fact, all the time management strategies that we've discussed can be applied to on-the-job tasks.

▶ *If you have slack time on the job, get some studying done.* Try to keep at least some of your textbooks, class notes, or notecards always with you so you can refer to them. Of course, you should never do schoolwork without your employer's prior agreement. If you don't get permission, you may jeopardize your job.

▶ *Use your lunch or dinner hour effectively.* Although it's important to eat a nutritious lunch and not to wolf your food down, you may be able to use some of the time allotted to you for lunch to fit in some studying.

▶ *Ask your employer about flextime.* If your job allows it, you may be able to set your own hours, within reason, as long as the work gets done. If this is an option for you, use it. Although it may create more time management challenges for you than would a job with set hours, it also provides you with more flexibility.

▶ *Always keep in mind why you're working.* If you're working because it's your sole means of support, you're in a very different position from someone who is working to earn a bit of extra money for luxuries. Remember what your priorities are. In some cases, school should always come first; in others, your job may have to come first, at least some of the time. Whatever you decide, make sure it's a thoughtful decision, based on consideration of your long-term priorities.

E | Evaluate Checking Your Time

Evaluating how you use your time is pretty straightforward: You either accomplished what you intended to do in a given period, or you didn't. Did you check off all the items on your daily to-do list? If you go over your list at the end of every day, not only will you know how successful your time management efforts have been, but you will be able to incorporate any activities you missed into the next day's to-do list.

The check-off is important because it provides an objective record of what you have accomplished on a given day. Just as important, it provides you with concrete reinforcement for completing the task. As we have noted, there are few things more satisfying than gazing at a to-do list with a significant number of check marks.

Of course, you won't always accomplish every item on your to-do list. That's not surprising, nor even particularly bad, especially if you've included some second- and third-level priorities that you don't absolutely have to accomplish and that you may not really have expected you'd have time for anyway.

Give yourself a virtual pat on the back for completing the things that you've accomplished. Successful time management is not easy, and if you've improved at all, you deserve to feel some personal satisfaction.

R | Rethink Reflecting on Your Personal Style of Time Management

At the end of the day, after you've evaluated how well you've followed your time management plan and how much you've accomplished, it's time to rethink where you are. Maybe you've accomplished everything you set out to do, and every task for the day is completed and every item on your to-do list has a check mark next to it.

Or maybe you have the opposite result. Your day has been a mess, and you feel as if nothing has been accomplished. Because of a constant series of interruptions and chance events, you've been unable to make headway on your list.

Or—most likely—you find yourself somewhere in between these two extremes. Some tasks got done, while others are still hanging over you. Now is the time to rethink in a broad sense how you manage your time by doing the following:

▶ **Reassess your priorities.** Are your long- and short-term goals appropriate? Are you expecting too much of yourself, given the constraints in your life?

Reassess your priorities to be sure you're attempting to do what is most important to you.

▶ **Reconsider your personal style of time management.** We've outlined one method of time management. Although it works well for most people, it isn't for everyone. Some people just can't bring themselves to be so structured and scheduled. They feel hemmed in by to-do lists.

If you're one of those people, fine. You don't need to follow the suggestions presented in this chapter exactly. In fact, if you go to any bookstore or office supply store, you'll find lots of other aids to help you manage your time. Publishing companies produce elaborate planners, such as DayTimers. In addition, software companies produce computerized time management software, such as Microsoft's Outlook or Apple's Calendar, that reside on a computer or on wireless handheld devices such as a smartphone or an iPad. Many cell phones contain a calendar system and alarm, and they can be set to provide periodic reminders.

> "Our costliest expenditure is time."
> **Theophrastus, quoted in Diogenes Laertius's *Lives and Opinions of Eminent Philosophers*, tr. R. D. Hicks (Loeb Classical Library, 1925).**

However you choose to manage your time, the important thing is to do so consistently. And remember that whatever approach to time management you take, it will work best if it is compatible with your own personal values and strengths. Keep experimenting until you find an approach that works for you.

▶ **Consider doing less.** If you keep falling behind, do less. There are only 24 hours in the day, and we need to sleep for about a third of the time. In the remaining hours, it may be nearly impossible to carry a full load of classes and work full time and care for a child and still have some time left to have a normal life.

Consequently, if you consistently fall behind in your work, it may be that you are just doing too much. Reassess your goals and your priorities, and make choices. Determine what is most important to you. It's better to accomplish less, if it is accomplished well, than to accomplish more, but poorly.

▶ **Do more.** Although it is a problem that many of us would envy, some people have too much time on their hands. Their classes may not be too demanding, or work demands may suddenly slacken off. If this happens to you, take advantage of your time. For example, you might use the extra time to simply relax and enjoy your more unhurried existence. There is a good bit to be said for having time to let your thoughts wander. We need to take time out to enjoy our friends, admire the flowers in the park, exercise, consider the spiritual side of our lives, and the like.

On the other hand, if you consistently have more time than you know what to do with, reflect on what you want to accomplish and add some activities that will help you reach your goals. For example, consider becoming involved in a service-learning activity. Volunteer your time to the community. Or you may consider taking an extra course during the next term.

But whatever you decide to do, make a real decision. Don't let the time slip away. Once it's gone, it's gone forever.

Speaking *of* Success

Courtesy of Javier Olivarez

NAME: **Javier Olivarez**

SCHOOL: **Southern New Hampshire University, Manchester, NH**

MAJOR: **Communications with concentration in Public Relations**

Imagine a world where your classroom is anywhere you happen to be at any given moment. For Javier Olivarez, a senior at Southern New Hampshire University, it is a reality he embraces.

"Being a full-time employee and a member of several committees at SNHU, it was important that I have the flexibility of attending classes on my time," he noted. "Now there are no excuses because college is wherever I want to be."

But there are special challenges that make online learning different from being in a traditional classroom.

"One of the challenges I encountered in pursuing my degree online was communicating electronically versus face-to-face in a campus environment," said Olivarez. "Electronic communication can be misinterpreted or be unclear especially when it comes to understanding an assignment or professor's expectations. As a student pursuing a communications degree, I took this as a challenge upon myself to understand my professor's communication style and bridge the gaps of communication.

"Usually a week before the new term starts, I e-mail my professors, introduce myself, and then ask a few standard questions to help me get a feel for the expectations.

This leads to a successful first week and sets the pace for the term," he added.

As an SNHU peer leader, Olivarez works closely with College of Online and Continuing Education (COCE) students guiding them through the initial processes of pursing a degree online.

"I share my tips for having a successful term, the most important being organization. For example, I have a picture of the binders I create for each course and the reminders that I have set up for important due dates," Olivarez said. "Life is busy and it helps to have these reminders to ensure success throughout the term. Taking online courses has enhanced my time management skills and helped me become more accountable."

While the idea of taking a course anywhere at any time is appealing, Olivarez stresses that it requires a strong commitment to the courses, and most importantly to oneself.

"My goal was to be a top student. In order to achieve success, you have to make it a priority," Olivarez added. "After a few terms, I became skilled at time management and now I am reaching my goal by graduating Summa Cum Laude this year."

[RETHINK]

- Why is it important for a student pursing an online degree to have especially solid skills in time management?

- Do you think that communication is more difficult in online classes than in face-to-face classes? Why, and how can you avoid such difficulties?

Looking Back

LO 2-1 Discuss strategies to manage your time effectively.

▶ Decide to take control of your time.

▶ Become aware of the way you use your time now.

▶ Find your time style and create a time log.

LO 2-2 Explain ways to balance competing priorities.

▶ Set clear priorities.

▶ Consider how your competing priorities relate to one another.

▶ Use time management tools such as a master calendar, a weekly timetable, and a daily to-do list.

LO 2-3 Identify ways to deal with surprises and distractions.

▶ Deal with surprises by saying no, getting away from it all, working in silence, taking control of communications, and leaving slack in your schedule to accommodate the unexpected.

▶ Avoid procrastination by breaking large tasks into smaller ones; starting with the easiest parts of a task first; working with other people; and calculating the true costs of procrastination.

▶ Learn strategies for balancing school and other life responsibilities.

▶ Manage work time carefully, use slack time on the job to perform school assignments, use flextime, accept new responsibilities thoughtfully, and assign the proper priority to work.

[KEY TERMS AND CONCEPTS]

Daily to-do list (p. 42)

Master calendar (p. 38)

Priorities (p. 37)

Procrastination (p. 47)

Time log (p. 35)

Weekly timetable (p. 41)

[RESOURCES]

ON THE WEB

The college official who determines when classes meet is known as the registrar. If you are having difficulty in scheduling your classes, it may be helpful to contact the registrar's office.

The *P.O.W.E.R. Learning* Connect website provides online versions of all the time management forms presented in this chapter. You can complete the forms online or download them and print out as many copies as you need.

▶ Penn State University offers helpful advice on time management at **http://pennstatelearning.psu.edu/time-management**.

▶ Useful tips for managing your time and prioritizing (and re-prioritizing) tasks can be found at the California Polytech website at **http://sas.calpoly.edu/asc/ssl/timemgmt-strategies.html**.

ON CAMPUS

If your college has a physical campus, consider consulting the on-ground learning center. The learning center provides help with such issues as planning a study schedule for the upcoming term, dealing with multiple assignments and obligations on the same date, or dealing with competing academic and work demands. The staff can help you sort out the various options you may have.

IN PRINT

Stephen Covey's *The Seven Habits of Highly Successful People* (Fireside, 2004) and Laura Stack's *What to Do When There's Too Much to Do* (Berrett-Koehler Publishers, 2012) offer practical, hands-on guides to time management.

Microsoft Outlook 2010 Step by Step (Microsoft Press), by Joan Lambert, provides a quick, hands-on introduction to Microsoft's Outlook software, a popular time management program that is part of the Microsoft Office Suite.

Finally, Veronique Vienne and Erica Lennard's *The Art of the Moment: Simple Ways to Get the Most Out of Life* (Clarkson Potter, 2002) is an antidote to the impulse to schedule every minute of our days. The book celebrates taking time out and devoting it to oneself, providing a practical guide to rest and relaxation.

ENDNOTES

1. National Survey of Student Engagement, 2004 *Annual Report*.
2. Adapted from J. D. Ferner, *Successful Time Management* (New York: Wiley, 1980), p. 33.

The Case of . . .
Time Crunched

Ed Goddard couldn't believe it. He was working over-time at his delivery job because one of his co-workers was taking vacation. During a break from his shift, he received an e-mail reminder from his college instructor, reminding him to study for the exam he had to take the following Monday. Ed had forgotten all about the exam.

Even worse, Ed couldn't study for the exam the next day because he'd promised his wife he would join her on her weekly visit to her mother. Although he wasn't looking forward to the two-hour drive, he knew his wife would be furious if he broke his promise. And on top of all that, he also had to find time in the next few days to work on a term paper due in one of his other classes.

As he was driving home thinking about all this, his car started to sputter and then stalled. He was unable to get it started. That was it. He sat there on the side of the road, feeling like his life had completely fallen apart and wondering how he'd ever get it back together again.

1. What might you tell Ed that could help solve his predicament?

2. Is there anything Ed could have done to prevent the situation he now faces from occurring in the first place?

3. What specific time management techniques might Ed have employed in the past to avoid these problems?

4. What strategies might Ed use now to take control over his limited time during the coming days?

5. What advice could you give Ed to try to prevent problems in time management for his next term?

Learning Outcomes

By the time you finish this chapter, you will be able to

» LO **3-1** Describe techniques for taking notes for an online class.

» LO **3-2** Apply techniques for taking notes from written materials.

» LO **3-3** Explain methods for effective notetaking.

Taking Notes

A s he opened to the first chapter of his marketing class textbook to start his second term of college, Matt Ortiz realized that something fundamental had changed.

For the whole first term, Matt rarely took notes in his online classes. He figured that notetaking was only necessary for classes he had to physically attend. What difference would notetaking make since his instructor could not see him?

But then he received mostly C's in his first-term courses.

In a notetaking webinar Matt enrolled in afterward, he learned the importance of taking good notes on his reading materials, podcasts, and recorded lectures. He also learned that one way to become more engaged in his online class is to regularly communicate with his instructor.

Trying out the strategies he was taught in the webinar, Matt found—a bit to his surprise—that they helped. By the end of the term, he'd pulled his grades way up.

Looking Ahead

Matt Ortiz's realization that online classes also require effective notetaking skills was both a source and a symbol of his academic success. Matt's ability to take good notes is also likely to pay beyond the classroom because notetaking skills not only help produce academic success in college, but also contribute to career success.

In this chapter, we discuss effective strategies for taking notes when listening to recorded lectures and other online media, as well as from written sources such as textbooks. There's a lot more to good notetaking than you probably think—and a lot less, if you view notetaking as essentially "getting everything down on paper." As we explore the ins and outs of notetaking, we'll pause along the way to discuss the tools of the notetaking trade, how to be an active learner, how to think your way to good notes, and how to deal with disorganized instructors.

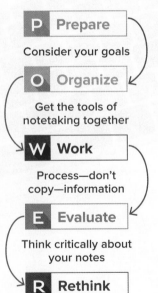

P **Prepare**
Consider your goals

O **Organize**
Get the tools of notetaking together

W **Work**
Process—don't copy—information

E **Evaluate**
Think critically about your notes

R **Rethink**
Review your notes shortly after class to activate your memory

P.O.W.E.R. Plan

»LO3-1 Taking Notes for an Online Class

Perhaps you know a student who desperately tries to write down everything from the textbooks, assigned podcasts, and recorded lectures, resulting in a set of notes that are virtually a transcript of every piece of material provided in an online class. And maybe you believe that if only you took such comprehensive notes, you'd be a much better student.

However, contrary to what you may think, good notetaking does not mean writing down everything from all of the online course materials. With notetaking, less is often more. We'll see why as we consider the basic steps in P.O.W.E.R. notetaking.

P **Prepare** Considering Your Goals

As with other academic activities, preparation is a critical component of notetaking. The following steps will prepare you for action:

▶ **Identify the instructor's—and your—goals for the course.** The first online post or communication you receive from your instructors often covers their objectives, what they hope you'll get out of the class, and what you'll know when it's over. Most restate the key information in the class syllabus, the written document that explains the assignments for the term. For example, they may write that they want you to "develop an appreciation for the ways that statistics are used in everyday life."

The information you receive from your instructor's first electronic communication with the class and through the syllabus is critical. If the instructor's goals aren't stated explicitly, you should attempt to figure them out. In addition to those "external" goals, you should have your own goals. What is it you want to learn from the course? How will the information from the course help you to enhance your knowledge, improve your career prospects, achieve your dreams?

▶ **Complete assignments on time.** Always be prepared and have all of your reading and other assignments completed before the instructor provides the next series of course materials. Instructors assume that their students have done what they've assigned, and the readings, podcasts, and recorded lectures are based upon that assumption. It's virtually impossible to understand the importance of those materials if you haven't completed the requisite assignments.

▶ **Accept the instructor, despite his or her limitations.** Not every instructor is superbly organized or clear in providing online instruction about which readings to complete, what materials to review, or which podcasts or recorded lectures to listen to. Accept the fact that just as there are differences in skills among students, some instructors are better at providing guidance than others. Ultimately, it's your responsibility to overcome an instructor's flaws. Don't let poor direction—or the fact that the instructor expects students to figure out how to take notes on course materials—get in the way of your education. You're going to notice these things, but don't let them interfere with your goals. Good notetaking requires being prepared and a willingness to ask for assistance if needed.

> "The highest result of education is tolerance."
>
> **Helen Keller, author**

▶ **Warm up.** No, this doesn't mean doing stretches just before reviewing class materials or posting to the online discussion board. Rather, prior to looking over the next set of assignments, podcasts, or recorded lectures, skim your notes from the previous week, looking over what topics were covered and where you left off. You should also briefly review the main headings or summary section of any reading you've been assigned.

The warm-up doesn't have to be long. The goal is simply to refresh yourself, to get yourself into the right frame of mind before learning about the new topics for that week.

▶ **Choose an environment that will promote good notetaking.** You should certainly choose an environment that enables you to focus and avoid distractions, but there's more to your choice than that. Picking the right environment can make a big difference.

Where is the best place to take notes? Usually it's in a quiet room, at a desk or table where you can spread out the course materials you have printed along with your textbook and laptop (or desktop) in order to easily look over and determine the most important information for your notes. An environment without distractions keeps you engaged in your notetaking.

Furthermore, a loud, crowded environment with various distractions makes it easier for your mind to wander and harder to take effective notes.

Journal Reflections

How Do I Take Notes?

1. Describe your typical notetaking techniques in a few sentences. Do you try to write down as much information as possible? Do you tend to take only a few notes? Do you often find you need a lot of time to write down notes?

2. Overall, how effective would you say your notetaking techniques are?

3. In which online classes do your techniques work best? Worst? Why?

4. Do your notes ever have "holes" in them—due to distractions causing your mind to wander or times when you didn't understand the information? When do you usually discover them? What do you do about them?

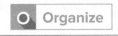 **Organize**

Getting the Tools of Notetaking Together

Do you have a favorite pen? Prefer an electronic tablet over a laptop?

Most of us have distinct tastes in the types of tools we use for various tasks: a favorite screwdriver, a preferred style of mouse, a brand of running shoes we find most comfortable. You should determine your preferred notetaking "tools," too. Using your favorite kind of notebook and pen or electronic tablet or laptop can give you the confidence and focus you need to take effective notes.

There are several things to consider as you prepare to take notes:

▶ **Choose the appropriate writing utensil.** Generally, using a pen is better than using a pencil. Ink is less likely to smudge, and what you produce with ink is usually brighter and clearer—and therefore easier to use when studying. Or consider typing all of your notes on your laptop or electronic device since you are already required to use either to complete work for your online classes. On the other hand, for your online math and accounting classes, where you work through formulas, a pencil might be better because it's easier to erase if you make a mistake when copying detailed, complex information.

Sometimes you may want to use a combination of pen and pencil. And in some cases you might use several different colors. One color—such as red—might signify important information that will be on the test. Another color might be reserved for definitions. And a third might be used for general notes. You can also apply this color-coding approach when taking notes using your laptop.

▶ **Choose a notebook that assists in notetaking.** Loose-leaf notebooks are particularly good for taking notes because they permit you to go back later and change the order of the pages or add additional material in the appropriate spot. But whatever kind of notebook you use, *use only one side of the page for writing: keep one side free of notes.* There may be times when you're studying when you'll want to spread your notes in front of you, and it's much easier if no material is written on the backs of the pages.

▶ **Consider the benefits of referring to your textbook while listening to podcasts or recorded lectures.** It's generally a good idea to have your textbook available to review when listening to a podcast or recorded lecture. Sometimes the content will refer to information contained in your textbook, and it's useful to have it handy to clarify information that is being delivered. You can also use it to look up key terms that may momentarily escape you.

▶ **Consider the pros and cons of using a laptop computer to take notes.** There are several advantages: Legibility problems are avoided, and it's easy to go back and revise or add material after you've taken the notes.

There are also potential pitfalls. You may end up typing more and thinking less. Or you may succumb to the temptation to check your e-mail or instant message your friends, rather than staying focused on notetaking.

From the perspective of . . .

A STUDENT Using a laptop is advantageous for students who type faster than they write. What are some of the advantages of taking handwritten notes?

© BJI/Blue Jean Images/Getty Images RF

Processing—Not Copying—Information

With pen poised, you're ready to begin the work of notetaking. As you start to write, you take down as much of the information from your course materials as possible.

Stop! You've made your first mistake. The central act in taking notes is not writing; thinking is far more important. The key to effective notetaking is to write down the right amount of information—not too much and not too little.

Successful notetaking involves processing and reflecting. When you are taking notes on podcasts or recorded lectures, it involves not just *hearing* what is said, but *listening actively.* **Hearing** is the involuntary act of sensing sounds. The annoying drip of a faucet or the grating sound of a co-worker's voice speaking on the phone in the next cubicle are two examples of how hearing is both involuntary and often meaningless. In contrast, **active listening** is the voluntary act of focusing on what is being said, making sense of it, and thinking about it in a way that permits it to

hearing
The involuntary act of sensing sounds.

active listening
The voluntary act of focusing on what is being said, making sense of it, and thinking about it in a way that permits it to be recalled accurately.

Determine Your Listening Style

Consider the following pairs of statements. Place a check mark next to the statement in each pair that more closely describes your listening style.

- ☐ 1a. When I'm listening in a meeting, I lean back and get as comfortable as possible.
- ☐ 1b. When I'm listening in a meeting, I sit upright and even lean forward a little.

- ☐ 2a. When listening to a recorded lecture, I let the instructor's words wash over me, generally going with the flow of the lecture.
- ☐ 2b. When listening to a recorded lecture, I try to guess in advance what the instructor is going to say and what direction the lecture is taking.

- ☐ 3a. I regard each recorded lecture as a separate event, not necessarily related to what the instructor has said before or will say the next time.
- ☐ 3b. As I listen, I regularly ask myself how this relates to what was said in previous recorded lectures.

- ☐ 4a. When I take notes, I try to reproduce the original information as closely as possible.
- ☐ 4b. When I take notes, I try to interpret and summarize the ideas behind the original information.

- ☐ 5a. I don't usually question the importance of what the instructor is saying in a recorded lecture or why it's the topic.
- ☐ 5b. I often ask why the content of the recorded lecture is important enough for the instructor to be speaking about it.

- ☐ 6a. I rarely question the accuracy or logic of a presentation, assuming that the presenter knows the topic better than I do.
- ☐ 6b. I often ask myself how the presenter knows something and find myself wondering how it could be proved.

- ☐ 7a. I just about never make eye contact with the individual presenting information.
- ☐ 7b. I often make eye contact with the individual presenting information.

If you tended to prefer the "a" statements in most pairs, you have a more passive listening style. If you preferred the "b" statements, you have a more active listening style. Based on your responses, consider ways that you can become a more active listener.

be recalled accurately. Listening involves concentration. And it requires shutting out competing thoughts, such as what we need to pick up at the grocery store or why our date last night went so badly wrong. (To get a sense of your own listening skills, complete **Try It! 1**.)

Keeping the importance of active listening in mind, consider the following recommendations for taking notes on podcasts, recorded lectures, or other online media:

▶ **Listen for the key ideas.** Not every sentence is equally important, and one of the most useful skills you can develop is separating the key ideas from supporting information. Good speakers strive to make just a few main points. The rest of what they say consists of explanation, examples, and other supportive material that expands upon the key ideas.

Your job, then, is to distinguish the key ideas from their support. To do this, you need to be alert and always searching for the **meta-message**—that is, the underlying main ideas that a speaker is seeking to convey, or the meaning behind the overt message you hear.

How can you discern the meta-message? One way is to *listen for key-words.* Speakers know what's important in the information they communicate; your job is to figure it out, not just from what they say but from how they say it.

meta-message
The underlying main ideas that a speaker is seeking to convey; the meaning behind the overt message.

For instance, listen for clues about the importance of material. Phrases like "don't forget . . . ," "be sure to remember that . . . ," "you need to know . . . ," "the most important thing that must be considered . . . ," "there are four problems with this approach . . . ," and—a big one—"this will be on the test . . ." should cause you to take notice. Another good sign of importance is repetition. If a speaker says the same thing in several ways, it's a clear sign that the material being discussed is important.

Finally, listen for what is not being said. Sometimes silence is not just golden, but informative as well. By noting what topics are not being covered, or are presented only minimally in the podcasts or recorded lectures, you can gauge the relative importance of ideas in comparison with one another.

This is where preliminary preparation and organization come in. The only way to know what's left out of a podcast or recorded lecture is to have done the assigned readings in advance. Also, don't be fooled into thinking that if a topic is not covered, it's unimportant: Most instructors believe students are responsible for all material that is assigned, whether or not it's explicitly covered.

▶ **Use short, abbreviated phrases—not full sentences—when taking notes.** Forget everything you've ever heard about always writing in full sentences. If you try to write notes in complete sentences, you'll soon become bogged down, paying more attention to your notes than to your online course materials. In fact, if you use full sentences, you'll be tempted to try transcribing every word you read or hear, which, as you now know, is not a good idea at all.

Instead, write in phrases, using only key words or terms. Save full sentences for definitions or quotes that your instructor clearly wants you to know word for word. For example, consider the following excerpt from a recorded lecture:

There are two kinds of job analyses used by human resource experts: First, there are job- or task-oriented analyses, and second, there are worker- or employee-oriented analyses. Job analyses just describe the tasks that need to be accomplished by a worker. For example, heart surgeons need to be able to operate on patients in order to carry out their jobs. In contrast, employee-oriented job descriptions need to describe knowledge, skills, and abilities the employee must have to get the job done. For example, surgeons need to understand the different types of blood vessels in the heart in order to be successful. Most job analyses include elements of both job-oriented and employee-oriented types.

If you were taking notes, you might produce the following:

2 kinds job analyses.
 1. Job-oriented (= task-oriented): tasks needed to get job done. Ex: heart surgeon operates
 2. Worker-oriented (= employee-oriented): knowledge, skills, abilities, etc. necessary to do job.
    Ex: surgeon knows blood vessels
 Most j.a. a combination

Note how the recorded lecturer used almost 120 words, while the notes used only around 35 words—less than one-third of the recorded lecture.

▶ **Use abbreviations.** One way to speed up the notetaking process is through the use of abbreviations. Among the most common:

and	*& or* +	with	*w/*	without	*w/o*
care of	*c/o*	leads to; resulting in	→	as a result of	←
percent	*%*	change	Δ	number	*#*
that is	*i.e.*	for example	*e.g.*	and so forth	*etc.*
no good	*n.g.*	question	*?*	compared with	*c/w*
page	*p.*	important!	*!!*	less than	*<*
more than	*>*	equals, same as	*=*	versus	*vs.*

▶ **Take notes in outline form.** It's often useful to take notes in the form of an outline. An outline summarizes ideas in short phrases and indicates the relationship among concepts through the use of indentations.

When outlining, it's best to be formal about it, using roman numerals, regular numbers, and capital and small letters (see the example in **Figure 3.1**). Or, if you prefer, you can also simply use outlining indentations without assigning numbers and letters.

Outlining serves a number of functions. It forces you to try to determine the structure of the podcast or recorded lecture or how to structure key information from your textbook, assignments, and course materials. Organizing the key points and noting the connections among them helps you remember the material better because you have processed it more.

Use **Try It! 2**, "Outline a Lecture," to practice your outlining skills.

figure 3.1
A Sample Outline

I. Difficulties faced by students seeking affordable child care
  A. Students subject to high costs of private child care
     1. Sometimes need to find alternative care
     2. Forced to take on part-time work to pay for child care
     3. Hard to find high-quality care
  B. Need to drop or reschedule classes due to child care limitations
II. Possible solutions
  A. College offers subsidized child care
     1. Advantage: Lower costs, convenience
     2. Potential problems
        a. Care may not be available for night classes
        b. School uses funds for child care instead of investing in education
  B. Using friends and family
     1. Advantage: Lower cost
     2. Disadvantages
        a. Availability may be inconsistent
        b. Care may not be available when needed
        c. Child may not be as secure if left with friends
III. Summary
  A. Advantages and disadvantages to both solutions
  B. May need new, creative solutions

Outline a Lecture

Slowly read the sections of the following recorded lecture.* As you read each paragraph, outline the main arguments on a separate piece of paper.

In 1985 Joseph Farman, a British earth scientist working in Antarctica, made an alarming discovery. Scanning the Antarctic sky, he found less ozone than should be there—not a slight depletion but a 30% drop from a reading recorded 5 years earlier in the Antarctic!

At first the scientist thought that this "ozone hole" was an as-yet-unexplained weather phenomenon. Evidence soon mounted, however, pointing to synthetic chemicals as the culprit. Detailed analysis of chemicals in the Antarctic atmosphere revealed a surprisingly high concentration of chlorine, a chemical known to destroy ozone. The source of the chlorine was a class of chemicals called chlorofluorocarbons (CFCs). CFCs have been manufactured in large amounts since they were invented in the 1920s, largely for use as coolants in air conditioners, propellants in aerosols, and foaming agents in making Styrofoam. CFCs were widely regarded as harmless because they were chemically unreactive under normal conditions. But in the thin atmosphere over Antarctica, CFCs condense onto tiny ice crystals; warmed by the sun in the spring, they attack and destroy ozone without being used up.

The thinning of the ozone layer in the upper atmosphere 25 to 40 kilometers above the surface of the earth is a serious matter. The ozone layer protects life from the harmful ultraviolet (UV) rays from the sun that bombard the earth continuously. Like invisible sunglasses, the ozone layer filters out these dangerous rays. When UV rays damage the DNA in skin cells, it can lead to skin cancer. Every 1% drop in the atmospheric ozone concentration is estimated to lead to a 6% increase in skin cancers. The drop of approximately 3% that has already occurred worldwide, therefore, is estimated to have led to as much as a 20% increase in skin cancers.

The world currently produces about 1 million tons of CFCs annually, three-fourths of it in the United States and Europe. As scientific observations have become widely known, governments have rushed to correct the situation. By 1990, worldwide agreements to phase out production of CFCs by the end of the century had been signed. Nonetheless, most of the CFCs manufactured since they were invented are still in use in air conditioners and aerosols and have not yet reached the atmosphere. As these CFCs, as well as CFCs still being manufactured, move slowly upward through the atmosphere, the problem can be expected to grow worse. Ozone depletion has now been reported over the North Pole as well, and there is serious concern that the Arctic ozone hole will soon extend over densely populated Europe and the northeastern United States.

Write your outline.

After you have outlined the passage, answer the following questions:

- Did you identify all of the main ideas of each passage?
- How do these notes differ from the types of notes you typically take?
- How might you improve your notes to better capture the main points?
- Would a different topic produce greater or fewer difficulties?

*Source: Adapted from G. Johnson, *The Living World*, 2nd ed. (New York: McGraw-Hill, 2000).

- **Copy key information from PowerPoint slides.** If your instructor posts to your class website PowerPoint slides that include definitions, quotations, or formulas, you probably should add this information to your notes. You can even print out the slides as the basis of your notes, filling in the details provided by other course materials. In fact, such prominently displayed material on your class website has "test item" written all over it. You might also want to highlight such material in some way in your notes. Ultimately, the combination of your notes and the PowerPoint slides will be invaluable when you are reviewing and studying the material.

- **Ask questions.** One of the most important things you can do is to ask questions. Raising questions will help you evaluate, clarify, and ultimately better understand the course materials. Even beyond these critical goals, questions serve several other purposes.

  For one thing, raising questions will help you personalize the material being covered, permitting you to draw it more closely into your own framework and perspective. Furthermore, when you ask a question and it is answered, you become more engaged in your academic performance.

  Questioning also increases your involvement in your online class as a whole. If you never raise questions, you are much less likely to feel connected. Becoming an active questioner in your online discussion boards will rightly make you feel like you have contributed something to the class.

  Finally, by posting questions to your class's online discussion board, you serve as a role model for other students. Your questions may help break the ice, making it easier for others to raise issues that they have about the material. And ultimately the answers that the instructor posts about others' questions may help you to better understand and/or evaluate your understanding of the material.

From the perspective of . . .

A MEDICAL ASSISTANT Learning abbreviations is an important aspect of life in a medical office. How can taking notes with abbreviations while in school help you learn important notations for your medical career?

© Tom Grill/Corbis RF

» LO 3-2 Strategies for Using Your Notes

The key to effective notetaking is to keep a balance between too many and too few notes.

Keep a Balance between Too Many Notes and Too Few Notes

The best way to achieve this balance is by paying close attention to the content in your online course materials. By being alert and engaged when taking notes,

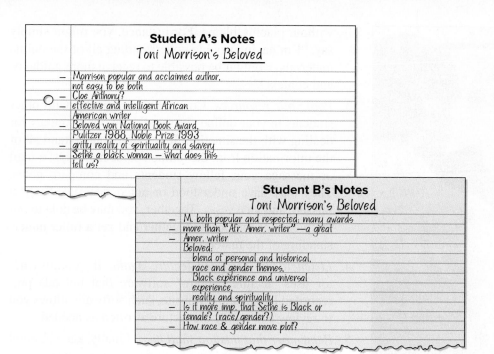

figure 3.2
Notes on a recorded lecture

Student A's Notes
Toni Morrison's <u>Beloved</u>

- Morrison popular and acclaimed author, not easy to be both
- Cloe Anthony?
- effective and intelligent African American writer
- Beloved won National Book Award, Pulitzer 1988, Noble Prize 1993
- gritty reality of spirituality and slavery
- Sethe a black woman — what does this tell us?

Student B's Notes
Toni Morrison's <u>Beloved</u>

- M. both popular and respected: many awards
- more than "Afr. Amer. writer" — a great
- Amer. writer
Beloved:
  blend of personal and historical,
  race and gender themes,
  Black experience and universal experience,
  reality and spirituality
- Is it more imp. that Sethe is Black or female? (race/gender?)
- How race & gender move plot?

you'll be able to make the most of the techniques we've discussed. The result: notes that capture the most important points and that will optimize your recall and mastery of the course subject matter (see a sample of two students' notes in **Figure 3.2**).

Use Special Techniques for Challenging Materials

Not every instructor provides online students with clear, compelling podcasts, recorded lectures, required reading, or additional course materials. All of us have suffered through online classes that are deficient in one or more ways. What should you do when you find yourself in such a situation?

1. *Ask questions about the material.* If you have questions, you need to contact your instructor—through e-mail or your class website. You probably are not the only one struggling with the instructor's shortcomings. You will be doing everyone in the class a favor if you admit you're confused and respectfully ask for clarification because your instructor may realize that further review of the topic is necessary and provide the entire class with online additional instruction.

2. *Ask—privately and politely—for the instructor to alter the way material is presented.* It is not bad etiquette, for example, to ask an instructor to provide more context on the PowerPoint slides he or she posts on the class website. Very often a reality check from a student will be welcome. But don't post your comment in the class discussion board where everyone can see it. Send your comment in an e-mail or private message through the class website. In addition, pay attention to the way you phrase your question. Avoid framing it in a way that makes the instructor feel inept ("The class materials are too confusing; you're completely losing me"). Instead, keep the comment neutral,

If you've ever been totally lost following a lecture, you may have discovered that speaking with your instructor immediately after class was helpful. Most instructors are very happy to go over and clarify key points that they've covered during class. They also appreciate your initiative and interest.
© Ariel Skelley/Blend Images LLC RF

without placing blame. For instance, you might simply say, "I'm having trouble understanding all of the online materials; would it be possible to receive more guidance and context?"

3. *Pool your resources.* Connect electronically with other students in your online class and work out a strategy for dealing with the situation. If you don't understand all of the information from the online course materials, e-mail or message your fellow students and compare notes. They may have understood or noted material that you missed, and vice versa. Together, you may be able to put the pieces of the puzzle together and get a fuller understanding of the material.

4. *Listen to the recorded lecture again.* If your instructor uses "lecture capture" software that uploads pre-recorded lectures to a website, such software allows you to review and replay the lecture as often as needed.

5. *Remember that this too shall pass.* Finally, keep in mind that this is a temporary condition; your experience usually won't last more than one term. Most online instructors are conscientious and well prepared, and unless you have enormously bad luck, the unpleasant experience you're having now will not be routine.

 **E Evaluate**

Thinking Critically about Your Notes

Take a moment to look over your notes—to evaluate what you've written.

After being sure you can answer yes to the most basic question—can I read what I've written?—ask yourself these questions:

▶ Do my notes do a good job of representing what was covered in the online course materials, including podcasts and recorded lectures?

▶ Are there any key points that are not entirely clear?

▶ Do I need help clarifying any of the key points?

Evaluating your notes is a critical part of the notetaking process. You can get a sense of how effective your notetaking has been and determine if you need to e-mail your instructor to clarify anything that is still not clear.

Perhaps, for example, you've left out a key word in a definition. Maybe you don't understand a concept fully, even though you've written about it in your notes. Possibly you've left out the third step in a list of six steps necessary to accomplish something.

Most instructors will be happy to answer questions from students who have obviously been engaged in the online course materials. Just make sure that you add what they tell you to your notes, so you'll be able to refer to them later. (To practice evaluating your notes, complete **Try It! 3**.)

Evaluate Your Notes

Take a set of notes you made recently for one of your online classes and evaluate it on the following criteria.

Statement	Not Even Slightly	Slightly	Moderately	Pretty Well	Very Well
1. I can read my notes (i.e., they are legible).					
2. Someone else can read my notes.					
3. My notes are complete; I missed nothing important.					
4. My notes represent the key points that were covered in the online materials.					
5. My notes reflect the emphasized content.					
6. The key points are clear and understandable.					
7. The notes contain only important points, with no extraneous material.					
8. I understand not only the notes but also the online class content they reflect.					
9. Using only the notes, I will be able to reconstruct the essential content of the online class in three months.					

What do your answers tell you about the effectiveness of your notetaking skills? What might you do differently the next time you take notes?

R Rethink | Activating Your Memory

Notetaking is finished. You put the top on your pen or close your laptop, set your textbook aside, and head out for a cup of coffee before going to work.

Wait! Before you close up your laptop, finish the P.O.W.E.R. process. Rethink the notes you just took. Spending 5 or 10 minutes reconsidering what you've written right now can save you *hours* of work later. The reason: Rethinking promotes the transfer of information into long-term memory. As you link the new information you've taken down to what you already know and then integrate it, you essentially plug this information into your memory in a much more meaningful way, which means you can remember it better and more easily.

If you looked over your notes to clarify and evaluate the information as soon as you finished writing them, you've already begun the process. But once you have set your notes aside for a period of time, you need to review the material more formally. Here's how to do it:

▶ **Rethink as soon as possible.** Time is of the essence! The rethinking phase of notetaking doesn't have to take long; 5 to 10 minutes are usually sufficient. The more critical issue is *when* you do it. The longer you wait before reviewing your notes, the less effective the process will be.

There's no doubt that the best approach is to review the material just after you finish writing. Stay seated and go over your notes. But what if you must hurry off to work? The next best thing is to find a quiet space during one of your breaks, take out your notes, and do your rethinking there.

In any case, don't let the day end without examining your notes. In fact, reconsidering material just before you go to sleep can be particularly effective.

▶ **Make rethinking an active process.** Some people feel the notes they take for an online class are akin to historical documents in a museum, with Do Not Touch! signs hanging on them. On the contrary, think of your notes as a construction project and yourself as the person in charge of the project.

When you review your notes, do so with an eye to improving them. If any information is not entirely clear, change the wording in your notes, adding to or amending what's there. If certain words are hard to read, fix them; it won't be any easier to read them the night before a test—in fact, chances are that you'll have even more trouble.

If, on rethinking the material, you don't understand something, e-mail your instructor to clarify it. And when you receive an explanation, add it to your notes so you won't forget it. (You might want to use a different-colored pen or different font color for additions to your notes, so you'll know they came later.)

▶ **Think critically about the material in your notes.** As you review the information, think about the material from a critical point of view. Go beyond the facts and pieces of information, integrating and evaluating the material.

In addition, as you rethink your notes, don't think of them only in terms of a single week's worth of online instruction. Instead, take a longer view. Ask yourself how they fit into the broader themes of the class and the goals that you and the instructor have for the term. How will the information be useful to you? Why did the instructor assign certain topics?

concept mapping
A method of structuring written material by graphically grouping and connecting key ideas and themes.

▶ **Create concept maps. Concept mapping** (sometimes called "mind mapping") is a method of structuring written material by graphically grouping and connecting key ideas and themes. In contrast to an outline, a concept map visually illustrates how related ideas fit together. The pictorial summary gives you another handle to store the information in memory, and it focuses your thinking on the key ideas from the online materials.

In a concept map, each key idea is placed in a different part of the map, and related ideas are placed near it—above, below, or beside it. What emerges does not have the rigid structure of an outline. Instead, a "finished" concept map looks something like a map of the solar system, with the largest and most central idea in the center (the "sun" position), and related ideas surrounding it at various distances. It has also been compared to a large tree, with numerous branches and subbranches radiating out from a central trunk. (**Figure 3.3** presents a sample concept map.)

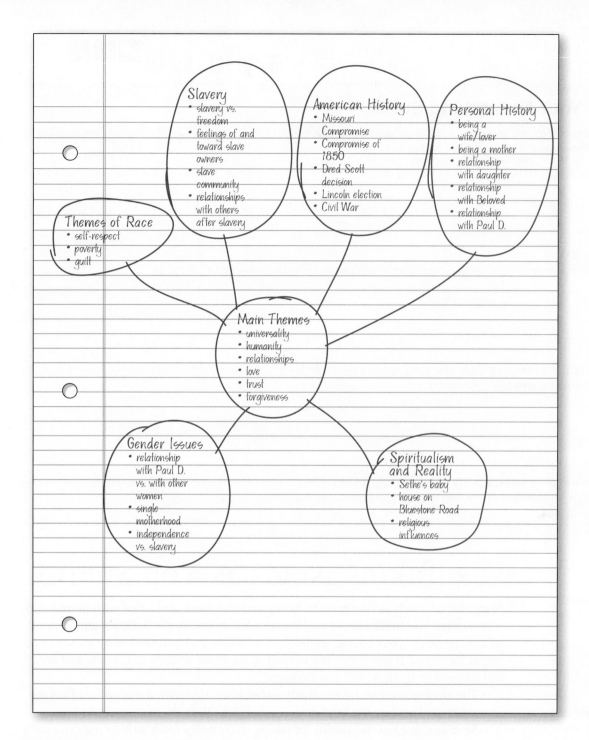

figure 3.3
A Concept Map of Toni Morrison's *Beloved*

Building a concept map has several advantages. It forces you to rethink the material in your notes in a new style—particularly important if you used traditional outlining while taking the notes. In addition, it helps you to tie together the material for a given week of online instruction. Finally, it will help you to build a master concept map later, when you're studying the material for a final exam. (To practice the techniques we've been discussing, see **Try It! 4**, "Practice Your Notetaking Skills.")

Practice Your Notetaking Skills

Practice your notetaking skills, using any techniques you find helpful, in one of the online classes in which you are enrolled this term. Use these notes to answer these questions:

1. Which specific techniques did I use in taking notes?

2. Which of the notetaking techniques detailed in this chapter was I unable to use, and why?

3. Could I take the notes I made in one of my online classes and redo them, using one of the techniques in this chapter, such as creating a concept map?

After you have taken notes, use the techniques discussed in this chapter to evaluate and rethink them. Creating a concept map on a separate sheet of paper may be particularly helpful.

»LO 3-3 Taking Notes as You Study

Weighing as much as five pounds, bulky and awkward, and filled with more information than you think anyone could ever need to know, it's the meat and potatoes of college work: your course textbook. You might feel intimidated by its size; you might think you'll never be able to read it, let alone understand, learn, and recall the material in it. How will you manage?

study notes

Notes taken for the purpose of reviewing material.

The answer involves taking **study notes**, notes taken for the purpose of reviewing material. They are the kind of notes that you take now to study from later.

Several strategies are useful for taking study notes from written material such as magazines, books, journals, and websites. Which approach works best depends on whether you're able to write on the material you wish to take notes on.

Taking Notes on Material You Can Write On or Annotate Digitally

Some forms of digital materials, such as the typical online textbook, have built-in software systems that allow you to create notes or to highlight the text. For such virtual material, as well as hard-copy materials that you own, here are some suggestions for creating study notes:

▶ **Use the annotation software capabilities on virtual material.** Most online textbooks or e-books allow you to highlight particular passages and to insert, and save, notes about the material. Some devices, such as certain tablets, permit you to use a stylus to physically write (and save) notes on the material in the e-book. Furthermore, in some cases, you can even share your notes with other online students, or view their notes. Be sure you understand the capabilities of the e-textbook software to get the most out of what it has to offer.

▶ **Integrate your text notes into your study notes.** Start by annotating the pages, using the techniques that work best for you: highlighting, underlining, circling, making marginal notes. (If you are using an e-textbook, the software will usually permit you to insert, and save, comments and different types of highlighting. Be sure you understand the capabilities of the e-textbook software to get the most out of what it has to offer.) Keep in mind that highlighting the text, by itself, is not sufficient to promote learning—it's what you do next that counts.

Specifically, after you've finished reading and annotating the material, create study notes. The study notes should provide a summary of the key points, in outline form or in the form of concept maps. Either form of summary should supplement the annotations you've made on the printed page.

Furthermore, any notes you take should stand on their own. For instance, they should include enough information to be useful whether or not you have the book or article on hand.

▶ **Use flash cards.** If you feel confident that the annotations you've written in the book are sufficiently comprehensive, you might consider taking notes on flash cards. **Flash cards** are simply index cards that contain key pieces of information that you need to remember.

Flash cards are particularly useful in subjects that present many small bits of information to remember, such as technical vocabulary words or math formulas. When you need to learn a new term, for instance, you can write the term on one side of a card and its definition on the other side.

One of the greatest virtues of flash cards is their portability. Because they are small, they can fit into your pocket or backpack, and you can look at them at odd times when you have a spare moment.

flash cards
Index cards that contain key pieces of information to be remembered.

Taking Notes on Material You Are Unable to Write On

Taking notes on materials that can't be written on or annotated digitally is a different story. Some digital textbooks and other online materials don't offer the opportunity of making online annotations. And traditional physical, hard-copy library books, magazines, journal articles, and materials on library reserve that are shared with others require a different approach.

▶ **Approach the written material as you would a podcast, recorded lecture, or other online media.** The techniques we discussed earlier for taking notes on podcasts and recorded lectures can all be adapted for taking notes from written material. In fact, the task is often easier because it's in black and white in front of you.

▶ **Use laptops, which can be especially helpful in creating study notes.** If you're a good keyboarder, it's often easier and quicker to take notes using

Taking Notes on the Job: Meetings of the Minds

The principles of good notetaking discussed in this chapter are useful not only in college. They can also help you as you make your way in your career. For instance, you may need to take notes on lengthy memos or reports that detail company procedures you will need to master to do your job.

Further, one of the most important settings where you'll want to take effective notes is in meetings. For many people, meetings take up a good part of their professional workdays, and being able to take effective notes can provide a significant career advantage.

Meetings are similar to online discussions. During a meeting you will want to look for key topics and make note of the ideas that receive the most emphasis or enthusiastic response. Note these areas and keep them in mind as likely priorities.

During meetings, tasks are often assigned. Not only do you want to clearly note what you are to do and when you are supposed to do it, but keeping track of what others are doing will also be helpful because you may need to get information from them or otherwise coordinate efforts. For instance, if you are assigned the task of managing the development of your company's website, you'll want to clarify in your notes who has agreed to do what portion of the task.

Taking notes when others are speaking also shows that you are paying attention to what the speaker is saying. It's a kind of compliment that suggests you find what the speaker is saying to be so important that you will want to refer to it later.

Finally, notetaking plays another role: It can make seemingly interminable meetings appear to proceed faster by providing something for you to do that's more active than simply listening. In short, not only can notetaking provide you with a clear record of what occurred in a meeting, but it can also keep you engaged in what is going on.

a word-processing program. On the other hand, don't be lured into typing too much. You need to be just as selective in what you input into your computer.

▶ **Use the tricks of the trade we discussed earlier.** Look for key ideas, definitions, quotations, and formulas, and include them in your notes. Use the headings that are included in the text, such as chapter and section titles. Bold or italic type is also a clue that an important point is being made. Graphs and charts often provide critical information.

▶ **Use the same form of notetaking that you use for podcasts, recorded lectures, or other online media.** If you write your notes in outline form, create an outline based on the written material. If you often create graphics such as concept maps, create them now. The point is to produce notes that are consistent.

Speaking *of* Success

© Mark Wilson/Getty Images News/Getty Images

NAME: **Sonia Sotomayor**

SCHOOL: **Princeton University, BA, 1976 (Summa Cum Laude); Yale Law School, JD, 1979**

U.S. Supreme Court Justice Sonia Sotomayor's educational journey was not an easy one, but hard work, determination, and a supportive family helped her become the first Latina and the third woman to serve in the Supreme Court's 220-year history.

Sotomayor's parents moved from Puerto Rico to New York City in the 1950s, and she grew up in a working-class Bronx neighborhood where both of her parents worked. At the age of 9, she experienced the emotional blow of her father's death, but she immersed herself in books—particularly the Nancy Drew series, which started her thinking about crime solving. That, and doing her homework in front of the TV while watching lawyer Perry Mason, ignited her goal of pursuing law.

She went on to graduate from Cardinal Spellman High School in New York City and was able to earn a scholarship to college. Although her undergraduate years were challenging, she was ultimately successful, graduating with honors. After graduation, she went on to law school.

"Although I grew up in very modest and challenging circumstances, I consider my life to be immeasurably rich," Sotomayor said.

"My mother taught us that the key to success in America is a good education," Sotomayor said at her Senate confirmation hearing. "And she set the example, studying alongside my brother and me at our kitchen table so that she could become a registered nurse."

Close to her family, the Supreme Court justice notes that her mother, who worked six days a week as a nurse to support her and her brother, is her greatest inspiration. And while her achievements have been attained through hard work, she points to an appreciation for the opportunities she has had.

"It is our nation's faith in a more perfect union that allows a Puerto Rican girl from the Bronx to stand here now," she said during her swearing-in ceremony. "I am struck again by the wonder of my own life and the life we in America are so privileged to lead."

[RETHINK]

- Why do you think Sotomayor's closeness to her family was important in helping her be academically successful?

- What do you think it was about the Nancy Drew books that proved inspirational to Sotomayor? (Look up "Nancy Drew" on the web if you are unfamiliar with the books.)

Looking Back

LO 3-1 Describe techniques for taking notes for an online class.

▶ The central feature of good notetaking is not writing down everything.

▶ Prepare for taking notes by identifying the instructor's and your own goals for the online course, completing all assignments on time, and "warming up" by reviewing the notes and assignments from the previous class.

▶ Before writing notes, first take the time to process the information.

▶ Notes should be brief phrases rather than full sentences and, if possible, in outline form.

LO 3-2 Apply techniques for taking notes from written materials.

▶ Once you finish your notes, evaluate them, verifying that they are complete and understandable.

▶ As soon as possible, actively rethink your notes.

LO 3-3 Explain methods for effective notetaking.

▶ Taking good study notes from written materials involves many of the principles that apply to taking good notes from oral sources, such as podcasts and recorded lectures, although with written materials, it can be easier to get the information down more accurately.

▶ Concept maps and flash cards can be helpful tools for notetaking from textbooks.

[KEY TERMS AND CONCEPTS]

Active listening (p. 61)
Concept mapping (p. 70)

Flash cards (p. 73)
Hearing (p. 61)

Meta-message (p. 62)
Study notes (p. 72)

[RESOURCES]

ON THE WEB

If you are having difficulty taking notes effectively on the online course materials, e-mail your instructor. Also consider attaching your notes to your e-mail so the instructor can assess what you are doing correctly and what could stand improvement.

If your problems persist, and you have great difficulty translating and summarizing the key points from your textbook and course materials into your own words, then there's a small possibility that you may suffer from a learning disability. Check your college website for resources and consider being tested by a specialist to rule this out.

The following sites on the Internet provide the opportunity to extend your learning about the material in this chapter. (Although the web addresses were accurate at the time the book was printed, check the *P.O.W.E.R. Learning* website for any changes that may have occurred.)

▶ Brigham Young University's Career and Counseling Center offers a page (**https://casc.byu.edu/note-taking**) on the Cornell Note-Taking System. This notetaking system can help you improve the organization of your notes, while allowing you to make use of your existing strengths as a notetaker.

▶ A learning style model formulated by Richard M. Felder and Linda K. Silverman from North Carolina State University, the Index of Learning Styles, is an online instrument used to assess preferences on four dimensions (active/reflective, sensing/intuitive, visual/verbal, and sequential/global) (**www.ncsu.edu/felder-public/ILSpage.html**).

IN PRINT

Fiona McPherson's *Effective Notetaking* (Wayz Press, 2012) and Judy Kesselman-Turkel and Franklynn Peterson's *Note-Taking Made Easy* (University of Wisconsin Press, 2003) provide broad overviews of how to take good notes in class.

In addition, Deana Hippie's *Note Taking Made Easy!* (Scholastic, 2010) and Bobbi DePorter and Mike Hernacki's *Quantum Notes* (Learning Forum, 2000) provide strategies for increasing your listening and notetaking expertise.

The Case of . . .

Not Missing a Thing

Some people write down a few key points from an important chapter in their textbook or from their course materials. Others write down most things. Jennifer Beck wrote down *everything*.

The woman was virtually a human dictation machine. She spent her time reviewing her class materials in a whirlwind of notetaking, writing down a clear, meticulous script of seemingly every word in the chapter, course handouts, and online lessons. By the end of a term, her notebooks were so lengthy that they approached the size of telephone books from a small city.

Yet despite her thorough notes, Jennifer was only a mediocre student. She was a hard worker and studied her many notes thoroughly before tests. But she never managed to get grades higher than a C+. It seemed unbelievable to her. She worked incredibly hard in taking good notes. Why wasn't it paying off?

1. How do you think Jennifer defines "good notetaking"?

2. Why does Jennifer's method of notetaking produce such poor results? What is she missing?

3. If you asked Jennifer to summarize the instructor's main ideas after a class lecture, how successful do you think she would be? Why?

4. Do you think it would be easy or hard to study for a final exam using Jennifer's notes? Why?

5. Do you think Jennifer evaluates her notes after she finishes writing them? Do you think she ever rethinks them? What questions would you ask to help her perform these steps?

6. In general, what advice would you give Jennifer on notetaking?

CHAPTER 4

Learning Outcomes

By the time you finish this chapter, you will be able to

» LO **4-1** Identify the kinds of tests you will encounter in college.

» LO **4-2** Explain the best ways to prepare for and take various kinds of tests.

» LO **4-3** Analyze the best strategies for answering specific kinds of test questions.

Taking Tests

Months of studying, reading, and online classes . . . and now it all came down to a test.

That was the thought that ran through Eddie Penn's head as he sat in front of his laptop to take the final exam in his online computer programming course. Eddie knew the test would end up counting for 65 percent of his final grade. If he passed, he would have enough credits to get the graphic design degree he'd been working toward for years. If he failed . . . Eddie tried not to think about that.

He'd taken tests before, but the stakes had never seemed so high for a single exam. Although he was fairly confident—he had studied hard—he couldn't relax altogether. He told himself that he had always done well on tests in the past; he wasn't going to fail now. But still—Eddie couldn't help but feel like his entire career, maybe his entire future, was on the line.

Looking Ahead

Although many tests are not as critical as Eddie Penn's computer programming final, tests do play a significant role in everyone's academic life. Students typically experience more anxiety over tests than over anything else in their college careers. If you are returning to college after a long break, or perhaps have struggled with tests earlier in your academic career, you may find the prospect of taking a test especially intimidating.

But tests don't have to be so anxiety producing. There are strategies and techniques you can learn to reduce your fear of test taking. In fact, learning how to take tests is in some ways as important as learning the content that they cover. Taking tests effectively does not just involve mastering information; it also requires mastering specific test-taking skills.

One of the most important goals of this chapter is to take the mystery out of the whole process of taking tests. To do that, you'll learn about the different types of tests and strategies you can start using even before you take a test. You'll gain insight into how different kinds of tests work and how best to approach them, and you'll also learn about the various types of test questions and strategies for responding most effectively to each type.

This chapter also explores two aspects of test taking that may affect your performance: test anxiety and cramming. You will learn ways to deal with your anxiety and keep cramming to a minimum—but you will also learn how to make the most of cramming, if you do have to resort to it.

The chapter ends with suggestions for evaluating your performance toward the end of a test and for using what you have learned to improve your performance the next time around.

»LO 4-1 Getting Ready

Tests may be the most unpopular part of college life. Students hate them because they produce fear, anxiety, apprehension about being evaluated, and a focus on grades instead of learning for learning's sake. Instructors often don't like them very much either because they produce fear, anxiety, apprehension about being evaluated, and a focus on grades instead of learning for learning's sake. That's right: Students and instructors dislike tests for the very same reasons.

But tests are also valuable. A well-constructed test identifies what you know and what you still need to learn. Tests help you see how your performance compares with that of others. And knowing that you'll be tested on a body of material is certainly likely to motivate you to learn material more thoroughly.

However, there's another reason you might dislike tests: You may assume that tests have the power to define your worth as a person. If you do badly on a test,

Journal Reflections

How I Feel about Tests

1. How do you feel about tests in general?

2. What are your first memories of being in a testing situation? What were your feelings, and why?

3. What makes a test "good" and "bad" from your perspective?

4. What factors contribute to your success or failure on a particular exam? Which of these factors are under your control?

5. What strategies do you use when taking tests to maximize your performance? Which have been particularly effective, and why?

you may be tempted to believe that you've received some fundamental information about yourself from the instructor and the college, information that says you're a failure in some significant way.

This is a dangerous—and completely wrong—assumption. If you do badly on a test, it doesn't mean you're a bad person. Or stupid. Or that you don't belong in college. If you don't do well on a test, you're the same person you were before you took the test—no better, no worse. You just did badly on a test. Period.

In short, tests are not a measure of your value as an individual. They are only a measure of how well (and how much) you studied, and your test-taking skills. Tests are tools; they are indirect and imperfect measures of what we know. Someone with a great deal of knowledge can do poorly on a test; tension or going at too slow a pace can lead to unwelcome results in some cases. Another person may know considerably less and still do better on the test simply because he or she may have learned some test-taking skills along the way.

How we do on a test depends on a number of considerations: the kind of test it is, the subject matter involved, our understanding of test-taking strategies, and, above all, how well we have prepared for it. Let's turn, then, to the first step in test taking: preparation. (The five steps are summarized in the P.O.W.E.R. Plan.)

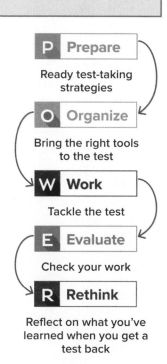

P Prepare
Ready test-taking strategies

O Organize
Bring the right tools to the test

W Work
Tackle the test

E Evaluate
Check your work

R Rethink
Reflect on what you've learned when you get a test back

P.O.W.E.R. Plan

Readying Your Test-Taking Strategies

Preparation for tests requires a number of strategies. Among the most important are the following.

Remember: Everything You Do in a Course Is Preparation for a Test

All the things you do during a course help to prepare you for a test. There is no surer way to get good grades on tests than to review all online course materials faithfully and to complete all class assignments seriously and on time.

Preparing for tests is a long-term proposition. It's not a matter of "giving your all" the night before the test. Instead, it's a matter of giving your all to every aspect of the course.

Know What You Are Preparing For

Determine as much as you can about the test before you begin to study for it. The more you know about a test beforehand, the more efficient your studying will be.

To find out about an upcoming test, ask these questions:

▶ Is the test called a "test," "exam," "quiz," or something else? As you can see in **Table 4.1**, the names imply different things. For simplicity's sake, we'll use the term "test" throughout this chapter, but know that these distinctions exist, and they should affect the way you prepare.

▶ What material will the test cover?

▶ How many questions will be on it?

▶ How much time is it expected to take? Will it be a timed test?

▶ What kinds of questions will be on the test?

▶ How will it be graded?

▶ Will sample questions be provided?

▶ Will the instructor post a study guide to the class website?

▶ How much does the test contribute to my final course grade?

Match Test Preparation to Question Types

Test questions come in different types (see **Table 4.2**), and each requires a somewhat different style of preparation.

▶ **Essay questions.** Essay tests focus on the big picture—ways in which the various pieces of information being tested fit together. You'll need to know not just a series of facts, but also the connections between them, and you will have to be able to discuss these ideas in an organized and logical way. A good study tactic is to play instructor: After carefully reviewing your notes and other course materials, think of likely exam questions. Then, without looking at your notes or your readings, answer each potential essay question, either aloud

table 4.1   Quizzes, Tests, Exams . . . What's in a Name?

Although they may vary from one instructor to another, the following definitions are most commonly used:

Quizzes. A *quiz* is a brief assessment, usually covering a relatively small amount of material. Some quizzes cover as little as one week's worth of reading. Although a single quiz usually doesn't count very much, instructors often add quiz scores together, and collectively they can become a significant part of your final course grade.

Tests. A *test* is a more extensive, more heavily weighted assessment than a quiz, covering more material. A test may come every few weeks of the term, often after each third or quarter of the term has passed, but this varies with the instructor and the course.

Exams. An *exam* is the most substantial kind of assessment. In many online classes, just one exam is given—a final exam at the end of the term. Sometimes there are two exams, one at the midpoint of the term (called, of course, a midterm) and the second at the end. Exams are usually weighted quite heavily because they are meant to assess your knowledge of all the course material covered up to that point.

table 4.2   Types of Test Questions

Essay	Requires a fairly extended, on-the-spot composition about some topic. Examples include questions that call on you to describe a person, process, or event, and questions that ask you to compare or contrast two separate sets of material.
Multiple-choice	Usually contains a question or statement, followed by a number of possible answers (usually 4 or 5 of them). You are supposed to choose the best response from the choices offered.
True–false	Presents statements about a topic that are either accurate or inaccurate. You are to indicate whether each statement is accurate (true) or inaccurate (false).
Matching	Presents two lists of related information, arranged in column form. Typically, you are asked to pair up the items that go together (e.g., a scientific term and its definition).
Short-answer	Requires brief responses (usually a few sentences at most) in a kind of mini-essay.
Fill-in	Requires you to add one or more missing words to a sentence or series of sentences.

or by writing out the major points an answer should include. After you've answered the questions, check yourself by looking at the notes and readings once again.

▶ **Short-answer and fill-in questions.** Short-answer and fill-in questions are similar to essays in that they require you to recall key pieces of information rather than finding it on the page in front of you. However, short-answer and fill-in questions—unlike essay questions—typically don't demand that you integrate or compare different types of information. Consequently, the focus of your study should be on the recall of specific, detailed information.

▶ **Multiple-choice, true–false, and matching questions.** While the focus of review for essay questions should be on major issues and controversies, studying for multiple-choice, true–false, and matching questions requires more attention to the details.

Almost anything is fair game for multiple-choice, true–false, and matching questions, so you can't afford to overlook anything when studying. True, these kinds of questions put the material right there on the page for you to react to—Did Columbus land in 1492, or not?—rather than asking you to provide the names and dates yourself (as in the case of the essay question). Nevertheless, to do well on these tests you must put your memory into high gear and master a great many facts.

It's a particularly good idea to record important facts on index cards. Either write them out by hand or use one of several smartphone apps that help you create them. In addition, if you are using an e-textbook, the software may make it easy for you to create index cards automatically. They can be reviewed on your smartphone or computer or you can print them out.

It also can be helpful to write the name of a particular concept or theory on one side of a note card, and then to generate and write an example of it on the other side. Studying the cards will help ensure that you fully understand the concepts and theories and can generalize them to different situations.

Deal with Test Anxiety

What does the anticipation of a test do to you? Do you feel shaky? Frantic, like there's not enough time to get it all done? Do you feel as if there's a knot in your stomach? Do you grit your teeth?

Test anxiety is a temporary condition characterized by fears and concerns about test taking. It's a sign of a very real physical reaction: Your body is producing stress hormones as a reaction to your mental state of concern.

Almost everyone experiences test anxiety to some degree, though for some people it's more of a problem than for others. The real danger with test anxiety is that it can become so overwhelming that it can hurt test performance. (To assess your own test-taking style and the degree of anxiety around tests that you experience, see **Try It! 1**.)

You'll never eliminate test anxiety completely, nor do you want to. A little bit of nervousness can energize us, making us more attentive and vigilant. Like any competitive event, testing can motivate us to do our best. You might think of moderate test anxiety as a desire to perform at your peak—a useful quality at test time.

On the other hand, for some, anxiety can spiral into the kind of paralyzing fear that makes their minds go blank. There are several ways to keep this from happening to you:

1. *Prepare thoroughly.* The more you prepare, the less test anxiety you'll feel. Good preparation can give you a sense of control and mastery, and it will prevent test anxiety from overwhelming you.

2. *Take a realistic view of the test.* Remember that your future success does not hinge on your performance on any single exam. Think of the big picture: Put the task ahead in context, and remind yourself of all the hurdles you've passed so far.

Measure Your Test-Taking Style

Do you feel anxious at the very thought of a test, or are you cool and calm in the face of testing situations? Get a sense of your test-taking style by checking off every statement below that applies to you.

- ☐ **1.** The closer a test date approaches, the more nervous I get.
- ☐ **2.** I am sometimes unable to sleep on the night before a test.
- ☐ **3.** I have "frozen up" during a test, finding myself unable to think or respond.
- ☐ **4.** I can feel my hands shaking as I open my laptop (or turn on my computer) to begin a test.
- ☐ **5.** The minute I read a tough test question, all the facts I ever knew about the subject abandon me and I can't get them back no matter how hard I try.
- ☐ **6.** I have become physically ill before or during a test.
- ☐ **7.** Nervousness prevents me from studying immediately before a test.
- ☐ **8.** I often dream about an upcoming test.
- ☐ **9.** Even if I successfully answer a number of questions, my anxiety stays with me throughout the test.
- ☐ **10.** I'm reluctant to submit my online test for fear that I can do better if I continue to work on it.

If you checked off more than four statements, you have experienced fairly serious test anxiety. If you checked off more than six statements, your anxiety is probably interfering with your test performance. In particular, statements 3, 5, 6, 7, and 10 may indicate serious test anxiety.

If, based on your responses to this questionnaire and your previous experience, your level of test anxiety is high, what are some of the steps described in this chapter that might be helpful to you?

3. *Eat right and get enough sleep.* Good mental preparation occurs when your body is well prepared.

4. *Learn relaxation techniques.* You can learn to reduce or even eliminate the jittery physical symptoms of test anxiety by using relaxation techniques. The basic process is straightforward: Breathe evenly, gently inhaling and exhaling. Focus your mind on a pleasant, relaxing scene such as a beautiful forest or a peaceful farm, or on a restful sound such as that of ocean waves breaking on the beach.

5. *Visualize success.* Think of an image of your instructor entering a big, fat "A" in the online grade book. Or imagine your family congratulating you on your fine performance the day after the test. Positive visualizations that highlight your potential success can help replace images of failure that may fuel test anxiety.

6. Just before you take a test, spend 10 minutes writing about your feelings regarding the upcoming exam. It's a way to help free yourself of negative emotions, allowing you to concentrate better on the exam.

What if these strategies don't work? If your test anxiety is so great that it's getting in the way of your success, consider consulting a professional counselor or therapist. Many colleges provide an online learning resource center or an online counseling center that can provide you with personalized help. (To focus on dealing with math test anxiety, see the **Course Connections** feature.)

Special Techniques for Dealing with Math Anxiety

For many students, the greatest test anxiety comes when they're taking a test involving math. Math seems to bring out the worst fears in some people, perhaps because it's seen as a discipline in which answers are either totally right or totally wrong, or because they feel they've "hit the wall" and they'll never be able to understand a new concept, no matter how hard they try.

Such feelings about math can be devastating because they can prevent you from doing well even if you know the material. If you suffer from math anxiety, keep these things in mind:

- Math is like any other subject: The greatest component of success is the effort you put in, not whether you have a "math gene" that makes you naturally good at math. It's not true that you either are born "good at math" or not. It's a cultural myth that "math is hard" and that somehow it's fine if you're not good at it.

- It's also not true that there's only one way to solve a math problem. Sometimes there are a variety of routes to coming up with a solution. And keep in mind that the solution to math problems often calls for creativity, not just sheer logic.

- It's a false stereotype that women are not as good at math as men, but it's a stereotype that many women buy into. Research has shown that when men do badly on a math test, they're most likely to think that they haven't put in enough effort. But when women don't do well on a math test, they're three times more likely than men to feel that they don't have enough ability to be successful.[1] That's an erroneous view of the world. Don't become a prisoner of stereotypes.

Use these special strategies to deal with math problems on exams:

BEFORE TESTS:

1. Math is cumulative, building on prior concepts and knowledge. Make sure you review math fundamentals before moving on to more advanced topics.
2. E-mail your instructor questions. Don't be afraid that you'll ask the wrong question in the wrong way. Instructors want you to understand their subject.
3. Make use of review materials and other study resources.
4. Practice, practice, practice. The more experience you have completing math problems under pressure, the better you'll do. Practice math problems using a timer in order to simulate an actual test.

DURING TESTS:

1. Analyze math problems carefully. What are the known quantities or constants, and what pieces of information are missing? What formula(s) or theorem(s) apply?
2. Consider drawing a diagram, graph, or probability tree.
3. Break down calculations into their component parts.
4. Check your math carefully.
5. Be logical in your presentation, and show every step as you solve problems. Your instructor may give you partial credit if you lay out every step you're going through. In addition, some instructors may require you to show your work.

Studying for the Test

A key part of preparing for a test is a trial run-through. Like running practice trials before you participate in an actual race, it makes sense to ready yourself for the real event by taking a practice test.

Test Yourself

Once you feel you've mastered the material, test yourself on it. There are several ways to do this. Often textbooks are accompanied by websites that offer automatically scored practice tests and quizzes.

You can also create a test for yourself. Make it as close as possible to what you expect the actual test to be. For instance, if your instructor has told you the online test will be made up primarily of short-answer questions, your test should reflect that.

You might also construct a test and e-mail it to a classmate. In turn, you could take a test that someone else has constructed. Constructing and taking practice tests are excellent ways of studying the material and cementing it into memory. (To be sure you're fully prepared for your next test, complete **Try It! 2**.)

virtual study groups
Small, informal groups of online students who connect electronically to share materials and notes in order to work together to study for a test.

© 68/Ocean/Corbis RF

From the perspective of . . .

A STUDENT You will take many types of courses during your academic career. Can you think of how test-taking strategies will work in an online English course versus an online science course?

Form a Virtual Study Group

Virtual study groups are small, informal groups of online students who connect electronically to share materials and notes in order to work together to study for a test. Forming such a group can be an excellent way to prepare for any kind of test.

For your online classes, you can form a virtual study group by using Skype, Facetime, or other applications that allow you to communicate face to face virtually. It may seem a bit awkward, but the benefits of even a virtual study group are very real.

Virtual study groups can be extremely powerful tools because they help accomplish several things:

▶ They help members organize and structure the material to approach their studying in a systematic and logical way.

▶ They allow students to share different perspectives on the material.

Virtual study groups are made up of a few online students who can help each other prepare for a test, organize material, provide new perspectives, and motivate members to do their best. Do you think you would function well in a virtual study group? Why or why not?
© Peter M. Fisher/Fuse/Getty Images RF

Complete a Test Preparation Checklist

It takes more than simply learning the material to prepare for a test. You also need a strategy that will help you understand what it is you are studying for. To do that, learn as much as you can about what the test will be like. The more you understand about the kind of test it is and what it will cover, the better you'll be able to target your studying.

To focus your studying, complete the following test preparation checklist before your next test.

TEST PREPARATION CHECKLIST

- [ ] I know whether it's a quiz, test, or exam.
- [ ] I know what kinds of questions will be on the test.
- [ ] I understand what material will be covered.
- [ ] I know how many questions will be on the test.
- [ ] I know how long I will have to complete the test.
- [ ] I know how the test will be graded, and how the grade contributes to my final course grade.
- [ ] I obtained sample questions and/or previous tests, if available.
- [ ] I have studied with the help of friends or family members.
- [ ] I used different and appropriate preparation strategies for different types of questions.
- [ ] I read and studied my class notes.
- [ ] I composed some questions of the kind that will be on the exam.
- [ ] I answered essay questions aloud.
- [ ] I actively memorized facts and details.
- [ ] I made and used index cards.
- [ ] I created and used a test like the real test.

After completing the checklist, ask yourself these questions: How can I use this checklist to study more effectively for tests? How might completing the checklist change the way I study for tests? What new strategies might I follow in order to prepare for tests more effectively in the future?

- ▶ They make it more likely that students will not overlook any potentially important information.
- ▶ They force members to rethink the course material, explaining it in words that other group members will understand.

There are some potential drawbacks to keep in mind. Virtual study groups don't always work well for students with learning styles that favor working independently. In addition, "problem" members—those who don't pull their weight—may cause difficulties for the group. In general, though, the advantages of virtual study groups far outweigh their disadvantages. (To set up your own virtual study group, see **Try It! 3**.)

Form a Virtual Study Group

The next time you have to prepare for a test, form a virtual study group with three to five of your online classmates. They may have a variety of study habits and skills, but all must be willing to take the group seriously.

The first time you communicate electronically, compare notes about what is likely to be on the test and brainstorm to come up with possible test questions. If the instructor hasn't given you detailed information about the test (e.g., number and types of questions, weighting), one of you should be delegated to ask for it. Plan to connect virtually once more closer to the test date to discuss answers to the questions you've come up with, or share any new insights on the material.

After you've taken the test and gotten your results, evaluate your experience by answering the following questions:

1. Did you find the experience useful?

2. Did participating in the virtual study group make you feel more confident prior to the test?

3. What aspects of the virtual study group were most effective?

4. What aspects of the virtual study group didn't work effectively?

5. What would you do differently the next time you use a virtual study group?

Use Your Campus Online Learning or Tutorial Center Resources

Many colleges have an online learning center or tutorial center that can help you study for a test. Don't wait until after you do badly on a test to seek out resources and support from your online learning or tutorial centers. Connecting with an online tutor prior to your first test is a good use of your time, even if you feel it's not essential. Just knowing what online resources are available can boost your confidence.

Cramming: You Shouldn't, But . . .

cramming
Hurried, last-minute studying.

You know, of course, that **cramming**, hurried, last-minute studying, is not the way to go. You know that you're likely to forget the material the moment the test is over because long-term retention is nearly impossible without thoughtful study. But . . .

. . . it's been one of those weeks where everything went wrong.

. . . the instructor sprang the test on you at the last minute.

. . . you forgot about the test until the night before.

Whatever the reason, there may be times when you can't study properly. What do you do if you have to cram for an exam?

Don't spend a lot of time on what you're unable to do. Beating yourself up about your occasional failings as a student will only hinder your efforts. Instead, admit you're human and imperfect like everyone else. Then spend a few minutes developing a plan about what you can accomplish in the limited time you've got.

The first thing to do is choose what you really need to study. You won't be able to learn everything, so you have to make choices. Figure out the main focus of the course and concentrate on it.

Once you have a strategy, prepare a one-page summary sheet with hard-to-remember information. Just writing the material down will help you remember it, and you can refer to the summary sheet frequently over the limited time you do have to study.

Next, read through your class notes, concentrating on the material you've underlined and the key concepts and ideas that you've already noted. Forget about reading all the material in the books and articles you're being tested on. Instead, read only the passages that you've underlined and the notes you've taken on the readings. Finally, maximize your study time. Using your notes, index cards, and concept maps, go over the information. Read it. Say it aloud. Think about it and the way it relates to other information. In short, use all the techniques we've talked about for learning and recalling information.

Just remember: When the exam is over, material that you have crammed into your head is destined to leave your mind as quickly as it entered. If you've crammed for a midterm, don't assume that the information will still be there when you study for the final. In the end, cramming often ends up taking more time for worse results than does studying with appropriate techniques.

Cramming can be exhausting, but it is on occasion necessary. With the many family and personal responsibilities many students face, sometimes it can't be avoided. There are, however, strategies you can use to help you make the best use of limited time.
© Ingram Publishing RF

 Organize ## Facing the Day of the Test

You've studied a lot, and you're happy with your level of mastery. Or perhaps you have the nagging feeling that there's something you haven't quite gotten to. Or maybe you know you haven't had enough time to study as much as you'd like, and you're expecting a disaster.

Whatever your frame of mind, it will help to organize your plan of attack on the day of the test. What's included on the test is out of your hands, but you can control how ready you are to take it.

For starters, have your computer set up with reliable access to the Internet. Have a backup charger with you in case your battery runs low or a plan B option if your computer crashes. It's usually best to have a backup plan when relying on technology to take your tests.

Be sure to know exactly when the test will be available online. You may be able to take the test only for a certain period. Miss that time, and you'll be out of luck. You should also ensure that you can see the clock on your computer: if not, have a watch or your cellphone with you. You will want to be able to pace yourself properly during the test.

For most online tests, instructors permit you to use notes and books. If you don't have them with you, they're not going to be much help. However, don't be lulled into thinking an open-book test is going to be easy. Instructors who allow you to use your notes and books during a test may not give you much time to look things up, so you still need to study.

In addition, you might want to plan on panicking. Although it sounds like the worst possible approach, permitting yourself the option of spending a minute feeling panicky will help you recover from your initial fears.

Finally, review the instructions carefully before beginning the test. The directions may tell you about a question that is optional or worth more points or inform you of a typographical error on the test. Any test instruction is information that you don't want to ignore.

» LO 4-3 Taking the Test

The online test is open, and it's time to start. Here are some proven strategies that will help you maximize your success.

W Work   Tackling the Test

Take a deep breath—literally.

There's no better way to start work on a test than by taking a deep breath, followed by several others. The deep breaths will help you to overcome any initial panic and anxiety you may be experiencing. It's OK to give yourself over for a moment to panic and anxiety, but to work at your best, use the relaxation techniques that we spoke about earlier to displace those initial feelings. Tell yourself, "It's OK. I am going to do my best."

Read test instructions carefully. It's critical to read the instructions for the test carefully. In fact, you should skim through the entire exam before you begin. Look at the kinds of questions and pay attention to the way they will be scored. If the point weighting of the various parts of the exam is not clear, ask your instructor to clarify it.

Knowing the point weighting is critical because it will help you to allocate your time. You don't want to spend 90 percent of your time on an essay that's worth only 10 percent of the points, and you want to be sure to leave time at the end of the test to check your answers.

An initial read-through will also help you verify that you have every page of the exam and that each one is readable. It may also provide you with "intratest knowledge," in which terms defined or mentioned in one part of a test trigger memories that can help answer questions in another part of the test.

If there are any lists, formulas, or other key facts that you're concerned you may forget, jot them down now on the back of a test page or on a piece of scrap paper. You may want to refer to this material later during the test.

Once this background work is out of the way, you'll be ready to proceed to actually answering the questions. These principles will help you do your best on the test:

► **Online test-taking best practices.** You'll be taking all of your online tests on a computer. Keep in mind that you shouldn't wait until the final deadline to start your test. Technical difficulties may prevent you from logging in or not allow you enough time to finish.

Be careful! A typo or misspelling can cause the computer software to misread your answers, producing errors in grading.

In addition, be sure to have paper and pencil available. Even though you use the computer to record your answers, you'll want to be able to jot down ideas, write notes, and do calculations the traditional way: by hand. This way you can also go back and check your answers easily—a step you should take frequently.

► **Answer the easiest questions first.** By initially getting the questions that are easiest for you out of the way, you accomplish several important things. First, you'll be leaving yourself more time to think about the tougher questions. In addition, moving through a series of questions without a struggle will build your confidence. Finally, working through a number of questions will build up a base of points that may be enough to earn you at least a minimally acceptable grade.

Use Strategies Targeted to Answering Specific Types of Test Questions

Every type of question requires a particular approach. Use the strategies below:

► **Essay questions.** Essay questions, with their emphasis on description and analysis, often present challenges because they are relatively unstructured. Unless you're careful, it's easy to wander off and begin to answer questions that were never asked. To prevent that problem, the first thing to do is read the question carefully, noting what specifically is being asked. If your essay will be lengthy, you might even want to write a short outline.

Pay attention to keywords that indicate what, specifically, the instructor is looking for in an answer. Certain action words are commonly used in essays, and you should understand them fully. For instance, knowing the distinction between "compare" and "contrast" can spell the difference between success and failure. **Table 4.3** defines common action words.

Use the right language in essays. Be brief and to the point in your essay. Avoid flowery introductory language. Compare the two sentences that follow:

"Management techniques have evolved to a point never before seen in the history of our country, or perhaps even our world."

"Many new management techniques have been developed in recent years."

The second sentence says the same thing much more effectively and economically.

table 4.3   Action Words for Essays

These words are commonly used in essay questions. Learning the distinctions among them will help you answer essay questions effectively.

Analyze: Examine and break into component parts.

Clarify: Explain with significant detail.

Compare: Describe and explain similarities.

Compare and contrast: Describe and explain similarities and differences.

Contrast: Describe and explain differences.

Critique: Judge and analyze, explaining what is wrong—and right—about a concept.

Define: Provide the meaning.

Discuss: Explain, review, and consider.

Enumerate: Provide a listing of ideas, concepts, reasons, items, etc.

Evaluate: Provide pros and cons of something; provide an opinion and justify it.

Explain: Give reasons why or how; clarify, justify, and illustrate.

Illustrate: Provide examples; show instances.

Interpret: Explain the meaning of something.

Justify: Explain why a concept can be supported, typically by using examples and other types of support.

Outline: Provide an overarching framework or explanation—usually in narrative form—of a concept, idea, event, or phenomenon.

Prove: Using evidence and arguments, convince the reader of a particular point.

Relate: Show how things fit together; provide analogies.

Review: Describe or summarize, often with an evaluation.

State: Assert or explain.

Summarize: Provide a condensed, precise list or narrative.

Trace: Track or sketch out how events or circumstances have evolved; provide a history or timeline.

Essays are improved when they include examples and point out differences. Your response should follow a logical sequence, moving from major points to minor ones, or following a time sequence. Above all, your answer should address every aspect of the question posed on the test. Because essays often contain several different, embedded questions, you have to be certain that you have answered every part to receive full credit. (After reviewing Table 4.3, complete **Try It! 4.**)

Understand Action Verbs in Essay Questions

Answer the following questions about the Second Amendment to the United States Constitution by outlining your responses to them, paying attention to the different action verbs that introduce the questions.

The Second Amendment states:

A well-regulated militia, being necessary to the security of a free State, the right of the people to keep and bear arms, shall not be infringed.

1. Summarize the Second Amendment to the Constitution.

2. Analyze the Second Amendment to the Constitution.

3. Discuss the Second Amendment to the Constitution.

How do your answers differ for each of the questions? Which of the questions provoked the lengthiest response? Which of the questions could you answer best?

▶ **Short-answer and fill-in questions.** Short-answer and fill-in questions basically require you to generate and supply specific information. Unlike essays, which are more free-form and may have several possible answers, short-answer and fill-in questions are usually quite specific, requiring only one answer.

Use both the instructions for the questions and the questions themselves to determine the level of specificity that is needed in an answer. Try not to provide too much or too little information. Usually, brevity is best.

▶ **Multiple-choice questions.** If you've ever looked at a multiple-choice question and said to yourself, "But every choice seems right," you understand what can be tricky about this type of question. However, there are some simple strategies that can help you deal with multiple-choice questions.

First, read the question carefully. Note any specific instructions. In most cases, only one answer will be correct, but some questions will ask you to select multiple items.

Then, *before you look at the possible answers, try to answer the question in your head.* This can help you avoid confusion over inappropriate choices.

Next, *carefully read through every possible answer.* Even if you come to one that you think is right, read them all—there may be a subsequent answer that is better.

Look for absolutes like "every," "always," "only," "none," and "never." Choices that contain such absolute words are rarely correct. For example, an answer choice that says, "A U.S. president has never been elected without having received the majority of the popular vote" is incorrect due to the presence of the word "never." On the other hand, less-absolute words, such as "generally," "usually," "often," "rarely," "seldom," and "typically," may indicate a correct response.

Be especially on guard for the word "not," which negates the sentence ("The one key concept that is not embodied in the U.S. Constitution is . . ."). It's easy to gloss over "not," and if you have the misfortune of doing so, it will be nearly impossible to answer the item correctly.

If you're having trouble understanding a question, underline key words or phrases, or try to break the question into different short sections. Sometimes it is helpful to work backwards, *Jeopardy!* style, and look at the possible answers first to see if you can find one that is clearly accurate or clearly inaccurate.

Use an educated guessing strategy—which is very different from wild or random guessing. Unless you are penalized for wrong answers (a scoring rule by which wrong answers are deducted from the points you have earned on other questions, rather than merely not counting at all toward your score), it always pays to guess.

The first step in educated guessing is to eliminate any obviously false answers. The next step is to examine the remaining choices closely. Does one response choice include an absolute or qualifying adjective that makes it unlikely ("the probability of war *always* increases when a U.S. president is facing political difficulties")? Does one choice include a subtle factual error? For example, the answer to a multiple-choice question asking why Columbus took his journey to the new world that says "the French monarchy was interested in expanding its colonial holdings" is wrong because it was not the French, but the Spanish, monarchy that funded his journey.

> **True–false questions.** Although most of the principles we've already discussed apply equally well to true–false questions, a few additional tricks of the trade may help you with this type of question. Begin a set of true–false questions by answering the ones you're sure you know. But don't rush; it's important to read every part of a true–false question because key words such as "never," "always," and "sometimes" often determine the appropriate response. If you don't have a clue about whether a statement is true or false, here's a last-resort principle: Choose "true." In general, more statements on a true–false test are likely to be true than false. (The reason for this? It's because it's easier for an instructor to think of true statements than to make up believable false statements.)

> **Matching questions.** Matching questions typically present you with two columns of related information, which you must link, item by item. For example, a list of terms or concepts may be presented in one column, along with a list of corresponding definitions or explanations in the second column. The best strategy is to reduce the size of both columns by matching the items you're most confident about first; this will leave a short list in each column, and the final matching may become apparent.

About Academic Honesty

It's tempting: A quick message or e-mail to a classmate during an online test may provide the one piece of information that you just can't remember. But you owe it to yourself not to do it. Getting answers from a classmate during a test is cheating. It is a violation of **academic honesty**, one of the foundations of civility in the classroom, as well as in society. Unless the work you turn in under your own name is your work, you are guilty of academic dishonesty.

Violations of academic honesty can take many forms. Academic dishonesty may involve **plagiarism**, taking credit for another's words, thoughts, or ideas. Academic dishonesty may also include using a calculator when it's not allowed, copying a computer file when it's unauthorized, taking an exam for another person,

educated guessing
The practice of eliminating obviously false multiple-choice answers and selecting the most likely answer from the remaining choices.

academic honesty
Completing and turning in only one's own work under one's own name.

plagiarism
Taking credit for someone else's words, thoughts, or ideas.

Tests for a Lifetime

If you think the last tests you'll ever have to take are the final exams just before you graduate from college, you're probably wrong.

Increasing numbers of professions require initial licensing exams, and some even require periodic exams to remain in good standing within the profession. For example, in some states, people who wish to become teachers must pass an exam. And even experienced teachers are required to take periodic tests throughout their careers to remain in the teaching field.

In short, good test-taking skills won't just bring you success in college. They're something that may benefit you for a lifetime as you pursue your career.

or stealing an exam. It can take the form of ripping a page out of a book in the library or lying to an instructor about the reason for a late paper. It includes using your textbook or messaging a classmate when taking a closed-book exam in an online, distance learning course.

You may feel that "everyone does it," so cheating is not so bad. Wrong. Everyone doesn't do it, just as most people don't embezzle from their companies or steal from others. Although you may know of a few cases of exceptionally dishonest classmates, most of your classmates try to be honest—you just don't notice their honesty.

Whatever form it takes, academic dishonesty is just plain wrong. It makes the grading system unfair, and it ultimately reduces the meaning of your grade. It certainly hinders academic and personal growth. It can't help but reduce one's self-esteem, and it robs the cheater of self-respect.

Finally, academic dishonesty violates the regulations of every college (rules that you should familiarize yourself with), and instructors feel it is their obligation to uphold standards of academic honesty. Violations of honesty policies will lead to any number of potentially devastating scenarios: failing the exam on which the cheating has taken place, failing the entire course, being brought before a disciplinary board, having a description of the incident permanently placed on your grade transcript, being placed on academic probation, or even being thrown out of school. A single instance of cheating can permanently prevent you from embarking on the career of your choice. Cheating is simply not worth it.

E Evaluate | Taking Your Own Final Examination

The last few minutes of a test may feel like the final moments of a marathon. You need to focus your energy and push yourself even harder. It can be make-or-break time.

Save some time at the end of a test so you can check your work. You should have been keeping track of your time all along, so plan on stopping a few minutes before the end of the test period to review what you've done. It's a critical step, and it can make the difference between a terrific grade and a mediocre one. It's a rare person who can work for an uninterrupted period of time on a test and commit absolutely no errors—even if he or she knows the material backwards and forwards. Consequently, checking what you've done is crucial.

Start evaluating your test by looking for obvious mistakes. Make sure you've answered every question and haven't skipped any parts of questions. Check to see that all your answers have been recorded in the online test and in the right spot.

If the test has included essay and short-answer questions, proofread your responses. Check for obvious errors—misspellings, missing words, and repetitions. Make sure you've responded to every part of each question and that each essay, as a whole, makes sense.

Check over your responses to multiple-choice, true–false, and matching questions. If there are some items that you haven't yet answered because you couldn't remember the necessary information, now is the time to take a stab at them. As we discussed earlier, it usually pays to guess, even randomly if you must. On most tests, no answer and a wrong answer are worth the same amount—nothing!

What about items that you initially guessed at? Unless you have a good reason to change your original answer—such as a new insight or a sudden recollection of some key information—your first guess is likely your best guess.

Know When to Stop

After evaluating and checking your answers, you may reach a point when there is still some time left. What to do? If you're satisfied with your responses, it's simply time to tell yourself, "Let it go."

Permit yourself the luxury of knowing that you've done your best, and submit your test. You don't have to review your work over and over just because there is time remaining. In fact, such behavior is often counterproductive because you might start overinterpreting questions and reading things into them that really aren't there.

Disaster! I've run out of time! It's a nightmarish feeling: The clock is ticking relentlessly, and it's clear that you don't have enough time to finish the online test. What should you do?

Stop working! Although this advice may sound foolish, in fact the most important thing you can do is to take a minute to calm yourself. Take some deep breaths to replace the feelings of panic that are likely welling up inside you. Collect your thoughts and plan a strategy for the last moments of the test.

If there are essays that remain undone, consider how you'd answer them if you had more time. Then type an outline of each answer. If you don't have time even for that, type out a few keywords. Typing anything is better than submitting a blank page, and you may get at least some credit for your response. The key principle here: Something is better than nothing, and even one point is worth more than zero points.

From the perspective of . . .

A LEGAL ASSISTANT Even though tests are uncommon in professional careers, deadlines are frequent occurrences. How might test-taking strategies help you when you are faced with a tight schedule?

The same principle holds for other types of questions. Even wild guesses are almost always better than not responding at all to an item. So rather than telling yourself you've certainly failed and giving up, do as much as you can in the remaining moments of the exam.

R Rethink | The Real Test of Learning

You are waiting for your instructor to post the grades for the exam. All sorts of thoughts run through your head: How did I do? Did I do as well as my classmates? Will I be happy with my results? Will the results show how much I studied? Will I be embarrassed by my grade?

Most of us focus on the evaluative aspects of tests. We look at the grade we've received on a test as an end in itself. It's a natural reaction.

But there's another way to look at test results: They can help guide us toward future success. By looking at what we've learned (and haven't learned) about a given subject, we'll be in a better position to know what to focus on when we take future exams. Furthermore, by examining the kinds of mistakes we make, we can learn to do better in the future.

When you receive your test score, you have the opportunity to reflect on what you've learned and to consider your performance. Begin by e-mailing your instructor about parts of the test you misunderstood. By asking for further clarification and support, you may also learn some important clues about what questions will be on future exams.

> "The test of any man lies in action."
>
> **Pindar, author, Odes**

Then examine your own mistakes. Chances are they'll jump out at you since they will be marked incorrect. Did you misunderstand or misapply some principle? Was there a certain aspect of the material covered on the test that you missed? Were there particular kinds of information that you didn't realize you needed to know? Or did you lose some points because of your test-taking skills? Did you make careless errors, such as forgetting to fill in a question or misreading the directions? Was your handwriting so sloppy that your instructor had trouble reading it?

Once you have a good idea of what material you didn't fully understand or remember, get the correct answers to the items you missed—from your instructor, your online course materials, or your book. If it's a math exam, rework problems you've missed. Then, summarize—in writing—the material you had trouble with. This will help you study for future exams that cover the same material.

Finally, if you're dissatisfied with your performance, e-mail or message your instructor—not to complain, but to seek help. Instructors don't like to give bad grades, and they may be able to point out problems in your test that you can address readily so you can do better in the future. Demonstrate to your instructor that you want to do better and are willing to put in the work to get there. The worst thing to do is crumple up the test and quickly leave the class in embarrassment. Remember, you're not the first person to get a bad grade, and the power to improve your test-taking performance lies within you. (Now, take a deep breath and complete **Try It! 5.**)

Take a Test-Taking Test

Take the following test on test-taking skills, which illustrates every question type discussed in this chapter.

Before taking the test, think of the test-taking strategies we've discussed in the chapter and try to employ as many of them as possible.

MULTIPLE-CHOICE SECTION

Choose one of the possible responses following each question.

1. Tests are useful tools for which of the following purposes?
   a. Determining people's likely level of future career success.
   b. Indicating strengths and gaps in people's knowledge.
   c. Defining people's fundamental abilities and potentials.
   d. Evaluating people's individual worth and contributions.

2. One of the main advantages of virtual study groups is that
   a. Every individual must contribute equally to the group.
   b. Group members can help each other during the test.
   c. Each member has to memorize only a fraction of the material.
   d. They allow each member to share different perspectives on the material.

3. Which of the following is a good way to deal with test anxiety?
   a. Visualizing success on the test.
   b. Drinking coffee or other stimulants.
   c. Telling yourself to stop worrying.
   d. Focusing on the importance of the test.

MATCHING SECTION

_____**1.** Essay question   **A.** A question in which the student supplies brief missing information to complete a statement.

_____**2.** Multiple-choice question   **B.** Hurried, last-minute studying.

_____**3.** Matching question   **C.** A question in which the student must link information in two columns.

_____**4.** Fill-in question   **D.** A question requiring a lengthy response in the student's own words.

_____**5.** Guessing penalty   **E.** Deduction of points for incorrect responses.

_____**6.** Cramming   **F.** Representing another's work as one's own.

_____**7.** Academic dishonesty   **G.** A question that requires selection from several response options.

FILL-IN SECTION

1. Fear of testing that can interfere with test performance is called _____.
2. The primary source of error on computer-scored tests is a misspelling or _____.

(continued)

TRUE–FALSE SECTION

1. The best way to prepare for an essay test is to review detailed factual information about the topic.
   T _____ F _____

2. True–false questions require students to determine whether given statements are accurate or inaccurate.
   T _____ F _____

3. You should never permit yourself to feel panicky during a test. T _____ F _____

4. A good evaluation strategy toward the end of a test is to redo as many questions as time permits.
   T _____ F _____

5. In a multiple-choice question, the words "always" and "never" usually signal the correct response.
   T _____ F _____

6. If you run out of time at the end of a test, it is best to type out brief notes and put ideas down in response to essay questions rather than to leave them completely blank. T _____ F _____

SHORT-ANSWER SECTION

1. What are five things you should find out about a test before you take it?

2. What is academic honesty?

ESSAY SECTION

1. Discuss the advantages of using a virtual study group to prepare for an examination.

2. Why is academic honesty important?

(Answers to all questions are at the end of this chapter.)

After you have completed the test, consider these questions: Did you learn anything from taking the test that you might not have learned if you hadn't been tested? How effective were the test-taking strategies you employed? Were any types of strategies easier for you to employ than others? Were any types of questions easier for you to answer than others?

Speaking *of* Success

Courtesy of Shayna J. Reinbold

NAME: **Shayna J. Reinbold**

SCHOOL: **Sullivan College of Technology and Design, Louisville, KY**

In high school, Shayna Reinbold studied hard to prepare herself for a future career in the medical profession. But a change of heart and consulting with her teachers helped guide her to pursue what she realized was her true passion: art.

"I have always been a very motivated person with a creative mind, and I am also patient and detail oriented," she said. "All my traits added up to the field of graphic design. As a result, I decided to go to college in order to have a career I will enjoy, as well as having a better future."

Enrolling in Sullivan College of Technology and Design, Reinbold, who graduated with an associate's degree in Computer Graphic Design, felt the school was perfectly suited for her personal and professional goals.

"I chose to go to SCTD because of the specialized degree programs they offer," she said. "All of the instructors that I had were extremely knowledgeable about the subject (because they were in the industry before becoming a teacher), and they gave us projects that heavily prepared us for our future careers."

"The school also had an excellent scholarship program," she added. But even with financial aid, Reinbold needed to work while earning her college degree, as the scholarship offered only half of the tuition. "It was totally worth it in the long run, though. I was able to work 20–35 hours a week and still focus on my classes for 10–12 hours or so a week," she said.

And while the school was generally very supportive, one still had to take advantage of the opportunities to succeed, according to Reinbold.

"Because I was paying for college myself, I was more driven to do well," she noted. She has advice for others: "Don't be afraid to challenge yourself, and take every opportunity that comes your way. If you don't challenge yourself, you will never get any better, and if you don't take any opportunity, you will never achieve greatness."

[RETHINK]

- What are the advantages of being as career driven and career oriented as Reinbold was in college? What kind of disadvantages might there be?

- Reinbold speaks of challenging oneself and following up on opportunities. Why would that be important in achieving success?

Looking Back

LO 4-1 Identify the kinds of tests you will encounter in college.

▶ Although tests are an unpopular fact of college life, they can provide useful information about one's level of knowledge and understanding about a subject.

▶ There are several types of tests, including brief, informal quizzes; more substantial tests; and even more weighty exams, which tend to be administered at the midpoint and end of a course.

LO 4-2 Explain the best ways to prepare for and take various kinds of tests.

▶ Good test preparation begins with doing the course assignments, attending class regularly, and paying attention in class. It also helps to find out as much as possible about a test beforehand and to form a study group to review material.

▶ If cramming becomes necessary, focus on summarizing factual information broadly, identifying key concepts and ideas, and rehearsing information orally.

▶ When you first receive the test, skim it to see what kinds of questions are asked, figure out how the different questions and sections will be weighted, and jot down complex factual information that is likely to be needed for the test.

▶ Answer the easiest questions first, write legibly, use only one side of each sheet of paper, mark answer sheets carefully, and record answers in the test book as well as the answer sheet.

LO 4-3 Analyze the best strategies for answering specific kinds of test questions.

▶ For essay questions, be sure to understand each question and each of its parts, interpret action words correctly, write concisely, organize the essay logically, and include examples.

▶ The best strategy for short-answer and fill-in questions is to be very sure what is being asked. Keep answers complete but brief.

▶ For multiple-choice questions, read the question very carefully and then read all response choices. Educated guessing based on eliminating incorrect response choices is usually a reasonable strategy.

▶ For true–false and matching questions, answer all the items that you are sure of quickly and then go back to the remaining items.

[KEY TERMS AND CONCEPTS]

Academic honesty (p. 95)   Educated guessing (p. 95)   Test anxiety (p. 84)
Cramming (p. 90)   Plagiarism (p. 95)   Virtual study groups (p. 87)

[RESOURCES]

ON THE WEB

College websites provide a variety of resources for students having difficulties with test taking. Some offer general webinar workshops for students, reviewing test-taking strategies. Furthermore, if you are planning to take a specific standardized test, you may be able to sign up for an online course offered through your college (or through such commercial organizations as Princeton Review or Kaplan).

The following sites on the Internet provide opportunities to extend your learning about the material in this chapter. (Although the web addresses were accurate at the time the book was printed, check the *P.O.W.E.R. Learning* Connect website.)

▶ "Taking Multiple Choice Exams" is an online presentation from the University of Wisconsin–Eau Claire outlining a series of strategies and approaches for taking multiple-choice exams. **http://people.uwec.edu/ivogeler/multiple.htm**

▶ The University of Reading, England, "Answering Exam Questions" site is a comprehensive collection of information on how to prepare for a variety of tests, including open-book and oral exams. **https://www.reading.ac.uk/internal/studyadvice/StudyResources/Exams/sta-answering.aspx**

▶ "Dealing with Text Anxiety," prepared by the University of Alabama's Center for Academic Success, presents a three-step strategy for confronting text anxiety. **http://www.ctl.ua.edu/CTLStudyAids/StudySkillsFlyers/TestPreparation/testanxiety.htm**

ON CAMPUS

If your college has a physical campus, and you are experiencing difficulties in a specific course, you may be able to find a tutor to help you. Some colleges have tutoring centers or campus learning centers that can provide one-to-one assistance. It's also important to communicate with your instructor, who more than likely has encountered many students with similar problems and may have some useful test-taking strategies.

If you find that you are experiencing significant test anxiety, talk to someone at your campus counseling center or health center. They can help you learn relaxation techniques and can provide counseling to help make your anxiety manageable.

IN PRINT

Ace Any Test (Cengage Learning PTR, 2011, 6th ed.), by educator Ron Fry, offers easy-to-follow strategies that can be used for all types of tests, from quizzes to the SAT.

Doc Orman's *The Test Anxiety Cure* (Stress Management Group, 2014) offers what the author describes as the 10 root causes of test anxiety and how to deal with them.

You can find test strategies for all types of questions in *Test Secrets,* by The Complete Test Preparation Team (CreateSpace Independent Publishing Platform, 2013).

[ANSWERS TO THE ITEMS IN TRY IT! 5]

Multiple-choice: 1b, 2d, 3a

Matching: 1D, 2G, 3C, 4A, 5E, 6B, 7F

Fill-in: test anxiety, typo

True–False: 1F, 2T, 3F, 4F, 5F, 6T

Short-answer:

1. Possible answers include what the test is called, what it will cover, how many questions will be on it, how much time it will take, what kinds of questions will be on it, how it will be graded, and whether sample questions will be provided.

2. Academic honesty is completing and turning in only one's own work under one's own name.

Essay:

1. Strong essays would include a brief definition of a virtual study group, followed by a discussion of the advantages of using virtual study groups (including such things as helping organize and structure material, providing different perspectives, and rethinking material). A mention of the disadvantages of virtual study groups would also be reasonable.

2. After starting with a brief definition of academic honesty, the bulk of the answer should concentrate on the reasons academic honesty is important and the consequences of academic dishonesty.

ENDNOTES

1. S. Tobias, *Overcoming Math Anxiety* (New York: W. W. Norton & Company, 1995).

The Case of . . .

That Sinking Feeling

This was going to be easy, Debbie Mallery said to herself as she sat down in front of her computer to take her test, a midterm exam covering the basics of restaurant management. She had spent a few hours the previous night and an hour right before the test studying key terms and concepts. She felt she knew the material. She felt ready.

Debbie was surprised to see, though, that the exam had two parts: a multiple-choice section and an essay section. Debbie hadn't really thought about what she might say in an essay. But she figured working on the multiple-choice questions might help give her some ideas.

The first two multiple-choice questions Debbie answered easily, but she got stuck on the third one. She went back and forth over two possible answers and finally decided just to leave that question blank. The pattern was the same for the rest of the multiple-choice questions. A few questions Debbie would answer easily, then she'd get stuck on a hard one.

Finally, Debbie finished the multiple-choice questions and came to the essay. Only then did she notice the instructions that indicated the essay was worth 50 points, and the multiple-choice questions 25 points. Then Debbie got another shock: She realized that only 10 minutes remained in her timed midterm for her to write her essay! Her mind froze—and Debbie had the horrible feeling that she didn't have enough time to complete the test. Even though she had studied, Debbie now felt certain she would fail.

1. What mistakes did Debbie make in her test preparation that probably harmed her performance?

2. What mistakes did Debbie make during the test that hurt her?

3. What was right about Debbie's initial approach to the test?

4. What should Debbie have done differently in calculating the amount of time to devote to each portion of the test? Why?

5. What specific strategies would have helped Debbie with the multiple-choice questions? What strategies could she have used on the essay?

6. If you were in Debbie's shoes, what would you do with only 10 minutes left in the test?

Learning Outcomes

By the time you finish this chapter, you will be able to

» LO **5-1**   Explain how reading style and attention span affect reading.

» LO **5-2**   Identify how to improve concentration and to read and remember more effectively.

» LO **5-3**   Discuss how best to retain what you have read.

Reading and Remembering

© Norman Pogson/Alamy Stock Photo RF

"Read the next chapter in the textbook by Tuesday." "Read the first two articles posted on the class website before your next writing assignment." "The test will cover the first hundred pages in your book, so be sure you've read it."

One day, three different reading assignments, Jeff Knowles thought as he checked the most recent posting from his online instructor on the class website. It would be hard enough for Jeff to complete all this reading during an ordinary week. But this week he had to finish painting his garage and had volunteered to help his brother move. On top of that, there was his part-time landscaping job—and, Jeff suddenly remembered, he'd agreed to work overtime on Friday.

Still, Jeff figured that even with all his work, family, and household obligations, he could still find time to do all his reading—except Jeff believed he was an unusually slow reader. When he pushed himself to read quicker and absorb more, he actually read and retained less. For Jeff, the problem wasn't just completing the reading—it was remembering it when test time rolled around.

Looking Ahead

For people like Jeff, reading assignments are the biggest challenge in college. The amount of required reading is often enormous. Even skilled readers may find themselves wishing they could read more quickly and effectively. On the job, too, many people struggle with all the memos, e-mails, manuals, and so forth that they need to read.

Fortunately, there are ways to improve your reading and memory skills. In this chapter, we'll first go over a number of strategies for reading more effectively. You'll assess your reading style and your attention span, consider what you should do before you even start reading an assignment, and discover some ways of getting the most out of your reading.

Then we'll focus on memory and retaining what you've read. You'll learn how you can improve the memory skills you already have. We'll examine what memory is and why it sometimes fails us. Finally, you will become acquainted with specific ways to learn information so that you can recall it when you need to.

» LO 5-1 Sharpen Your Reading and Memory Skills

One of the reasons many people struggle with reading, especially in college, is that they feel they *shouldn't* have to struggle with it. Reading, after all, is something almost all of us master as children . . . right?

In fact, it is not so simple. Reading, as we will see in this chapter, involves more than just recognizing words. The task of reading large amounts of information and remembering the essential points takes time to master.

To begin, consider the way you read now. In other words, what kind of reader are you? Ask yourself first of all about your reading *preferences:* What do you *like* to read, and why? What makes you pick up a book and start reading—and what makes you put one down?

Before going any further, think about your own reading preferences by completing the **Journal Reflections**.

Journal Reflections

My Reading Preferences

Think about what you like and don't like to read by answering these questions.

1. Do you read for pleasure? If so, what do you read (e.g., magazines, newspapers, novels, humor, short stories, nonfiction, illustrated books)?

2. What makes a book enjoyable? Have you ever read a book that you "couldn't put down"? If so, what made it so good?

3. What is the most difficult book you are reading this semester? Why is it difficult? Are you enjoying it?

4. Think about when you read for pleasure compared with when you read material for a class. How does the way you read differ between the two types of material?

5. How well do you remember the last book or magazine you read for pleasure? Do you remember it better than your last college reading assignment? Why do you think this might be?

Read for Retention, Not Speed

You may have come across advertisements on the web promoting reading "systems" that promise to teach you to read so quickly that you'll be reading entire books in an hour and whizzing through assigned readings in a few minutes.

Unfortunately it's not going to happen. Research has shown that claims of speed-reading are simply groundless. But even if it were physically possible to read a book in an hour, ultimately it probably doesn't matter very much. If we read too fast, comprehension and retention plunge. Reading is not a race, and the fastest readers are not necessarily the best readers.

The act of reading is designed to increase our knowledge and open up new ways of thinking. It can help us achieve new levels of understanding and get us to think more broadly about the world and its inhabitants. Speed matters far less than what we take away from what we've read. That's not to say we shouldn't try to become more efficient readers who comprehend and recall more effectively. Ultimately, though, the key to good reading is understanding—not speed.

In describing how you can use the principles of P.O.W.E.R. Learning to become a better reader with a more complete memory of what you read, we'll focus on the type of reading that is typically called for in academic pursuits—textbook chapters, articles, handouts, and the like. However, the same principles will help you get more benefit and enjoyment out of your recreational reading as well. Crucially, the reading skills you learn and employ in the classroom will also help you read more efficiently and effectively on the job.

 **Prepare** ## Approaching the Written Word

Preparation to begin reading isn't hard, and it won't take very long, but it's a crucial first step in applying P.O.W.E.R. Learning (summarized in the P.O.W.E.R. Plan here). Your aim in preparation is to become familiar with **advance organizers**—outlines, overviews, section objectives, or other clues to the meaning and organization of new material—provided in the material you are reading. Most textbooks have them built in; for an example, look at the start of every chapter in this book, which includes a "Learning Outcomes" list and a "Looking Ahead" section. You can also create your own advance organizers by skimming material to be read and sketching out the general outline of the material you'll be reading.

Advance organizers pave the way for subsequent learning. They help you tie information that you already know to new material you're about to encounter. This connection between old and new material is crucial in helping build memories of what you read. If you approach each new reading task as something entirely new and unrelated to your previous knowledge, you'll have enormous difficulty recalling it. On the other hand, if you connect it to what you already know, you'll be able to recall it far better.

In short, the more we're able to make use of advance organizers and our own prior knowledge and experiences, the better we can understand and retain new material. (To prove the value of advance organizers, complete **Try It! 1**, "Discover How Advance Organizers Help.")

What's the Point of the Reading Assignment?

Before you begin an assignment, think about what your goal is. Will you be reading a textbook on which you'll be thoroughly tested? Is your reading supposed to provide background information that will serve as a context for future learning but that won't itself be tested? Is the material going to be useful to you personally? Realistically, how much time can you devote to the reading assignment?

Your goal for reading will help you determine which reading strategy to adopt. You aren't expected to read everything with the same degree of intensity. Some material you may feel comfortable skimming; for other material, you'll want to put in the maximum effort.

Understand the Point of View of the Material Itself

What are you reading—a textbook, an essay, an article? If it is an essay or article, why was it written? To prove a point? To give information? To express the author's personal feelings? Knowing the author's purpose (even if his or her specific point and message aren't yet clear) can help you a great deal as you read.

advance organizers
Outlines, overviews, objectives, and other clues to the meaning and organization of new material in what you are reading, which pave the way for subsequent learning.

P **Prepare**
Approach the written word

O **Organize**
Gather the tools of the trade

W **Work**
Get the most our of your reading

E **Evaluate**
Consider what it means and what you know

R **Rethink**
Get it the second time

P.O.W.E.R. Plan

Discover How Advance Organizers Help

Read this passage. What do you think it means?

The procedure is actually quite simple. First you arrange items into different groups. Of course, one pile may be sufficient, depending on how much there is to do. If you have to go somewhere else due to lack of facilities, that is the next step; otherwise, you are pretty well set. It is important not to overdo things. That is, it is better to do too few things at once than too many. In the short run this may not seem important but complications can easily arise. A mistake can be expensive as well. At first, the whole procedure will seem complicated. Soon, however, it will become just another facet of life. It is difficult to foresee any end to the necessity for this task in the immediate future, but then one can never tell. After the procedure is completed, one arranges the materials into different groups again. Then they can be put into their appropriate places. Eventually, they will be used once more and the whole cycle will then have to be repeated. However, this is a part of life.*

If you're like most people, you don't have a clue about what this all means and won't be able to remember anything about it in five minutes. But suppose you had been given some context in advance, and you knew before reading it that the description had to do with washing laundry. Now does it all fall into place? Do you think it will be easier to remember? Read the passage once more, and see how having an advance organizer (in this case, *washing laundry*) helps out.

*Source: J. D. Bransford and M. K. Johnson, "Contextual Prerequisites for Understanding: Some Investigations of Comprehension and Recall," *Journal of Verbal Learning and Verbal Behavior* 11, 1972, p. 722.

Start with the Frontmatter

If you'll be using a text or other book extensively throughout the term, start by reading the preface and/or introduction and scanning the table of contents—what publishers call the **frontmatter**. Instructors often don't formally assign the frontmatter, but reading it can be a big help because it is there that the author has a chance to step forward and explain, often more personally than elsewhere in an academic book, what he or she considers important. Knowing this will give you a sense of what to expect as you read.

frontmatter
The preface, introduction, and table of contents of a book.

Create Advance Organizers

To provide context for your reading, create your own advance organizers by skimming through the table of contents, which provides the main headings of what you will be reading. Textbooks often have chapter outlines, listing the key topics to be covered, which also provide a way of previewing the chapter content. As you read over the outline, you can begin to consider how the new material in the book may relate both to what you know and to what you expect to learn—from the reading assignment itself and from the course.

Textbooks also often have end-of-chapter summaries, and many articles include a final section in which the author states his or her conclusions. Take a look at these ending sections as well. Even though you haven't read the material yet and the summary probably won't make complete sense to you, by reading the summary, you'll get an idea of what the author covers and what is important.

Your instructor may also provide an advance organizer for readings. Sometimes instructors will post instructions to pay particular attention to or to look for, such as "When you read Thomas Paine's *Common Sense,* notice how he lays out his

Create an Advance Organizer

Use any information you have available to create an advance organizer for a chapter in a text that you are using this term. Skim the section headings in the chapter, read the chapter summary, consult the book's frontmatter, and recall anything your instructor may have posted about the chapter.

Complete the following statements to prepare your organizer:

1. The general topics that are covered in the chapter are . . .

2. The most critical topics and concepts in the chapter are . . .

3. The most difficult material in the chapter includes . . .

4. Words, phrases, and ideas that are unfamiliar to me include . . .

5. Ways that the material in this chapter relates to other material that I've previously read in the text include . . .

Use this Try It! as a starting point for advance organizers for future chapters in the book.

---

argument and what his key points are." Sometimes they will explain in their post why they assigned a reading. Such information provides clues that can help you develop a mental list of the reading's key ideas.

However you construct advance organizers, be sure they provide a framework and context for what you'll be reading; this framework and context can spell the difference between fully comprehending what you read and misunderstanding it.

Now it's time to put all this practice to good use. Create an advance organizer for a textbook chapter in **Try It! 2**.

Identify What You Need to Remember

Memorize what you need to memorize. Forget about the rest.

The average textbook chapter has something like 20,000 words. If you had to recall every word of the chapter, it would be nearly impossible. Furthermore, it would be a waste of time. Being able to spew out paragraphs of material is quite different from the more important ability to recall and deeply understand material in meaningful ways.

Within those 20,000 words, there may be only 20 different concepts that you need to learn. And perhaps there are only 10 keywords. *Those* are the pieces of information that should be the focus of your efforts to memorize.

How do you know what's so important that you need to recall it? One way is to use the guides built into most textbooks. Key concepts and terms are often highlighted or in boldface type. Chapters often have summaries that recap the most important information. Use such guideposts to understand what's most critical in a chapter.

Write down what you determine is important. Not only does putting critical information in writing help you manage what you need to remember, but the very act of writing it down makes it easier to memorize the information later.

In short, the first step in building a better memory of your reading is to determine just what it is that you wish to recall. By extracting what is important from what is less crucial, you'll be able to limit the amount and extent of the material that you need to recall. You'll be able to focus, laserlike, on what you need to remember.

⊙ Organize | Gathering the Tools of the Trade

It's obvious that the primary item you'll need to complete a reading assignment is the material that you're reading. But there are other essential tools you should gather, potentially including the following:

▶ A copy of the assignment, so you'll be sure to read the right material.

▶ A pad of paper and/or index cards for notetaking if the material is particularly complex. If you use a computer to take notes, get it ready.

▶ Pencils or pens to write notes in the margin, if it's a traditional paper book, and highlighters to indicate key passages in the text.

▶ Access to a dictionary, either online or as a hard copy. You never know what new words you'll encounter while you're reading. If a dictionary isn't easily accessible, you'll be tempted to skip over unfamiliar words—a decision that may come back to haunt you. All word processing software includes a dictionary, and there are also many good dictionaries available online (e.g., Merriam-Webster's at **www.m-w.com**, where you will also find an online thesaurus).

Give Yourself Time

There's one more thing you need to prepare successfully for a reading assignment: enough time to complete it. The length of reading assignments is almost never ambiguous. You will typically be given a specific page range, so you will know just how much material you will need to cover.

Now get a watch and time yourself as you read the first three pages of your assignment, being sure to pay attention to the material, not the time! Timing how long it takes to read a representative chunk of material provides you with a rough measure of your reading speed for the material—though it will vary even within a single reading assignment, depending on the complexity of the material.

You'll also need to consider an aspect of your personal learning style: your reading attention span. **Attention span** is the length of time that a person usually is able to sustain attention. People with long attention spans can read for relatively lengthy periods without getting jumpy, while those with shorter ones can only maintain attention for a short while. You can get a general sense of this by using **Try It! 3**, "Discover Your Attention Span."

attention span
The length of time that attention is typically sustained.

Discover Your Attention Span

You should be aware of your attention span, the length of time you usually are able to sustain attention to a task, as you prepare for reading assignments. To get an idea of the length of your current attention span for reading, perform this exercise over the next few days.

1. Choose one of the textbooks that you've been assigned to read this semester.
2. Start reading a chapter, without any preparation, noting in the chart below the time that you start reading.
3. As soon as your mind begins to wander and think about other subjects, stop reading and note the time on the chart below.
4. Using the same textbook, repeat this process four more times over the course of a few days, entering the data on the chart below.
5. To find your reading attention span, calculate the average number of minutes across the five trials.

Trial #1	Starting time:_____ Ending time: _____ Number of minutes between start and end times: _____
Trial #2	Starting time:_____ Ending time:_____ Number of minutes between start and end times: _____
Trial #3	Starting time:_____ Ending time:_____ Number of minutes between start and end times: _____
Trial #4	Starting time:_____ Ending time:_____ Number of minutes between start and end times: _____
Trial #5	Starting time:_____ Ending time:_____ Number of minutes between start and end times: _____

Reading attention span (the average of the length of time on each trial, found by subtracting the ending time from the starting time on each trial, adding the times together, and dividing by 5) = _____ minutes.

Ask yourself these questions about your reading attention span:

1. Are you surprised by the length of your reading attention span? In what way?
2. Does any number in the set of trials stand out from the other numbers? For instance, is any number much higher or lower than the average? If so, can you account for this? For example, what time of day was it?
3. Do the numbers in your trials show any trend? For instance, did your attention span tend to increase slightly over the course of the trials, did it decrease, or did it stay about the same? Can you explain any trend you may have noted?
4. Do you think your attention span times would be very different if you had chosen a different textbook? Why or why not?
5. What things might you do to improve your attention span?

Use the three pieces of information you now have—the length of the assignment, your per-page reading speed at full attention, and your typical attention span—to estimate roughly how long it will take you to complete the reading assignment. For example, if you are asked to read 12 pages, you have found that you need approximately 4 minutes to read a page, and your reading attention span is, on average, 25 minutes long, you can expect your reading to take at least 60 minutes, assuming you'll take a short break when your attention begins to fade after 25 minutes.

In addition, you may need to interrupt your reading to look up words in the dictionary, get a drink, stretch, or answer the phone. You may also decide to break your reading into several short sessions, in which case your total reading time may be greater because you will have to get reacquainted with the reading assignment each time you sit down again.

Remember that you can use this strategy for estimating the amount of time reading will take you for reading tasks outside the classroom, too. If your employer asks you to read a set of customer feedback forms, for example, you can figure out how much time in your day you'll need to block off to complete the work by factoring in the total length of all the forms, your per-page reading speed, and your attention span. Remember, though, that reading on the job is different from reading in a college library or at your desk at home. You can expect many more distractions as you try to read—co-workers asking questions, e-mails coming in, the phone ringing. Take into account these inevitable workplace distractions when making your reading time estimate.

》LO**5-2**

W Work

Getting the Most Out of Your Reading and Using Proven Strategies to Memorize New Material

Once you've familiarized yourself with the material as a whole and gathered the necessary tools, it's time to get down to work and start reading. Here are several things that will help you get the most out of the reading process.

Stay Focused

The TV show you watched last night . . . your husband forgetting to meet you at the bus stop . . . the new toothbrush you need to buy for your daughter . . . your grumbling stomach. There are a million and one possible distractions that can invade your thoughts as you read. Your job is to keep distracting thoughts at bay and focus on the material you are supposed to be reading. It's not easy, but the following are things you can do to help yourself stay focused:

▶ **Read in small bites.** If you think it is going to take you 4 hours to read an entire chapter, break up the 4 hours into more manageable time periods. Promise yourself that you'll read for 1 hour in the afternoon, another hour in the evening, and the next 2 hours spaced out during the following day. One hour of reading is far more manageable than a 4-hour block.

If you are reading a long assignment, taking a break can be a reward and reinvigorate you.

▶ **Take a break.** Actually, plan to take several short breaks to reward yourself while you're reading. During your break, do something enjoyable—eat a snack, watch a bit of a ball game on television, text message a friend, or the like. Just try not to get drawn into your break activity to the point that it takes over your reading time.

▶ **Deal with mental distractions.** Sometimes problems have a way of popping into our minds and repeatedly distracting us. If a particular problem keeps interrupting your concentration—such as a difficulty you're having on the job— try to think of an action-oriented strategy to deal with it. You might even write your proposed solution down on a piece of paper. Putting it down in words can get the problem off your mind, potentially making it less intrusive.

▶ **Manage interruptions.** You can't prevent your children from getting into a fight and needing immediate attention. But there are some things you can do to reduce interruptions and their consequences. For instance, you can schedule reading to coincide with periods when you know you'll be alone. You can also plan to read less critical parts of assignments (such as the summaries or book frontmatter) when distractions are more likely, saving the heavier reading for later. Or, if you are a parent with small children, you can get them involved in an activity that they can perform independently so you'll be free to concentrate.

Write While You Read

Writing is one of the most important aspects of reading. If you haven't underlined, jotted notes to yourself, placed check marks on the page, drawn arrows, constructed diagrams, and otherwise defaced and disfigured your book while you're reading, you're not doing your job as a P.O.W.E.R. reader.

The idea of writing on a book page may go against everything you've been taught in the past. (And, of course, you should never write on a library book or one that you've borrowed.)

However, once you've bought your book, *you own it and you should make it your own.* Don't keep your textbooks spotless on the off chance they will fetch a higher price if you sell them later. Instead, think of textbooks as documents recording your active learning and engagement in a field of study. In addition, you should look at your textbooks as the foundation of your personal library, which will grow throughout your lifetime. In short, writing extensively in your book while you're reading is an important tactic for achieving success. (For more on using textbooks, see the **Course Connections** feature.)

The ability to add your own personal notes, underlining, and other annotations to a clean text while you're reading is one of the reasons it usually pays to buy new, rather than used, textbooks. Why would you want a stranger's comments on

Textbook Tips: Starting Off on the Right Page

You've just received your online book orders and other materials for the upcoming term. Now is the time to take some preliminary steps to make the most of your investment.

- Make sure you've bought the correct textbooks. Look at each syllabus from your classes to ensure you've bought the appropriate text and the right edition. Sometimes there are multiple sections of a course, and each section uses a different text. Be sure the book you've bought matches the description in the syllabus.

- Make the book your own. Write your name, e-mail address, and/or telephone number in the front of the book. If you misplace your book during the term, you want the person who finds it to be able to return it to you.

- Orient yourself to each of your textbooks. Take a quick look at each of the books, examining the table of contents, introduction, and/or preface (as we discussed earlier). Get a sense of the content and the general reading level of the book.

- Get yourself online. Many textbooks contain a card or insert with a password that gives you access to online material, sometimes including access to the complete book in an online format. Follow the directions and enter the book's website, making sure the password allows you to register. If you have trouble making the site work, call the tech support number that should be included with the password.

---

something you own? Can you really trust that person's judgment over your own regarding what's important to underline? New books allow you to mark them up in your own personal style, without the distraction of competing voices.

If you have purchased an *electronic textbook,* or *e-book,* you'll be able to read it on a laptop computer, an iPad, or even a smartphone. E-books have several advantages over traditional books. You can easily follow links to visuals and interactive exercises, search for key terms, listen to music, watch embedded videos, and manipulate 3-D images. And, as with traditional textbooks, you can highlight and take notes as you are reading and save (and organize) your notes for future study.

© Jose Luis Pelaez Inc/Blend Images/SuperStock RF

Writing the Right Way

What should you be writing while you are reading? There are several things you should write down (or—if you are using an e-book—type into your electronic text):

> "What is reading but silent conversation?"
>
> **Walter Savage Landor, author, 1824–53, "Aristoteles and Callisthenes,"** *Imaginary Conversations.*

▶ **Rephrase key points.** Make notes to yourself, in your own words, about what the author is trying to get across. Don't just copy what's been said. Think about the material and rewrite it in words that are your own.

Writing notes to yourself in your own words has several consequences, all good. First, you make the material yours; it becomes something you now understand and part of your own knowledge base. This is an essential aid to memorization. When you try to recollect your reading, you won't be trying to summon the thoughts of someone else—you'll be trying to remember *your own* thinking.

Second, trying to summarize a key point in your own words will make it very clear whether you truly understand it. It's easy to be fooled into thinking we understand something as we're reading along. But the true test is whether we can explain it to ourselves (or someone else) on our own, without referring to the book or article.

Third, the very act of writing engages an additional type of perception—involving the physical sense of moving a pen or pressing a keyboard. This will help you learn the material in a more active way.

Finally, writing notes and phrases will help you study the material later. Not only will the key points be highlighted, but your notes will also quickly bring you up to speed regarding your initial thoughts and impressions.

▶ **Highlight or underline key points.** Very often the first or last sentence in a paragraph, or the first or last paragraph in a section, will present a key point. Before you highlight anything, though, read the whole paragraph through. Then you'll be sure that what you highlight is, in fact, the key information. Topic sentences do not always fall at the beginning of a paragraph.

Be selective in your highlighting and underlining. A page covered in yellow highlighter may be artistically appealing, but it won't help you understand the material any better. Highlight only the key information. You might find yourself highlighting only one or two sentences or phrases per page. That's fine. *In highlighting and underlining, less is more.* One guideline: No more than 10 percent of the material should be highlighted or underlined.

Keep in mind, too, as you highlight and underline, that the key material you are marking is the material you will likely need to remember for exams or writing assignments. To aid in your recall of such material, read it over a time or two after you've marked it, and consider also reading it aloud. This will reinforce the memories you are building of the essential points in the assignment.

▶ **Use arrows, diagrams, outlines, tables, timelines, charts, and other visuals to help you understand and later recall what you are reading.** If there are three examples given for a particular point, number them. If a paragraph discusses a situation in which an earlier point does not hold, link the original point to the exception by an arrow. If a sequence of steps is presented, number each step.

For example, after you have annotated *this* page of *P.O.W.E.R. Learning,* it might look something like what is shown in **Figure 5.1.**

Particularly if your learning style is a visual one, representing the material graphically will get you thinking about it—and the connections and points in it—in new and different ways. Rather than considering the material solely in verbal terms, you now add visual images. The act of creating visual annotations will not only help you to understand the material better but also ease its later recall. Practice this technique on the sample textbook page in **Try It! 4.**

▶ **Look up unfamiliar words in a dictionary.** Even though you may be able to figure out the meaning of an unfamiliar word from its context, use a dictionary anyway. This way you can be sure that what you think it means is correct. A dictionary will also tell you what the word sounds like, which may be important if your instructor uses the word in class.

Writing notes to yourself in your own words has several consequences, all good. First, you make the material yours; it becomes something you now understand and part of your own knowledge base. This is an essential aid to memorization. When you try to recollect your reading, you won't be trying to summon the thoughts of someone else—you'll be trying to remember *your own* thinking.

Second, trying to summarize a key point in your own words will make it very clear whether you truly understand it. It's easy to be fooled into thinking we understand something as we're reading along. But the true test is whether we can explain it to ourselves (or someone else) on our own, without referring to the book or article.

Third, the very act of writing engages an additional type of perception—involving the physical sense of moving a pen or pressing a keyboard. This will help you learn the material in a more active way.

Finally, writing notes and phrases will help you study the material later. Not only will the key points be highlighted, but your notes will also quickly bring you up to speed regarding your initial thoughts and impressions.

Topic sentence

Read whole paragraph before highlighting

① **Highlight or underline key points.** Very often the first or last sentence in a paragraph, or the first or last paragraph in a section, will present a key point. Before you highlight anything, though, read the whole paragraph through. Then you'll be sure that what you highlight is, in fact, the key information. Topic sentences do not always fall at the beginning of a paragraph.

Be selective in your highlighting and underlining. A page covered in yellow highlighter may be artistically appealing, but it won't help you understand the material any better. Highlight only the key information. You might find yourself highlighting only one or two sentences or phrases per page. That's fine. *In highlighting and underlining, less is more.* One guideline: No more than 10 percent of the material should be highlighted or underlined.

Reread key points to help memory

Keep in mind, too, as you highlight and underline, that the key material you are marking is the material you will likely need to remember for exams or writing assignments. To aid in your recall of such material, read it over a time or two after you've marked it, and consider also reading it aloud. This will reinforce the memories you are building of the essential points in the assignment.

② **Use arrows, diagrams, outlines, tables, timelines, charts, and other visuals to help you understand and later recall what you are reading.** If there are three examples given for a particular point, number them. If a paragraph discusses a situation in which an earlier point does not hold, link the original point to the exception by an arrow. If a sequence of steps is presented, number each step.

 Use visuals

For example, after you have annotated *this* page of *P.O.W.E.R. Learning,* it might look something like what is shown in **Figure 5.1**.

Particularly if your learning style is a visual one, representing the material graphically will get you thinking about it—and the connections and points in it—in new and different ways. Rather than considering the material solely in verbal terms, you now add visual images. The act of creating visual annotations will not only help you to understand the material better but also ease its later recall. Practice this technique on the sample textbook page in **Try It! 4.**

▶ **Look up unfamiliar words in a dictionary.** Even though you may be able to figure out the meaning of an unfamiliar word from its context, use a dictionary anyway. This way you can be sure that what you think it means is correct. A dictionary will also tell you what the word sounds like, which may be important if your instructor uses the word in class.

figure 5.1
Sample of Annotated Page

▶ **Use your own reading system.** If you've already learned a reading system in the past and it works for you, use it. Many students have been taught the *SQ4R* method, which consists of six steps, designated by the initials *S-Q-R-R-R-R:*

• *Survey.* Give yourself an overview of the major points of the material.

• *Question.* Formulate questions about the material—either aloud or in writing—prior to actually reading a section of text.

• *Read.* Read the material carefully and, even more important, actively and critically. While you are reading, answer the questions you have asked yourself.

Mark Up a Book Page

Read the excerpt in **Figure 5.2**. Then use the techniques we've discussed for marking up a page to highlight its key points.

1. What types of annotations did you use?

2. How might these annotations help you to remember what is important?

3. If there were different sorts of material presented on the page, such as mathematical formulas, would you use different kinds of annotations?

The more parents speak to their children, the better their children's language skills.

Understanding Language Acquisition: Identifying the Roots of Language

Anyone who spends even a little time with children will notice the enormous strides that they make in language development throughout childhood. However, the reasons for this rapid growth are far from obvious. Two major explanations have been offered: one based on learning theory and the other on innate processes.

The **learning-theory approach** suggests that language acquisition follows the principles of reinforcement and conditioning discussed in Chapter 6. For example, a child who utters the word "mama" is hugged and praised by her mother, which reinforces the behavior and makes its repetition more likely. This view suggests that children first learn to speak by being rewarded for making sounds that approximate speech. Ultimately, through a process of shaping, language becomes more and more like adult speech (Skinner, 1957).

The learning theory approach is supported by research that shows that the more parents speak to their young children, the more proficient the children become in language usage (see Figure 8-11). In addition, higher levels of linguistic sophistication in parents' speech to their young children are related to a greater rate of vocabulary growth, vocabulary usage, and even general intellectual achievement by the time the children are 3 years of age (Hart & Risley, 1997).

On the other hand, the learning theory approach is less successful when it comes to explaining the acquisition of language rules. Children are reinforced not only when they use proper language, but also when they respond incorrectly. For example, parents answer the child's "Why the dog won't eat?" as readily as they do the correctly phrased question "Why won't the dog eat?" Both sentences are understood equally well. Learning theory, then, has difficulty in providing the full explanation for language acquisition.

Pointing to such problems with learning theory approaches to language acquisition, Noam Chomsky (1968, 1978, 1991), a linguist, provided a ground-breaking alternative. Chomsky argued that humans are born with an innate linguistic capability that emerges primarily as a function of maturation. According to his analysis, all the world's languages share a similar underlying structure called a **universal grammar.** Chomsky suggests that the human brain has a neural system, the **language-acquisition device,** that both permits the understanding of the structure of language and provides strategies and techniques for learning the unique characteristics of a given native language.

learning-theory approach: The theory suggesting that language acquisition follows the principles of reinforcement and conditioning

universal grammar: Noam Chomsky's theory that all the world's languages share a similar underlying structure

language-acquisition device: A neural system of the brain hypothesized to permit understanding of language

figure 5.2
Sample Page to Annotate
Source: © Sonda Dawes/Image Works

- *Recite.* Describe and explain to yourself the material you have just read and answer the questions you have posed earlier.
- *Record.* Write in your textbook, make notes, or create flash cards.
- *Review.* Review the material, looking it over, reading end-of-chapter summaries, and answering the in-text review questions.

In addition to *SQ4R,* you can also make up your own system. The truth is that it doesn't matter what system you use, as long as you use a system. What does matter is that you're systematic in the work of reading.

From the perspective of...

A STUDENT To truly retain what you are reading, you must give your reading your undivided attention. Make a list of your biggest distractions and consider strategies for avoiding those distractions when you read.

© CMCD/Getty Images RF

Memorize Key Material

Many of the reading strategies discussed above will help fix key material in your mind. Rephrasing key points, highlighting or underlining essential material and then rereading it, and creating visuals will all help you recall the information you've read.

Sometimes, though, these strategies are not enough. You may need to memorize a great deal of information, more than you'll be able to recall just through the process of reading, underlining, and so forth. Many people find extensive memorization daunting. But one of the good things about the work of memorization is that you have your choice of literally dozens of techniques. Depending on the kind of material you need to recall and how much you already know about the subject, you can turn to any number of methods.

As we sort through the various options, keep in mind that no one strategy works by itself. (And some strategies don't seem to work: For example, forget about supplements like gingko biloba—there's no clear scientific evidence that they are effective.[1]) Instead, try the following proven strategies and find those that work best for you. Feel free to devise your own strategies or add those that have worked for you in the past.

Rehearsal

Rehearsal. Think it again: rehearsal. Say it aloud: rehearsal. Think of it in terms of the three syllables that make up the word: re—hear—sal. OK, one more time—say the word "rehearsal."

If you're scratching your head over the last paragraph, it's to illustrate the point of **rehearsal**: to transfer material that you encounter into memory. If you don't

rehearsal
The process of practicing and learning material.

rehearse information in some way, it will end up like most of the information to which we're exposed: on the garbage heap of lost memory.

To test if you've succeeded in transferring the word "rehearsal" into your memory, put down this book and go off for a few minutes. Do something entirely unrelated to reading this book. Have a snack, catch up on the latest sports scores on ESPN, or read the front page of the newspaper.

Are you back? If the word "rehearsal" popped into your head when you picked up this book again, you've passed your first memory test. You can be assured that the word "rehearsal" has been transferred into your memory.

Rehearsal is the key strategy in remembering information. If you don't rehearse material, it will never make it into memory. Repeating the information, summarizing it, associating it with other memories, and, above all, thinking about it when you first come across it will ensure that rehearsal will be effective in pushing the material into memory.

Mnemonics

This odd word (pronounced in an equally odd fashion, with the "m" silent—"neh MON ix") describes formal techniques used to make material more readily remembered. **Mnemonics** are the tricks of the trade that professional memory experts use, and you too can use them to nail down the sort of information you will often need to recall for tests.

Among the most common mnemonics are acronyms. You're already well acquainted with **acronyms**, words or phrases formed by the first letters of a series of terms. For instance, though you may not have known it, the word "laser" is actually an acronym for "light amplification by stimulated emissions of radiation," and "radar" is an acronym for "radio detection and ranging." If you took music lessons, you may know that FACE spells out the names of the notes that appear in the spaces on the treble clef music staff ("F," "A," "C," and "E," starting at the bottom of the staff).

The benefits of acronyms is that they help us to recall a complete list of steps or items. P.O.W.ER. stands for—well, by this point in the book, you probably remember.

After learning to use the acronym "FACE" to remember the notes on the spaces of the music staff, many beginning musicians learn that the names of the lines on the staff form the acrostic, "Every Good Boy Deserves Fudge." An **acrostic** is a sentence in which the first letters spell out something that needs to be recalled. The benefits—as well as the drawbacks—of acrostics are similar to those of acronyms. (You can explore acronyms and acrostics in **Try It! 5**.)

Although mnemonics are helpful, keep in mind that they have a number of significant shortcomings. First, they don't focus on the meaning of the items being remembered. Because information that is learned in terms of its surface characteristics—such as first letters that form a word—is less likely to be retained than information that is learned in terms of its meaning, mnemonic devices are an imperfect route to memorization.

There's another problem with mnemonics: Sometimes it takes as much effort to create a mnemonic device as it would to memorize the material in the first place. And because the mnemonic itself has no meaning, it can be forgotten.

Despite their drawbacks, mnemonics can be useful. They are particularly helpful when the material being memorized includes a list of items or a series of steps.

mnemonics
Formal techniques used to make material more readily remembered.

acronym
A word or phrase formed by the first letters of a series of terms.

acrostic
A sentence in which the first letters of the words correspond to material that is to be remembered.

Do-It-Yourself Acronyms and Acrostics

In the first part of this Try It!, create an acronym and an acrostic.

1. Figure out an acronym to remind you of the names of the five Great Lakes, using the first letters of their names (which are Erie, Huron, Michigan, Ontario, Superior).

2. Devise an acrostic for the nine planets in order of their average distance from the sun. Their names, in order, are Mercury, Venus, Earth, Mars, Jupiter, Saturn, Uranus, Neptune, Pluto. (Bonus question: Because many astronomers no longer believe Pluto is a planet, devise an acrostic that omits Pluto and just contains the first eight planets.)

After you've tried to create the acronym and acrostic, respond to these questions: How successful were you in devising effective acronyms and acrostics? Is the act of creating them an important component of helping to remember what they represent, or would having them created by someone else be as helpful in recalling them? For your information, a common acronym for the Great Lakes is HOMES (**H**uron, **O**ntario, **M**ichigan, **E**rie, **S**uperior), and a traditional acrostic for the order of the planets is **M**y **V**ery **E**ducated **M**other **J**ust **S**erved **U**s **N**ine **P**izzas. (As for the bonus question that omits Pluto, future generations may use the acrostic **M**y **V**ery **E**ducated **M**other **J**ust **S**erved **U**s **N**oodles.)

Chunking Material

When we learn new material, we face a physical limitation of our brains: We can hold only a limited amount of information in our heads at the same time. Although the specific amount varies, it's generally around five to nine individual bits of information.

But there's a way around that limitation, known as chunking. A *chunk* is a grouping of information that can be stored in working memory, the memory store where information is processed before it moves into long-term memory. For example, a chunk can be a group of seven individual letters or numbers, permitting us to hold a seven-digit phone number (such as 226-4610) in working memory.

But a chunk also may consist of larger categories, such as words or other meaningful units. For example, consider the following list of 21 letters:

P B S F O X C N N A B C C B S M T V N B C

Because the list of individual letters exceeds seven items, it is difficult to recall the letters after one exposure. But suppose they were presented as follows:

PBS FOX CNN ABC CBS MTV NBC

In this case, even though there are still 21 letters, you'd be able to store them in working memory since they represent only seven chunks.

The principle of chunking can help us to store information more efficiently. Rather than considering individual bits of information, try to link them into meaningful groups. The larger the meaningful groupings, the more information you'll be able to recall.

Involve Multiple Senses

The more senses you can involve when you're trying to learn new material, the better you'll be able to remember. Here's why: Every time we encounter new information, all of our senses are potentially at work. For instance, if we witness a car crash, we receive sensory input from the sight of the two cars hitting each other, the sound of the impact, and perhaps the smell of burning rubber. Each piece of sensory information is stored in a separate location in the brain, and yet all the pieces are linked together in extraordinarily intricate ways.

What this means is that when we seek to remember the details of the crash, recalling a memory of one of the sensory experiences—such as what we heard—can trigger recall of the other types of memories. For example, thinking about the *sound* the two cars made when they hit can bring back memories of the way the scene looked.

When you learn something, use your body. Don't sit passively at your desk. Instead, move around. Stand up; sit down. Touch the page. Trace figures with your fingers. Talk to yourself. Think out loud. It may seem strange, but doing this increases the number of ways in which the information is stored.

Visualization

Visualization is a technique by which images are formed to ensure that material is recalled. For instance, memory requires three basic steps: the initial recording of information, the storage of that information, and, ultimately, the retrieval of the stored information. As you read the three steps, you probably see them as logical and straightforward processes. But how do you remember them?

You might visualize a computer, with its keyboard, flash drives, and monitor (see **Figure 5.3**). The keyboard represents the initial recording of information, the flash drive represents the storage of information, and the monitor represents the display of information that has been retrieved from memory. If you can put these images in your mind, it will help you to remember the three basic memory steps later.

Overlearning

Overlearning. Think back to when you were learning your basic multiplication facts ($1 \times 1 = 1$; $2 \times 2 = 4$; and so forth). Let's suppose you had put each multiplication problem on a flash card, and you decided to go through your entire set of cards, trying to get every problem right.

The first time you went through the set of cards and answered all the problems correctly, would you feel as if you'd memorized them perfectly and that you'd never again make an error? You shouldn't. You would need several instances of perfect performance to be sure you had learned the multiplication facts completely.

Lasting learning doesn't come until you have overlearned the material. **Overlearning** consists of studying and rehearsing material past the point of initial mastery. Through overlearning, recall becomes automatic. Rather than searching for a fact and going through mental contortions until perhaps the information surfaces, overlearning permits us to recall the information automatically, without even thinking

visualization
A memory technique by which images are formed to help recall material.

overlearning
Studying and rehearsing material past the point of initial mastery to the point at which recall becomes automatic.

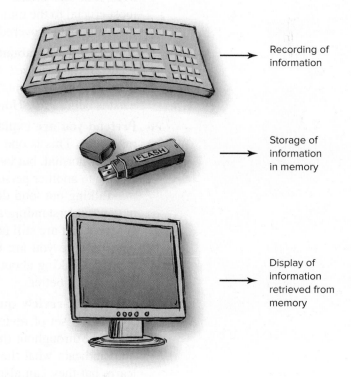

Recording of information

Storage of information in memory

Display of information retrieved from memory

figure 5.3
Visualizing Memory

about it. The more facts and mental operations that you have memorized through overlearning, the more quickly you can move through a test.

To put the principle of overlearning to work, don't stop studying at the point when you can say to yourself, "Well, I'll probably pass this test." You may be right, but that's all you'll do—pass. Instead, spend extra time learning the material until it becomes as familiar as an old pair of jeans.

≫ LO 5-3
E Evaluate

What Does It Mean? What Do I Know?

Evaluation is a crucial step in reading. You need to be able to answer the seemingly simple question: "What does all this mean?"

But there's another aspect to evaluation. You need to evaluate, truthfully and honestly, your own level of understanding. What do you know as a result of your reading? Evaluation, then, consists of the following steps:

▶ **Identify the main ideas and themes and their value *to you personally*.** Try to determine the take-home message of the material you've read. For example, the take-home message of a chapter on accounting ethics might be, "In the long run, honest accounting practices benefit the long-term health of any business."

Sometimes the main ideas and themes are spelled out, and at other times you will have to deduce them for yourself. Evaluating the main ideas and themes in terms of how they relate to you personally will help you understand and remember them more easily.

▶ **Prioritize the ideas.** Of all the information that is presented, which is the most crucial to the main message and which is the least crucial? Make a list of the main topics covered and try to rank them in order of importance.

▶ **Think critically about the arguments presented in the reading.** Do they seem to make sense? Are the author's assertions reasonable? Are there any flaws in the arguments? Would authors with a different point of view dispute what is being said? How would they build their own arguments?

▶ **Pretend you are explaining the material (talking—out loud!—about the material).** This is one time when talking out loud when no one is around is not only normal, but beneficial. Summarize the material aloud, as if you were talking to another person.

Talking out loud does two things. First, it helps you identify weak spots in your understanding and recall. Talking to yourself will help you nail down concepts that are still not clear in your own mind. Second, and equally important, because you are transforming the written word into the spoken word, you are thinking about the information in another way, which will help you remember it better.

▶ **Use in-text review questions and tests.** Many textbook chapters end with a quiz or a set of review questions about the material. Some have questions scattered throughout the chapter. Don't ignore them! Not only do such questions indicate what the writer of the book thought was important for you to learn, but they can also provide an excellent opportunity for evaluating your memory.

▶ **Use a virtual study group.** When it comes to evaluating your understanding of a reading, two heads (or more!) are often better than one. Working with a virtual study group can help you test the limits of your understanding and memory of material and assess areas in which you need work.

▶ **Be honest with yourself.** Most of us are able to read with our minds on cruise control. But the net result is not much different from not reading the passage at all. If you have drifted off while you've been reading, go back and reread the passage.

From the perspective of . . .

AN EDITORIAL ASSISTANT The ability to discern what is important within what you read is a key job function for editors. How might you apply your reading evaluation skills to an author's first draft?

© Comstock/SuperStock RF

Dealing with Learning Disabilities

If you, like millions of people in the United States, have a learning disability of one sort or another, reading and remembering may prove to be particularly challenging. **Learning disabilities** are defined as difficulties in processing information when listening, speaking, reading, or writing; in most cases, learning disabilities are diagnosed when there is a discrepancy between learning potential and actual academic achievement.

One of the most common kinds of learning disabilities is *dyslexia,* a reading disability that produces the misperception of letters during reading and writing, unusual difficulty in sounding out letters, spelling difficulties, and confusion between right and left. Although its causes are not yet completely understood, one likely explanation is a problem in the part of the brain responsible for breaking words into the sound elements that make up language.

Another common disability is *attention deficit hyperactivity disorder* (or *ADHD*), which is marked by an inability to concentrate, inattention, and a low tolerance for frustration. For the 1 to 3 percent of adults who have ADHD, planning, staying on task, and maintaining interest present unusual challenges. These challenges not only are present in college, but also affect job performance.

People with learning disabilities are sometimes viewed as unintelligent. Nothing could be farther from the truth: There is no relationship between learning disabilities and IQ. For instance, dozens of well-known and highly accomplished individuals suffered from dyslexia, including physicist Albert Einstein (pictured on the following page), U.S. general George Patton, poet William Butler Yeats, and writer John Irving.

By the time they reach college, most people with learning disabilities have already been diagnosed. If you do have a diagnosed learning disability and you need special services, it is important to disclose your situation to your online instructors and other college officials.

learning disabilities
Difficulties in processing information when listening, speaking, reading, or writing, characterized by a discrepancy between learning potential and actual academic achievement.

Career Connections

The Job of Reading

Memos. Annual reports. Instructions. Continuing education assignments. Professional journals.

Each of these items illustrates the importance of developing critical reading skills for on-the-job success. Virtually every job requires good reading expertise, and for some professions, reading is a central component. Polishing your reading skills now will pay big dividends when you enter the world of work. The better you are at absorbing and remembering written information, the better you'll be at carrying out your job.

For instance, in many corporations, vital information is transmitted through the written word, via e-mails, hard-copy memos, technical reports, or web-based material. The job of repairing broken appliances or automobiles requires reading numerous service manuals to master the complex computer diagnostic systems that are now standard equipment. Nurses and others in the healthcare field must read journals and reports to keep up with the newest medical technologies.

Furthermore, because not all supervisors are effective writers, you'll sometimes need to read between the lines and draw inferences and conclusions about what you need to do. You should also keep in mind that there are significant cultural differences in the ways in which people write and the type of language they use. Being sensitive to the cultural background of colleagues will permit you to more accurately interpret and understand what you are reading.

In short, reading is a skill that's required in virtually every profession. Developing the habit of reading critically while you are in college will pave the road for future career success.

A disability in no way dictates what sort of accomplishments you are capable of.
Library of Congress Prints and Photographs Division

In some cases, students with learning disabilities have not been appropriately evaluated prior to college. If you have difficulties such as mixing up and reversing letters frequently and suspect that you have a learning disability, your college may provide online resources that can provide you with guidance. If your college has a physical campus, one place to start is their counseling or health center.

Many sorts of treatments, ranging from learning specific study strategies to the use of medication, can be effective in dealing with learning disabilities. In addition, colleges that accept support from the federal government have a legal obligation to provide people diagnosed with learning disabilities with appropriate support. This obligation is spelled out in the Americans with Disabilities Act, and it provides important legal protections.

However, just because you are having trouble with reading assignments doesn't automatically mean that you have a learning disability. Not only is the kind of reading you do in college more difficult than in other contexts, but there's also more of it. It's only when reading represents a persistent, long-term problem—one that won't go away no matter how much work you do—that a learning disability becomes a possible explanation.

 **Rethink** Getting It the Second Time

You're human, so—like the rest of us—when you finish a reading assignment you'd probably like nothing more than to heave a sigh of relief and put the book away.

By now you know that there's a crucial step you should take that will assist you in cementing what you've learned into memory: rethinking what you've read. If you do it within 24 hours of first reading the assignment, it can save you hours of work later.

The best way to rethink an assignment is to reread it, along with any notes you've taken. "Yeah, right," you're probably thinking. "Like I have time for that." The goal, though, is not a literal rereading. In fact, it isn't necessary to reread word for word. You already know what's important and what's not important, so you can skim some of the less important material. But it is wise to reread the more difficult and important material carefully, making sure that you fully understand what is being discussed and that you'll remember the key details.

What's most critical, though, is that you think deeply about the material, considering the take-home message of what you've read. You need to be sure that your understanding is complete and that you're able to answer any questions that you had earlier about the material. Rethinking should be the central activity as you reread the passage and your notes.

The benefits of rethinking the material can't be overstated. Rethinking transfers material from your short-term memory to your long-term memory. It solidifies information so that it will be remembered far better over the long haul.

> "Reading furnishes the mind only with materials of knowledge; it is thinking that makes what we read ours."
>
> **John Locke, author, *Of the Conduct of the Understanding*, 1706.**

Speaking *of* Success

Courtesy of Sarah J. Wilson

NAME: **Sarah J. Wilson**

EDUCATION: **National American University**

DEGREE: **Business Administration with emphasis on tourism and hospitality**

For Sarah Wilson, going to college not only gave her the chance to get an education—it also provided her the opportunity to promote her Native American heritage.

While pursuing a degree in Business Administration at National American University, Wilson is working at the Dahl Art Center to support local Native American artists.

"I recently worked at a cultural event that helped Native artists get their work evaluated so they could get into major art festivals," says Wilson, an enrolled member of the Oglala Sioux. "Another one of our biggest projects is developing a website for Native artists on the Pine Ridge Reservation."

Wilson's work is also tied to promoting tourism and small business development for the reservation. "Our culture is one of the most positive things we have," she explains. "My work allows me to see and interact with it every day, and to make it an even greater support for the community."

Wilson is already thinking about her next moves following graduation.

"I would like to get a nonprofit organization going and am also interested in microloans," she says. "I'd especially like to focus on helping artists get the financial support they need. I've seen 19-year-olds with fully developed business plans who could use the help. I would like to create something that doesn't exist yet, to develop something positive and sustainable."

By admission a poor student in high school, Wilson says that her time in college has been different from anything else she had experienced before. Through hard work and determination, she's made the honor roll every quarter with straight A's.

"The first thing I do during the start of a new semester is review the syllabi for all of my classes, write down all important due dates, and prioritize how much time I need to dedicate to every class each week," Wilson describes. "I'm extremely focused on staying on top of my work. I also take really good notes on all of the course materials."

When preparing for tests, Wilson also stays motivated by keeping in mind the work she has done before. "I consider everything I've done during the quarter and through all of college," she explains. "I think about how much I'm paying for college and the sacrifices of time I've made. That helps me make the final push to ensure I'm ready on test day."

[RETHINK]

- What do you think Wilson means when she says she "prioritizes how much time she needs to dedicate to every class each week"?

- Why does thinking about the sacrifices she's made lead Wilson to be motivated when she prepares for tests?

Looking Back

LO 5-1 Explain how reading style and attention span affect reading.

▶ The most important aspect of reading is understanding, not speed. Finishing a reading assignment quickly is far less important than understanding it fully.

▶ One problem people have with reading is a limited attention span. However, attention span can be increased with self-awareness and practice.

LO 5-2 Identify how to improve concentration and to read and remember more effectively.

▶ Reading should be approached with a clear sense of purpose and goals, which will vary from assignment to assignment. Examining the frontmatter of a book and creating advance organizers is also useful.

▶ As you read, identify and focus on the key material you will need to remember later. Don't try to memorize everything you read.

▶ Maintain focus by breaking down the reading into small chunks, taking breaks as needed, dealing with distractions, and writing while reading.

▶ Many memory techniques are available to improve memorization. Rehearsal is a primary one, as is the use of mnemonics, such as acronyms and acrostics.

▶ Overlearning is a basic principle of memorization.

LO 5-3 Discuss how best to retain what you have read.

▶ Understanding of reading assignments can be cemented in memory by identifying the main ideas, prioritizing them, thinking critically about the arguments, using in-text questions and tests, and explaining the writer's ideas to someone else.

▶ Quickly rereading assignments and notes taken on them can greatly help in solidifying memories of what has been read.

[KEY TERMS AND CONCEPTS]

Acronym (p. 121)

Acrostic (p. 121)

Advance organizers (p. 108)

Attention span (p. 111)

Frontmatter (p. 109)

Learning disabilities (p. 125)

Mnemonics (p. 121)

Overlearning (p. 123)

Rehearsal (p. 120)

Visualization (p. 123)

[RESOURCES]

ON THE WEB

The following sites on the Internet provide opportunities to extend your learning about the material in this chapter. (Although the web addresses were accurate at the time this material was published, check the *P.O.W.E.R. Learning* Connect website or contact your instructor for any changes that may have occurred.)

- ▶ "Editor Eric's Greatest Literature of All Time: The Works" (**http://editoreric.com/greatlit/indexB.html**): Check out this lengthy list of books. While it is one person's interpretation of what constitutes great books, it nevertheless contains a variety of great literature, with links to outlines of each work.

- ▶ SQ3R—Improving Reading Comprehension is the title of this site offered by Virginia Tech University (**http://www.ucc.vt.edu/academic_support_students/online_study_skills_workshops/SQ3R_improving_reading_comprehension/index.html**). It offers a clear and detailed outline on how to use the SQ3R method, as well as links to other reading comprehension aids such as critical reading, proofreading, and selective reading.

- ▶ Need a mnemonic? Have one you'd like to share? Then just go to **www.mnemonic-device.com/**, a site devoted entirely to mnemonics. This fun and educational site covers a variety of subjects from astronomy to weather.

- ▶ Mind Tools, a bookstore specializing in works on memory, offers a number of free online articles (**www.mindtools.com/memory.html**) detailing methods for improving memory. It includes examples of how each technique can be applied to such topics as remembering lists and foreign languages.

ON CAMPUS

If you are experiencing unusual difficulties in reading or remembering material, you may have a learning disability. If you suspect this is the case, take action. If your college has a physical campus, there is an office that deals specifically with learning disabilities. You can also talk to someone at your college's counseling center; he or she will arrange for you to be tested, which can determine whether you have a problem.

IN PRINT

The seventh edition of Joe Cortina and Janet Elder's book, *Opening Doors: Understanding College Reading* (McGraw-Hill, 2015), provides complete guidelines for reading textbooks and other kinds of writing that you will encounter during college. Another useful volume is *Breaking Through: College Reading* (Longman, 2015, 11th ed.), by Brenda Smith. In *Improving Your Memory* (Johns Hopkins, 2014, 4th ed.), Janet Fogler and Lynn Stern provide an overview of practical tips on maximizing your memory. Finally, Forrest King provides numerous memory improvement techniques in *How to Improve Memory* (CreateSpace Independent Publishing Platform, 2014).

ENDNOTES

1. P. E. Gold, L. Cahill, and G. L. Wenk, "The Low-Down on Ginkgo Biloba," *Scientific American*, April 2003, pp. 86–91..

The Case of . . .
The Five-Hundred-Pound Reading Packet

The instructor posted a large packet of course readings on the class website. Student Delila Meade printed out the entire packet and dropped it on her desk. It landed with a loud *thunk*.

Delila realized that she would be reading this packet over the next four weeks in her online class.

But staring at the packet, all Delila could think was, *I don't think I could even lift that, let alone read it in just a month!*

Sure, Delila thought, she was interested in the topics of the readings. They all dealt with the history of computer programming, and Delila was in college to get her online degree in that same field. She told herself a lot of the information in the readings would probably be very useful, both in college and throughout her programming career.

But still—all Delila could focus on as she stared at the packet were nagging questions. How could she possibly read all of it in four weeks? How would she remember all that material for tests or on the job?

1. How would you advise Delila to prepare for her course reading?

2. How would you suggest Delila organize her time so she can finish the readings in the allotted four weeks?

3. How might Delila stay focused on her reading? How might she most effectively use writing as a way to accomplish her task?

4. What techniques might Delila use to memorize long lists or other key material from her reading?

5. In what ways can Delila use rethinking techniques to improve her understanding of the readings in the packet?

Careers

Learning Outcomes

By the time you finish this chapter you will be able to

>> LO **6-1** Identify your career goals and ideal job.

>> LO **6-2** Describe how to create a career portfolio and its advantages.

>> LO **6-3** Discuss strategies for identifying references and interviewing well.

Michelle Edmunds felt ready for her first job interview. In fact, she felt more than ready.

The interview, for a position as a medical assistant, had been scheduled the week before. And ever since then, Michelle had been mentally preparing answer after answer about her background and about the position. She'd researched the medical practice online, reviewed her own job experience, and even scanned some websites for medical practices in the local area, to get a sense of the overall market.

But when the interviewer, seemingly out of the blue, asked her, "How many piano tuners are there in your home state?" she was clueless. How should she know? And, more to the point, what did that question have to do with being a medical assistant?

Looking Ahead

Luckily for Michelle, what she later called the "piano crisis" was a turning point. Once she got beyond her initial shock, she realized that the aim of the question was to test not her knowledge of piano tuners but her problem-solving skills. After first considering the population of her home state, and then guessing how many of those people might own pianos, she was able to come up with a rough estimate of how many piano tuners there might be. The interviewer, clearly satisfied, moved on to other, more predictable questions.

Job interviews can be anxiety-producing events. But they are just one of a series of challenging activities that are part of the process of finding a job. In the last few chapters of *P.O.W.E.R. Learning*, we've been looking at skills that are usually applied in your online classes: notetaking, test taking, and so forth. In this chapter, we explore strategies that will help you in the world of work. We address ways to identify your career goals and the best methods to achieve them. To put it simply, we consider the things you need to know to get the job you want.

»LO 6-1 Career Planning

At this point, you're in college to learn the skills to start down a specific career path. That means you've made up your mind about your career . . . right?

In fact, the answer is no. Even those on their way to acquiring training to work within a particular field need to think and plan carefully with regard to their professional ambitions.

For instance, imagine you are on your way to earning a degree in accounting. Clearly, you've made an important decision about your career. But consider these questions: Do you want to work independently or as an employee of a business? If you want to work for a business, would you rather it be a small company or a large corporation? Do you want a job that will pay less initially but at which you can advance, or would you rather trade the possibility of moving up the ladder for a better starting salary?

Further, do you want to work locally, or would you be willing to relocate for the right job? What kind of hours are you willing to work? What kind of hours *can* you work, given demands of family and other obligations?

These are just some of the questions people need to answer as they approach their careers. Keep in mind that you don't need to have all the answers right now. Few people know *exactly* how they'd like their professional lives to unfold. What's important to realize is that even if you've chosen a field, you still have lots of decisions to make and options to choose from as you pursue your career. Remember: Career planning is not a decision you make once. Rather, it is an ongoing process. (To explore your thinking about work and careers, complete the **Journal Reflections**.)

P Prepare
Identify your career goals

O Organize
Find career opportunities

W Work
Create a career portfolio

E Evaluate
Get feedback on your resume and cover letter

R Rethink
Reconsider your career choices

P.O.W.E.R. Plan

Journal Reflections

Thinking about Work

At some point in your life, you've almost surely had a job. Maybe you have one right now. And whether you realize it or not, there's no doubt you have developed some strong ideas about what it's like to work. Take some time now to consider your thoughts about work more fully.

1. What was most rewarding about the best job you ever had: the ability to earn money, social aspects involving your fellow employees, enjoyment of the work itself, or something else?

2. What would you see as the positive and negative aspects of supervising other people? Would you like to supervise others at some point in your career?

3. How important is the amount of money that you're paid for the work you do?

4. Do you see work as something you must do in order to earn a living, or something that is a central and important aspect of life in and of itself?

5. How important is variety in what you do? How important is stability in what you do?

P Prepare   Identifying Your Career Goals

Some people take a job for the money. Some people take a job for the health benefits. Some people show up at work because they love to crunch numbers or treat patients or cook filet mignon. Other people go to the office because they believe that hard work is the key to happiness.

These are all valid reasons for doing a job. As you think about the kind of job you want to find, it's essential to consider your own goals. Apart from what you might do during the day, do you want a job that helps others? A job that pays very well? One with flexible hours? Is having an impact on future generations important to you? Use **Try It! 1** to identify your long-term career goals.

Identifying Your Long-Term Career Goals

Consider each of these areas as you determine your long-term goals:

- Achievement
- Advancement opportunities
- Challenge
- Contribution to society
- Control, power
- Creativity

- Financial security
- Friendships with co-workers
- Helping others
- Independence
- Leadership
- Learning new things

- Loyalty
- Prestige
- Recognition from others
- Security
- Variety
- Working with others

Using this list, create a set of your three most important occupational goals. For example, three primary goals might be to (1) be challenged to reach my potential, (2) work with others in a cooperative environment, and (3) make a lasting contribution to society. However, don't be influenced by these examples—choose goals that are your own.

My Primary Career Goals Are to:

1.

2.

3.

Stating your career goals up front, even before you consider the range of jobs that you have to choose from, is important. Identifying your goals helps you know what it is that *you* want out of work. Future employers are interested in what you bring to your job, rather than how well a job fulfills your important goals. It's crucial that you consider what has significance to you before making career decisions. If a career opportunity doesn't fulfill your major goals, it will not be a good choice for you.

○ Organize | Finding Career Opportunities

Research, research, research. That's the name of the game when it comes to charting your career. Even if you know the general direction you want your career to take, you'll want to get a feel for the specific opportunities within your chosen field, as well as how your field is developing and changing.

Be sure to keep notes about what you find. Your notes don't have to be elaborately written. Just keep them simple, legible, and organized, and make sure that they include the source of the information you're describing.

Books and Websites

A good first step in obtaining career information is the U.S. Department of Labor's *Occupational Outlook Handbook (OOH)*. The *OOH,* revised every two years, categorizes occupations into 11 broad groupings. It provides information on kinds of work, working conditions, job outlook, earnings, education and training requirements, and expected job prospects.

The Department of Labor website at **www.bls.gov/oco/** not only provides the *OOH* online, but offers a wealth of additional information as well. Among the most interesting features of the website is a compilation of the most up-to-date information on the hottest professions, in terms of projected future growth. (This information, summarized in **Table 6.1**, must be used with care: The mere fact that a job is expanding rapidly doesn't necessarily mean that there are huge numbers of openings. A quickly growing profession may have only a few openings, and even with rapid growth, the absolute number of jobs may still be relatively small in coming years.)

From the perspective of . . .

A STUDENT Part of your growth as a student involves an honest assessment of career possibilities. What careers appeal to you most?

© Rubberball Productions/Getty Images RF

You are likely to find links to a wealth of career information either at the online career center of your college or in its online library. In addition, almost every public library has a reference section on careers, and state employment centers often have extensive materials to help identify careers.

In addition to books, you may find CDs, pamphlets, and other helpful material at career centers, libraries, and employment centers. These resources also may offer on-site computers with software that can help you gather job-related information. For example, the *Discover Career Guidance and Information System* and *SIGI PLUS (System of Interactive Guidance and Information)* are widely used computer programs that have proven helpful to those engaged in career searches.

© Jeff Cadge/Photographer's Choice/Getty Images

© Brand X Pictures/Punchstock RF

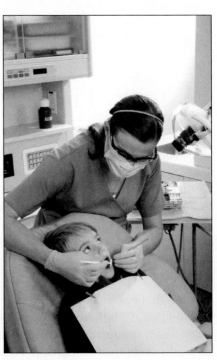
© UpperCut Images/Getty Images RF

Home healthcare aides, forensic science technicians, and dental hygienists are all career areas on the rise. Have you considered any of the careers on this list?

table 6.1	Occupations with the Fastest Growth, Projected 2012–2022	
OCCUPATION	**GROWTH RATE, 2012–2022**	**2012 MEDIAN PAY**
Industrial-organizational psychologists	53%	$83,580 per year
Personal care aides	49%	$19,910 per year
Home health aides	48%	$20,820 per year
Insulation workers, mechanical	47%	$39,170 per year
Interpreters and translators	46%	$45,430 per year
Diagnostic medical sonographers	46%	$65,860 per year
Helpers—brickmasons, blockmasons, stonemasons, and tile and marble setters	43%	$28,220 per year
Occupational therapy assistants	43%	$53,240 per year
Genetic counselors	41%	$56,800 per year
Physical therapist assistants	41%	$52,160 per year
Physical therapist aides	40%	$23,880 per year
Skincare specialists	40%	$28,640 per year
Physician assistants	38%	$90,930 per year
Segmental pavers	38%	$33,720 per year
Helpers—electricians	37%	$27,670 per year
Information security analysts	37%	$86,170 per year
Occupational therapy aides	36%	$26,850 per year
Health specialties teachers, postsecondary	36%	$81,140 per year
Medical secretaries	36%	$31,350 per year
Physical therapists	36%	$79,860 per year

Source: U.S. Bureau of Labor Statistics (2014). *Occupational Outlook Handbook, 2012–2022: Labor Statistics Bureau Bulletin 2800.* Washington, DC: U.S. Government Printing Office.

Personal Interviews

To get an up-close-and-personal look at a profession, another strategy is to talk with people who are already in it. People love to talk about their jobs, whether they love them or hate them, so don't be afraid to ask for a meeting or information session regarding their profession. You don't need a lot of their time—just enough to get an inside view of what it's like to work in their profession. Some questions you might want to ask:

▶ What's your typical day like?

▶ How did you find your job?

▶ What are the best and worst aspects of being in your profession?

▶ What do you look for in someone who wants to enter your field?

Keep in mind, of course, that the answers you get will be the opinions of one individual, reflecting his or her unique, personal experience. That's why it is a good idea to talk to several practitioners of a particular occupation, and to consider what they say in the context of other research that you have conducted.

Be sure to write a thank-you note following an interview. Not only is it a common courtesy, but it also serves the additional purpose of reinforcing who you are and your interest in their profession. You never know: One day, they might have a job opening, and you might want to ask them for a job!

》 LO 6-2 W Work

Creating a Career Portfolio

career portfolio

A dynamic record that documents your skills, capabilities, achievements, and goals, as well as providing a place to keep notes, ideas, and research findings related to careers.

The research you've done on career options forms the foundation for creating a career development portfolio. A **career portfolio** is a dynamic record that documents your skills, capabilities, achievements, and goals; it also provides a place to keep notes, ideas, and research findings related to careers. Such a portfolio will provide an easy-to-access history of your job-related activities, and it will include material that will be helpful for you and, later, for potential employers. You'll want to keep and update your career portfolio for as long as you are pursuing a career.

Your career portfolio will consist of two main parts. The first part, background information, will hold information to help you keep track of your accomplishments and notes on your research; the second part, which includes your resume and cover letter, will be material that you share with potential employers.

Your career portfolio can be in the form of a traditional, hard-copy version, or you can create an e-portfolio online. Some colleges provide online templates or "wizards" that guide you through the process of creating a career portfolio. E-portfolios have the advantage of being easily modified, and—because they reside on the web—they are accessible anywhere you have access to the web.

Career Portfolio Part I: Background Information

The information in this section of your portfolio is meant to help you make career-related decisions and record your thinking about your career. This part is for your eyes only. Although you will draw on the material for the "public" part of your portfolio that potential employers will see, think of it as your own private repository of information.

- ▶ **Basic personal data.** Keep a record of data and identification numbers that you think you'll never forget—but that, even with the best intentions, you probably will not remember at the least opportune moment. For example, include your social security number, addresses (home and college), college ID number, and telephone numbers. If you're a renter, keep a record of your landlord's name and address; you might need a credit reference one day.

- ▶ **Career research notes.** Whether you have notes collected from books, web-based research, or interviews with people in a particular occupation, they belong in your career portfolio. They will provide a record of your career-related activities.

- ▶ **Syllabi and outlines from courses you have taken.** Include a copy of the syllabus and course outline of every course you have taken, along with the grade you received in the course. The information contained in a course syllabus and outline will serve to jog your memory about the material the course covered. Without these materials, you're at the mercy of your memory when you're trying to recall the content of a course you may have taken several years earlier that has direct relevance to your career.

  For further documentation relating to a course, you could include a copy of the course description from the college catalog and, if the class had a list of competencies that students were to attain, a copy of these as well.

- ▶ **Transcripts.** Include the most recent version of your transcript, listing the courses that you took, credits earned, and grades you received in your classes.

- ▶ **Your personal history.** If someone were to write your biography, what are the key events that you'd want him or her to know about?

  The events that would be included in your biography can form the core of a list that you should make of every significant experience you've had. Although the list should include every employment-related experience you've had, even part-time jobs or summer jobs when you were in high school, don't limit yourself only to job experiences. Also include other accomplishments, such as the military service or community service you perform. Personal events that have had a major impact on who you are, such as notable athletic achievements, should also earn a place in your personal history. Use **Try It! 2** to help make this list, which you'll use later to create a resume.

- ▶ **Long-term career goals.** Your career portfolio should have the statement of your long-term career goals that you developed in **Try It! 1**.

- ▶ **Writing samples.** Add examples of your best writing. These can be papers that you've submitted for classes or other writing you have done on your own or on the job. The idea is to have a sample of your writing easily available should a potential employer ask for one.

- ▶ **Credentials.** Include copies of any credentials you have earned. For example, place in the portfolio a copy of diplomas you have earned, certificates of workshop or training participation you have received, proof of noncredit continuing education courses you have taken, and the like. You never know when an employer might want to see documentation of your accomplishments.

Instructors as Career Guides

Each of your instructors has a job—that of a college instructor. But despite the similarity in their job titles, each got that job in a different way, using different tactics and strategies. Each followed his or her own particular career path and has a distinct educational background. Furthermore, your instructors may have had a variety of positions, and possibly a number of previous careers, prior to becoming a college instructor.

You can learn a great deal about career opportunities and the process of getting a job by communicating with your online instructors about their own careers. Consider asking (via e-mail, chat, or Skype) your online instructors these questions:

- What is your educational and professional background?
- How did you get your current job?
- What students have you had that have been particularly successful careerwise? What qualities did they have that set them apart from other students of yours?
- What general advice do you have for someone looking for a job?
- Knowing me from your course, what skills would you encourage me to work on and develop in order to increase my chances of successfully getting a job?

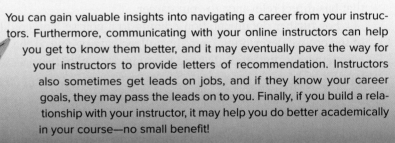

You can gain valuable insights into navigating a career from your instructors. Furthermore, communicating with your online instructors can help you get to know them better, and it may eventually pave the way for your instructors to provide letters of recommendation. Instructors also sometimes get leads on jobs, and if they know your career goals, they may pass the leads on to you. Finally, if you build a relationship with your instructor, it may help you do better academically in your course—no small benefit!

Career Portfolio Part II: Resume and Cover Letter

This section of your career portfolio encompasses information that you will share with potential employers. Whereas the material in the first part of your portfolio provides the background for your career planning, this is the public face of your portfolio.

Think of the components of the first part as the equivalent of the backstage of a play, with a director and crew working behind the scenes to pull things together. In contrast, this second part of the portfolio is the play the audience sees, the part that should proceed flawlessly. You want the critics to offer nothing less than raves for your production.

The two primary elements that belong in the second part of your career portfolio are your resume and your cover letter.

Resume

A resume (pronounced res-oo-may) is a brief summary of your qualifications for a job. It is the first thing that potential employers see and should serve to arouse their interest. Actually, a human may not even initially see it: An increasing number of employers use computers to screen resumes. The computers look for key skills, and if they are lacking, they send an automatic rejection.

Cataloging Your Personal History

	Activity or Event	When Activity or Event Took Place	Where Event Occurred (e.g., company, hospital, social agency)	Responsibilities or Actions Performed	Skills or Talents Used	Achievements, Results, or Insights
Did you work during or before high school?						
Were you a member of any clubs or other organizations in high school?						
How many paid jobs have you held since high school?						
Have you performed any community service?						
Have you provided any services to a religious institution?						
Are you working while at college?						
Are you in any clubs or organizations at college?						
Have you had any personally significant life experiences?						
Have you ever been called upon to exercise skills or talents you didn't know you had?						
Have you ever solved a tough problem and felt great satisfaction?						
Have you ever worked in a group to solve a problem?						
Have you ever organized a complex task on your own?						
Have you ever led a group in the performance of a large task?						
What is the best thing you have ever done?						

Consequently, the resume must be crafted with great precision and care. If you've created a personal history statement earlier for Part I of your career portfolio, use it to get started.

The key elements of a resume include the following and are illustrated in a sample resume in **Figure 6.1**.

▶ **Contact information.** Include your name, address (current and permanent if they're different), phone number(s), and e-mail address. *Don't* include your sex, age, race, or marital status. Not only are they irrelevant, but employers who take them into consideration are breaking antidiscrimination laws.

ALEJANDRO D. WEBB
1334 Russel Lane, Brooksville, FL 34603
352 - 555 - 1877 e: alejwebb@gmail.com

JOB OBJECTIVE—To obtain a position as a paralegal

WORK EXPERIENCE
Law offices of Brandon and Shields, Brooksville, FL
Office Manager
May 2006–Present

- Oversaw logistics of law office of twelve people; was responsible for scheduling, filing, copying, and managing administrative staff.
- Devised new office-wide filing system for records of completed cases.
- Researched and implemented new office-wide benefits package.
- Responsible for balancing monthly facilities budget.
- Occasionally accompanied attorneys to court to provide organizational support.

Amelia D. Rafael, P.A., Jacksonville, FL
Administrative Assistant
October 2010–April 2012

- Managed schedule, correspondence, and files for high-profile Jacksonville attorney.
- Aided in creating documents and organizing evidence for $13 million class action case.

EDUCATION
Central Florida University
AD Paralegal Studies, June 2015

HONORS AND AWARDS
Academic Dean's List
Frederick Stein Prize for Outstanding Writing

CAMPUS AND COMMUNITY ACTIVITIES
Latino Students Organization
Volunteer, Holling Street Soup Kitchen

PROFESSIONAL MEMBERSHIP
Florida Paralegal Association

PARTICULAR SKILLS
Proficient in all Microsoft Office programs
Fluent in Spanish

REFERENCES
Available upon request

---

figure 6.1
Sample Resume

- ▶ **Job objective.** If you are targeting a specific job, include a specific objective (such as "to obtain a position as a buyer for a major retail department store"). However, if you're willing to be flexible, provide a more general job objective (for example, "to obtain an entry-level position in retail sales").

- ▶ **Education.** Include the colleges you've attended or are currently attending, with the actual or anticipated year of graduation and degree earned.

- ▶ **Awards and honors.** If you've won any awards or honors (such as membership in an honors program or inclusion on the Dean's List), mention them. If you have none that you want to include, leave this category off your resume.

- ▶ **Campus and community activities.** Include activities in which you've participated, and indicate any in which you've had a leadership role. You want to demonstrate that you are an involved, contributing member of your community.

- ▶ **Professional memberships.** Do you belong to any professional organizations that are relevant to the job you'll be seeking? If so, include them.

- ▶ **Work experience.** List your experience, starting with your most recent job and working backward. Include the job title, dates, and your major on-the-job responsibilities.

  Don't feel you need to include every job you've ever held (for example, leave out the occasional pet sitting). Instead, focus on the key positions that illustrate your ability to hold a job and carry out responsibilities. In fact, it is sometimes appropriate to use what is known as a *functional resume,* in which you organize your experience according to specific skills or functions, rather than chronologically.

  Functional resumes are particularly helpful if you are changing careers or are reentering the job force after a long period in which you weren't working. Whether you use a traditional, chronologically organized resume or a functional resume to present your work experience, always remember that the focus should be on how your past work can get you a job in the profession you want in the future.

- ▶ **Particular skills.** Do you know how to program in Linux? Can you speak Spanish fluently? Are you a certified lifeguard? Can you use an Excel spreadsheet or PowerPoint?

  Include a brief list of the special skills you have. Once again, make sure that the skills you list are related to the job you're seeking. For example, if you're seeking a job in information technology, Linux programming is relevant, but it may not be if you're looking for a job in medical services.

- ▶ **References.** A "reference" category is optional, but if you include it, simply say, "References available upon request." Don't list specific names, but have them available should you be asked for them. (We'll discuss whom to ask and how to obtain references later in the chapter.)

As you create a resume, keep in mind some general rules. First, keep it short. In a resume, less is more. Generally, resumes should be no longer than one page.

Second, make it look good. Your resume should appear professional. Use plenty of white space, with one-inch margins on every side. Use strong action words, such as those in **Table 6.2**. Avoid articles (such as "the," "a," and "an") and pronouns (such as "I" or "we"); don't write in full sentences.

Third, you should prepare several versions of your resume: edit-ready and PDF versions. *Edit-ready* versions are in word processing programs such as Word, Google Docs, or OpenOffice. An edit-ready version can be printed

table 6.2   Action Words

Using strong action words and making sentences short will help you prepare a professional and eye-catching resume. Here is a list of action words to get you started. Use words that best describe what you do and who you are.

Achieved	Directed	Investigated
Administered	Discovered	Launched
Advised	Drafted	Led
Aided	Edited	Managed
Approved	Educated	Moderated
Archived	Enabled	Monitored
Arranged	Established	Negotiated
Assigned	Evaluated	Operated
Assisted	Examined	Organized
Authored	Expanded	Oversaw
Budgeted	Expedited	Performed
Built	Extracted	Recommended
Calculated	Facilitated	Recruited
Cataloged	Fashioned	Regulated
Chaired	Forecasted	Remodeled
Classified	Formulated	Reported
Coached	Founded	Restored
Collected	Generated	Reversed
Compiled	Granted	Reviewed
Computed	Guided	Saved
Conducted	Identified	Scheduled
Contracted	Illustrated	Solved
Controlled	Improved	Strengthened
Coordinated	Increased	Summarized
Counseled	Influenced	Supervised
Created	Informed	Trained
Critiqued	Initiated	Translated
Delegated	Inspected	Trimmed
Demonstrated	Installed	Tutored
Designated	Instituted	Upgraded
Designed	Instructed	Validated
Developed	Integrated	Worked
Devised	Interviewed	Wrote
Diagnosed	Invented	

as a hard copy or sent online as an e-mail attachment. You should also save your edit-ready version as a *PDF file,* using your word-processing software or Adobe. The advantage of a PDF file is that it maintains the formatting precisely, ensuring that your resume looks its best.

Finally, proofread, proofread, proofread. And then ask someone else to proofread your material. You want to be absolutely sure that no typographical errors or misspellings find their way into your resume.

The same rules hold for the second element of Part II of your career portfolio, your cover letter, which we discuss next. Before moving on, though, get a start on creating a resume by completing **Try It! 3**.

Creating a Resume

It's time to use some of the pieces you have been thinking about and working on to create a resume. You have explored your ideas about your occupational goals (**Try It! 1**), and you have gathered important elements of your personal history (**Try It! 2**). Now put the pieces together by filling in the worksheet below. Then use the worksheet to create a clean, one-page resume that you can have reviewed and proofread.

Contact Information:

Your name, address, phone number(s), and e-mail address.

Job Objective:

Use your ideas about your occupational goals. Write one statement, beginning with the word "To," that sums up your goals. Be specific ONLY if you are applying for a job you understand and want to focus on; otherwise, state your goals broadly and generally.

Education:

List any colleges attended, including your current college, starting with the most recent. If you have taken college courses without being formally enrolled, list those too.

Awards and Honors (Optional):

List any honors you have received. Academic honors are of primary importance, but honors and awards from social, religious, and community groups (e.g., 4-H, Red Cross, Rotary Club) may be worth including if they testify to personal characteristics that may help you gain employment, such as leadership, perseverance, or a sense of civic duty.

Campus and Community Activities (Optional):

List any clubs, teams, or activities in which you have participated since high school. Include high school activities only if they were significant and are related to your career goals. Also list community activities in which you have participated, especially those in which you had a leadership role.

(continued)

Professional Memberships (Optional):

List any professional organizations related to your career goals of which you are or have been a member. Professional organizations are groups such as the Modern Language Association; any of a number of national honor societies; the National Student Speech, Language, and Hearing Association; National Art Education Association; Student Sports Medicine Association; and the like.

Work Experience (If You've Had Any):

List all jobs you have had, including paid jobs, apprenticeships, internships, and similar "real" jobs. List your most recent work experience first and work backward through time. Include the title of the job, organization for which you worked, dates of work, and major responsibilities. Understand that you may be asked about any of the jobs you list, including your reasons for moving to the next job.

Particular Skills (Optional):

List anything you are particularly good at that might transfer to a work setting, for example, the ability to speak a foreign language, to fix computer hardware problems, to write and debug software programs, to repair engines, to create websites, and so forth. You can draw this list from your academic, work, and even personal/recreational life.

References:

Available on request.

Cover Letter

Although your resume is the centerpiece of your presentation to potential employers, your cover letter is no less important. It shows that you can string words together into well-crafted sentences, and it gives you the opportunity to bring life to the list of qualifications on your resume. It also gives you the opportunity to say how enthusiastic you are about the job for which you're applying and to illustrate how well your qualifications match the job requirements.

In writing a cover letter, keep in mind the perspective of the person who is reading it. Potential employers have a problem that they need to solve: identifying someone to do work that they need done so much that they're willing to pay someone to do it. The better you can provide them with a solution to this problem, the more attractive you will be.

What this means is that your cover letter should be oriented toward helping employers solve *their* problem, not toward how the job will solve *your* problems. Consequently, don't talk about how you think the job will fulfill you as a person or how much you need it to pay your bills. Instead, orient your letter toward describing how well your own unique qualifications match the specific job requirements.

Although every cover letter should be tailor-written to a specific position (see the two sample letters in **Figure 6.2**), they typically contain the following elements:

▶ **Introduction: Catching the reader.** Describe why you are writing, how you learned about the job, and why you are interested in it. Emphasize the connection between the position requirements and your qualifications.

▶ **Letter body: Drawing in the reader.** Here's where you describe, in very brief terms, who you are and what makes you unique. Highlight major accomplishments and qualifications from your personal history, making the argument that your skills are a close match to the job. Show enthusiasm!

  You can also include information that does not appear on your resume; for instance, if you paid for your education entirely on your own, mention that fact. In addition, you can write about what you hope to accomplish on the job.

  Finally, show that you know something about the organization to which you are applying. Do some homework to learn about the employer, and state specifically what you find attractive about it.

▶ **Conclusion: A call for action.** End the letter by restating your interest in the position and suggesting that you would like to discuss the position further. State that you are available to meet for an interview. Thank the employer for considering your application.

Like your resume, the cover letter should read well and look good. Before you send it, be sure to proofread it carefully.

The point of including a sample cover letter in your career portfolio is to be ready at a moment's notice to revise the sample and send it off. Job opportunities sometimes appear unexpectedly, and it will be much easier for you to respond quickly, and respond well, if you already have a sample letter on file.

Unless you are certain of the job you'll be seeking in the future, you might want to prepare several cover letters, targeted at the different job possibilities you are considering. In addition, the act of writing cover letters for a variety of professions may actually help you come to a decision regarding the path you ultimately choose to follow.

July 29, 2017

Mr. Reginald Pelly
Assistant Vice President
WorldWide Publishing Corp.
New York, NY 10011

Dear Mr. Pelly:

Jennifer Windsor, Director of Editorial Development at WorldWide Publishing, advised me of an opening in your company for an entry-level trade book editor. From my enclosed resume, you will find that both my experience and my education fully meet the requirements you have outlined for the position.

My current position as a copy editor at a medium-sized daily newspaper has given me experience in dealing with deadlines and working closely with others. Having served as a reporter for six years, I can relate to the needs of writers as well. My colleagues consider me both outgoing and diplomatic, traits that have served me well in my work as an editor.

I will contact you Monday to learn when we can meet for an interview.

Sincerely,

Martina L. Veschova

Enclosure: Resume

figure 6.2
Two Sample Cover Letters

One final note about your career portfolio: Keep in mind that it is a work in progress, a living document that is meant to be revised as your interests and aspirations change. That's why it is a good idea to keep your career portfolio both in a virtual format and as a hard copy. By creating an e-portfolio, you will be able to make revisions easily. An e-portfolio also simplifies the process of producing an updated version of your resume and cover letter for an actual job opening.

Martin L. Chen

14A Orchard Street
Boise, Idaho 83702   email: marlchen@mrnr.com   Phone: 207 889-3763

January 29, 2017

Ms. Arlene Washington
Director, Human Services
Mercy General Hospital
18 Medical Plaza
Chicago, IL 60604

Dear Ms. Washington:

I am writing in response to the position advertised July 22, 2017, in the *Chicago Tribune* seeking a Lead Cost Analyst Accountant. My professional experience and education match well with the position requirements listed. Enclosed is my resume.

In addition to being self-motivated, I work well under pressure and welcome new challenges and opportunities. Among some of my accomplishments are the following:

- Analyzed, defined, and produced appropriate budgets for wages and salary costs, materials, expenses, and workload.
- Provided extensive, timely, and appropriate reporting for all aspects of the various budgets.
- Investigated variations from budget.
- Performed cost-benefit analyses and assisted with capital expenditure proposals.

My experience in supervising a team of four co-workers has taught me patience and has strengthened my organizational skills. My greatest satisfaction in a job comes from selecting, training, and motivating personnel. I believe I have the qualities that can help a department become more efficient and productive.

I am familiar with Mercy General Hospital from news stories on breakthrough cancer research conducted there, and I have further researched your hospital and its contributions to medicine. I feel there is a good fit between my career goals and your needs. I welcome the opportunity to discuss the position further, and look forward to hearing from you soon. Thank you for your consideration.

Yours truly,

Martin L. Chen

Enclosure

figure 6.2
Two Sample Cover Letters (*continued*)

 **Evaluate** | ## Getting Feedback on Your Resume and Cover Letter

After you have created the key elements of your career portfolio—your resume and cover letter—it's time to evaluate their effectiveness. Start by asking a trusted person, such as one of your instructors or someone on the staff of your college's online career center, to review what you've created. Ask them to provide honest and concrete suggestions because the more feedback you receive, the better the finished product will be.

Once you've received an initial review, one of the best strategies is to ask individuals working in the field in which you're interested to review your resume and cover letter. Requesting feedback from one or two people who are already working in your desired profession, particularly if they have hired people in the past, serves several purposes. Your reviewers will be in the best position to know what employers are looking for, and they can tell you how to present yourself most effectively. Not only can they help you say the right things, but they can also help you avoid saying the wrong thing.

But there's an extra bonus from seeking advice from someone currently working in the field: You become a known quantity to them, and at some point in the future, they may have a job opening, and you may spring to mind. Or if you contact them in the future, they may be able to steer you to a job opening.

R Rethink — Reconsidering Your Career Choices

Going through the process of identifying your goals, researching careers, and building a career portfolio may lead you to solidify your ideas about which occupation you'd like to pursue. That's great—that's the point of career exploration.

But even if you are sure about what you intend to do professionally, it's important to take some time to reconsider your choices. The most important thing is to avoid what psychologists call "foreclosure." Foreclosure is making a premature decision and sticking with it so persistently that you ignore other possibilities, even ones that hold considerable promise. Keeping an open mind by reconsidering your choices will help you be sure that you've made the best decisions.

From the perspective of . . .

A SECOND-CAREER EMPLOYEE It is possible to work for years in one field before deciding on a new career path. What are some things to consider if you are contemplating a second career?

What if you haven't been able to narrow things down? What if you're still completely up in the air about what path you'd like to pursue? First, realize that it's natural to be undecided. It's almost inevitable that you'll have some uncertainty with regard to decisions as important as where you work.

Also, keep in mind that even if you are certain about the general shape you want your career to take, there will inevitably be moments of backtracking and reconsideration. Very few people take one job at one organization and work there until they retire. The point is that you will

© Jack Hollingsworth/Getty Images RF

have many opportunities to rethink your decisions. Don't feel that any one decision will forever shape the rest of your career, or your life.

If you're close to the point of graduating and are ready to begin your career, and you still don't have a clue about what you want to do, then maybe you need to rethink your approach. Assuming you've considered various possibilities, you may want to reconsider the career-planning strategies you've been using. Ask yourself these questions:

▶ Have you been too restrictive or too selective in considering possibilities?

▶ Have you done sufficient research?

▶ Have you rejected job opportunities that seem somewhat interesting without carefully considering what they have to offer?

▶ Have you underestimated (or overestimated) your skills?

▶ Have you taken full advantage of all the online resources your college offers in terms of career planning?

> "Far and away the best prize that life has to offer is the chance to work hard at work worth doing."
> **Theodore Roosevelt**

» LO 6-3 Acting on Your Career Plans

Your References: Who Says What about You

Getting the job you want sometimes can hinge less on what you say about yourself and more on what others say about you. A good reference can make the difference between getting a job and getting passed over. A bad reference can destroy your chances of being offered a position.

That's why finding just the right people to supply potential employers with a reference can be the key to obtaining the job you want. That's why it's critical to identify people who are willing to speak on your behalf well before you face a deadline.

Identifying People to Provide References

Several categories of individuals can provide you references, including

▶ Former job supervisors

▶ Colleagues in previous positions

▶ Online instructors

▶ Community service supervisors

▶ Coaches, club advisors, or heads of professional groups to which you belong

▶ People who can provide character references (e.g., clergy)

The most effective references come from people who know you well—very well—and can speak to your skills, abilities, accomplishments, motivation, and character. In addition, people who can speak to the specific requirements of the job you're seeking (especially those who have worked with you in environments similar to that of the potential job) are highly effective.

The least effective references are those from family members or friends or, even worse, friends of friends. For instance, a reference from someone famous who happens to play tennis occasionally with your uncle will rarely be helpful, unless that person knows you well. Remember a key rule of references: The ability of a reference provider to describe in detail *your* strengths and *your* accomplishments is considerably more important than the identity of the reference provider, whatever his or her strengths and accomplishments.

The necessity of having people to act as references points to the importance of networking. Even while you're in college, it's critical to build up a network of people who can vouch for you. To network effectively, be sure to keep in touch with people who know and like you. And try to expand your network of contacts. For example, whenever you're at a social event, talk to people you don't know and don't just hang out with people you're familiar with.

Asking for a Reference

When choosing someone to be a reference, *always ask permission.* Never give out the names of people who you think will provide references without asking them beforehand. Not only is seeking permission common courtesy, but asking first avoids violating another rule of references: *No reference is better than a bad reference.* You need to check that the reference someone provides will be an explicitly positive one.

Although you can't directly ask someone if they can provide a positive reference (it's very hard for someone to tell you straight out that they can't), you can approach the issue indirectly. When asking someone to serve as a reference, ask them if they have any reservations. If they do, no matter how minor, turn to someone else to provide the recommendation.

You should also offer some guidelines for those providing recommendations. Let them know why you're asking them in particular, and remind them of the context in which they've known you. If there is something you'd like them to specifically address in providing you with a reference—such as the unusual creativity you showed in a previous position or the fact that you wrote exceptionally good papers in a class—let them know. The more explicit information you can provide them, the better.

Using the Web in Your Job Hunt

The web has changed the rules for conducting a job search. It permits you to post your resume and have the potential for thousands of possible employers to screen it. It also permits employers to post their job needs and have the potential for thousands of possible employees to see them. You can even apply for jobs online. Internet services can help you conduct automated searches, exposing you to job listings in your chosen field and letting you receive e-mails containing job postings that fit your skills.

The advantages of electronic job searches—such as the potentially wide exposure of your resume—come at some potential costs. First, your resume quite likely will be scanned initially by a computer. That means you must be extremely precise and follow some specific stylistic rules to avoid its being misread or ignored. Second, there are security issues since you never know who may be reading your resume.

In using the web for a job search, you need to cast your net widely. Although general interest job sites such as monster.com and careerbuilder.com post millions of jobs each year, there are more focused boards that can help you identify possible jobs in specific industries (see **Table 6.3**). In addition, most large companies post job openings on their own websites.

Starting Over: Once You Have a Job You Want

What's the best time to start looking for a job? When you already have one and don't need to find a new position.

Even if you feel happy and secure in your job, it makes sense to be prepared for the unexpected. Perhaps you'll get a new boss whom you find it difficult to work with, or your current job's activities and requirements will change for the worse. Or maybe the company will downsize or be merged with another corporation, causing widespread layoffs.

For a variety of reasons, then, you'll want to keep your resume and career portfolio updated, even if you've just started a new job. You will want to stay in contact with the people who have provided you with references in the past.

Above all, take every opportunity to learn new skills. As the economy and technology change, you'll want to have cutting-edge skills that will allow you to compete effectively.

In short: Be prepared!

There are several general guidelines to follow when posting your resume on an online employment site:

▶ Be very precise in the words you employ. For example, use action verbs and other words that are standard within an industry.

▶ Use simple type styles, such as Arial, Calibri, or Times New Roman.

▶ Avoid elaborate formatting, such as tabs or italics.

▶ Use a standard 80 characters per line.

▶ As always, proofread, proofread, proofread. A typographical error is more than embarrassing: Computers screening your resume may reject your application before a human ever sees it because they do not recognize a misspelled word.

table 6.3	Finding the Right Site on the Web
Specific Sites	
www.HigherEdJobs.com	Teaching
www.EngineerJobs.com	Engineering
www.ShowBizJobs.com	Acting
www.Medzilla.com	Doctors, nurses
www.RXCareerCenter.com	Pharmaceuticals
www.HR.com	Human resources
www.dice.com	Information technology
www.LegalStaff.com	Legal
www.AgCareers.com	Agriculture

Source: L. Farquharson, "Find a Job," *The Wall Street Journal,* September 15, 2003, p. R8.

Social Networking and Job Searches

A key strategy for finding a job is to make use of your online social networks. Membership in sites such as LinkedIn, Facebook, and Twitter allows you to alert others that you are seeking a job. For example, you can use LinkedIn's professional headline or status box to say that you are seeking a new position. You can also use a status update in Facebook to alert others that you're in the job market.

When looking for a job, it's important to expand your social network as much as you can. Think hard about everyone you know and invite them to join your network. Remember that it's not just those whom you know that may lead to a job, but the friends of your friends that may lead to a job. So the wider your social network, the better your chances of coming in contact with someone who knows about a job opportunity.

Job Interviews: Putting Your Best Foot Forward

For a potential employer who has never met you, a job interview puts a face to what has previously been an impression based on mere words written on a page. The interview is your chance to show who you are, to demonstrate your enthusiasm for a potential position, and to exhibit what you can bring to that position.

The fact that interviews are so important may make them seem intimidating and overwhelming. However, remember that the mere fact that you've been invited to an interview means you've overcome some of the highest hurdles already. Furthermore, you can follow a variety of concrete strategies to ensure that you maximize the opportunity an interview presents. Among the most important are the following.

Interviews can be a nerve-wracking experience, but preparation and a coolheaded approach can make all the difference. Don't forget that you are interviewing a potential employer, as well as being interviewed as a potential employee!
© Jupiterimages/Getty Images RF

Before the Interview

▶ **Learn about the potential employer.** It's important to learn as much as you can about the position and the company that is offering it. Go to the potential employer's website and find out as much as you can about the organization's management style and company culture. Then try to find magazine and newspaper articles to gain a sense of the success and effectiveness of the organization. The bottom line: If an interviewer asks, "What do you know about our organization?" be prepared to answer, "Quite a bit because I've researched it thoroughly."

▶ **Prepare with questions.** Come to the interview prepared with questions. Think up a set of questions and write them down so you can remember them—it's perfectly fine to refer to them during the interview. Having targeted questions shows that you've spent time thinking about the position. (Don't ask about salary during the interview; salary issues are usually addressed if you get an actual job offer.)

▶ **Prepare answers.** Finally, come prepared with answers to likely questions. For instance, it shouldn't be a surprise if an interviewer asks you to "tell me about yourself." So have an answer ready, a two- or three-minute response that touches on your career goals, your skills, your experiences, and your personal traits. Obviously, this is a lot to cover in just a few minutes, so practice it until you can do it comfortably within that short time frame. Going longer than three minutes runs the risk of boring your interviewer. Furthermore, don't just practice it by yourself. Have someone else listen to it and give you feedback.

Other favorite interview questions include "What are your major strengths and weaknesses?" "Why do you want to leave your current position?" "What are your major qualifications?" "What are your short-term and long-range goals?" and "Why should I hire you?" Although you can't prepare for every possible question in advance, thinking through some of the most likely possibilities will help you feel more confident and ready to deliver polished responses.

During the Interview

▶ **Be punctual.** Allow yourself enough time to arrive well ahead of the scheduled interview. That will help you find a parking space, locate the building and room, and generally get composed.

▶ **Dress appropriately.** Wear the right clothes for the interview. Stop by beforehand to see how people dress. If you're unsure of how formal to be, keep in mind that it's almost always better to be overdressed than to be underdressed. This is not the time to make a fashion statement. You want to look professional.

▶ **Use your social skills effectively.** Shake hands firmly and look the interviewer in the eye. Show that you're interested in the interviewer as a fellow human being, not just as someone who might give you a job. Listen attentively to what he or she has to say and be responsive. Above all, try to think confidently. Thinking positive, confident thoughts will help you appear positive and confident.

▶ **Ask questions.** If you have prepared for the interview, you've got some questions to ask about the organization with which you're looking for a job. Be sure to ask them. Interviewers almost always ask if you have any questions, but if they don't, try to work them in when you sense that the interview is almost over. It's also a good idea to ask about the hiring process the employer is using. Ask how long it will be before they will be making a decision and when you are likely to be hearing from them again.

▶ **Above all, be yourself and be honest.** You do yourself no favor by pretending to be someone other than who you are. Getting a job under false pretenses virtually guarantees that neither you nor your employer ultimately will be satisfied with your job performance. You may end up doing things you don't like to do and may not be very good at, and neither you nor your employer will find that acceptable for very long. (To get experience interviewing, complete **Try It! 4**.)

> "Rule No. 1: Just be yourself. Unless, of course, you're sloppy, lazy, or otherwise undesirable, in which case, be someone else. Be ready to humbly sell yourself, and if someone asks about your weak points, say, 'Occasionally I just work too hard.'"
>
> **Rainbow Rowell, *The Daily Nebraskan*, in P. Combs, *Major Success* (Berkeley, CA: Ten Speed Press, 1998), p. 103.**

Interviewing

Nothing will prepare you better for an upcoming interview than a number of prior interviews. To get practice interviewing, ask a person who has had experience in hiring, or even a friend, to role-play an interview with you in which they will interview you, the potential job applicant. Tell them that you will prepare for your role carefully and that you will treat the practice interview seriously.

Follow these steps:

- Choose a company or organization that you would like to work for, and provide the person who will interview you with some details about it, such as information from the company website.

- Also, research your chosen company as a potential interviewee would, to gain enough knowledge to answer potential interview questions well.

- Hold the interview. You should be serious and try to play your role well. If you like, you can "dress the part" to help you set the right tone. You may also want to tape-record the session.

- After you've concluded the interview, ask your interviewer for a critique of your performance. Ask the interviewer to make as candid a judgment as he or she can as to which category you would fit into based solely on the interview: (A) Offer a job; (B) Don't offer a job; or (C) Call back for another interview to follow up with additional questions.

After you've completed the steps outlined above, answer the following questions:

1. What did you learn from the interview?

2. Critically assess your performance as an interviewee. What was your greatest strength as an interviewee? Your greatest weakness?

3. What would you do differently during an actual interview?

4. How can you better prepare for an actual interview in the future?

After the Interview

▶ **Evaluate your interview performance.** Are you pleased with how you presented yourself in the interview? What did you do particularly well? What things could you have done better?

Jot down your impressions of the interview while they're still fresh in your mind and place them in your career portfolio. These notes will be valuable when you prepare for future interviews.

▶ **Consider if you still want the position.** Suppose, for a moment, you were actually offered the job. Do you really want it?

It's important to ask yourself whether, given what you learned about the position, you would accept it if it were actually offered to you. You probably found out things about the position that interested you, and others that may be worrisome. Evaluate the job, and if there are too many negatives, rethink whether you'd actually want it.

However, unless there are so many negatives that you're certain that under no circumstances would you take the job, don't withdraw your application. It may be that if you are offered the job, you could negotiate with your potential employer to eliminate the factors that you find undesirable.

▶ **Write a thank-you note.** It's common courtesy to thank someone for giving you his or her time during an interview.

It's also strategically important. It shows that you are polite and can be counted on to do the right thing. It demonstrates your interest in the job. And it gives you one more opportunity to show you have the "right stuff."

Although you shouldn't turn your thank-you note into a sales pitch, do indicate your continued interest in the position. Write about the aspects of the job that were of particular interest to you and explain how you can see yourself fitting in well with the company.

▶ **Follow up.** If you haven't heard from the employer in a few weeks, and it's past the point where you were told you'd be contacted, it's perfectly reasonable to e-mail or call. The purpose is not to badger the employer into hiring you—that's not going to work—but to simply check up on where the process stands. Of course, it also serves another purpose: to remind a potential employer of your continued interest in the position. You can also use the opportunity to provide additional information or to inform the employer of another job offer.

Speaking *of* Success

NAME: **Jason M. Jno-Lewis**

SCHOOL: **Alaska Career College, Anchorage, Alaska**

College means many things to many people, but for Jason Jno-Lewis, seeking a better life for his family was the primary reason.

"My biggest motivation to go to college was my family, first and foremost . . . wanting a better life for my wife and two boys," he said. "And the best choice for me was the field of business administration and computer technology, which would allow me to work in multiple fields."

Jno-Lewis, who had attended the University of Alaska for several years, decided a career-oriented college would better suit his needs.

"A deciding factor for transferring to Alaska Career College was the structure and programs they offer," he explained. "I was very interested in organizational psychology and business law and ethics. I liked how job-specific the courses were, and how I was able to learn real-life applications that better prepare you for the workforce."

But in spite of a more job-centric structure, the process was not without its challenges, according to Jno-Lewis.

"With the grueling academic demands, it's easy to get distracted or make an excuse," he noted. "Juggling work and home life can make studying for five classes, and doing your best even when you don't feel like it, very hard.

"But the one thing that helped me meet that challenge was focusing on the 'WHY' I was there. That helped me overcome every obstacle that came my way," Jno-Lewis said.

[RETHINK]

- What are the advantages and disadvantages of having a course of study that is strictly structured and career oriented?

- Jno-Lewis said that his strongest motivation for attending college was to seek a better life for his family. What would you say is your strongest motivation behind your decision to attend college?

Looking Back

LO 6-1 Identify your career goals and ideal job.

▶ Careful and systematic research is the key to identifying possible career options.

▶ Books, websites, and informational interviews provide useful information about careers.

▶ The Internet not only provides substantial information about potential jobs and companies but also can play an important role in getting a job.

LO 6-2 Describe how to create a career portfolio and its advantages.

▶ A career portfolio can document a job seeker's skills, capabilities, achievements, and goals, as well as provide a place to keep notes and research findings relating to jobs.

▶ A career portfolio also includes the person's resume and cover letter.

LO 6-3 Discuss strategies for identifying references and interviewing well.

▶ It is important to find appropriate references.

▶ Job interviews require a significant amount of preparation.

▶ Useful interview strategies include being punctual, dressing appropriately, using social skills effectively, asking questions, being oneself, and being honest.

▶ After an interview, follow up with the interviewer.

[KEY TERMS AND CONCEPTS]

Career portfolio (p. 138)

[RESOURCES]

ON THE WEB

The following sites on the web provide opportunities to extend your learning about the material in this chapter. (Although the web addresses were accurate at the time this material was published, check the *P.O.W.E.R. Learning* Connect website or contact your instructor for any changes that may have occurred.)

▶ The "Planning Your Career" section of Mapping Your Future's website (**www.mappingyourfuture.org/PlanYourCareer/**) offers guidance on finding the right path toward pursuing a career. Also available are numerous links on finding and building a career.

▶ Welcome to Resumania (**www.resumania.com/**)—a fun but practical look at those things you shouldn't put into a resume. The term "Resumania" was coined by Robert Half, founder of the specialized staffing firm Robert Half International Inc. (RHI), to describe errors made by job seekers on resumes, applications, and cover letters.

▶ From Virginia Tech, the site **https://www.career.vt.edu/Interviewing/AskQuestions.html** is full of comprehensive tips and strategies on preparing for a job interview, covering everything from handshakes to behavioral interviewing.

AT SCHOOL

If your college has a physical campus, check if there is an office devoted to career planning. In addition, any public library should have books that can help you research careers and find a job.

IN PRINT

If you're planning a career, writing a resume, or getting ready to look for work, you can't go wrong with Richard Bolles' classic, *What Color Is Your Parachute? 2016: A Practical Manual for Job-Hunters and Career-Changers* (Ten Speed Press, 2016).

For tips and solid guidance on pursuing that first job just out of college, *The Career Playbook: Essential Advice for Today's Aspiring Young Professional,* by James M. Citrin (Crown Business, 2015), offers solid advice on entering the professional world.

Don't Wear Flip-Flops to Your Interview: And Other Tips (Career Press, 2015) by Paul Powers presents several approaches to job hunting and interviewing, including personal experiences of successful professionals.

The Case of . . .
Interviewophobia

Dale had found his dream job.

A few weeks before finishing college with his degree in fitness training, Dale found an online job posting for an entry-level training job with the professional basketball team that played in his area. Dale had long been a fan of the team. The salary and benefits were excellent. The facility where the team trained was only ten minutes from Dale's house. In short, the job was perfect, and Dale was thrilled when, a week after submitting his resume, he received a call about scheduling an interview.

But then Dale started to get nervous. He had failed miserably at the only job interview he had ever had, for a sales position at a retail company after he finished high school. He'd actually gotten into an argument with his interviewer. What if the interview for the fitness trainer position went just as poorly?

Other worries started creeping into Dale's mind. What if the interviewer asked questions about Dale's limited training experience? What if Dale forgot to mention the key experiences on his resume? What if he wore the wrong clothes?

As the interview approached, Dale went from excited to terrified. He was certain he would blow the interview. So much for my dream job, he thought.

1. What advice would you give Dale? How is this interview different from the one he experienced just after finishing high school?

2. What steps could Dale take to ready himself for the interview? How could he build his confidence?

3. What could Dale do to prepare for questions about his work experience?

4. What tactics could Dale employ to make sure the interview remains cordial, and to get on his interviewer's good side?

Technology and Information Competency

Learning Outcomes

By the time you finish this chapter you will be able to

» **LO 7-1**   Explain how technology impacts you and your education.

» **LO 7-2**   Describe strategies for effective distance learning.

» **LO 7-3**   Discuss approaches for developing information competency.

Tara Mallory had never been comfortable with technology. Raised in a small rural community, she'd never had a computer—much less the Internet—in her home growing up. Now, unlike most of her friends, she rarely used e-mail. She wasn't even sure she knew what an "Instant Message" was.

So when Tara's admissions advisor informed her that her psychology class would be entirely online, Tara was not very enthusiastic. And when the instructor sent her the class syllabus, outlining that the course would involve mandatory participation in online discussion groups, Tara became downright nervous.

Tara struggled with the required computer-based assignments for the first few weeks. But then something happened that Tara didn't expect. Not only did she get the hang of surfing the web and communicating with classmates online—she actually started to enjoy it. She saw that it was easier to keep up with friends and family via e-mail than through phone calls. And the fact that there were computers in her office at work and in her apartment made it easy for her to do schoolwork when she found she had a spare 20 minutes.

In short, Tara realized technology was not something that should intimidate her. In fact, she found that in many ways, it was a powerful ally.

Looking Ahead

The technology that Tara utilized in her psychology course didn't even exist 15 years ago. Education is changing, just like every other aspect of society, as "virtual" resources—e-mail, the web, texting, and so forth—become more and more a part of how we live our lives. Today, businesspeople hold meetings and many instructors teach courses without even being in the same room with their co-workers or students.

Technology is making a profound difference in how we are taught, the ways we study and carry out our work, and how we communicate with our loved ones. It is changing the way you can access the vast quantities of information published each year—tens of thousands of books, journals, and other print materials, and literally billions of web pages. But successfully wading through all that information requires significant new skills in information competency that weren't necessary in the past.

In this chapter, we discuss how technological advances increase your opportunities to achieve success in college and on the job. We'll first consider the basic educational uses of technology. We'll also talk about distance learning, the approach you are taking to education that involves studying with an instructor who may be thousands of miles away. Finally, we'll consider how you can use technology to develop information competency—locating and using both the information traditionally held in print *and* information created for, and in, the virtual world of cyberspace. Information competency is an essential skill in our increasingly technology-driven classrooms and offices.

»LO 7-1 You and Technology

It's a great tool that if wielded effectively, will help you achieve success in your online classes. It can save you hours of time on your job, whether you work in a cubicle or a garage. At the same time, it can be extremely frustrating, annoying, and maddening. And sometimes instead of saving time, it can eat up hours of your time.

"It," of course, is technology. Today, it's as much a necessity to use technology as it was for you to learn to write using pen and paper earlier in your schooling. No one facing the job market in the 21st century will want to leave college without a strong working knowledge of a variety of technologies and what they can do for you.

And if using technology is as familiar to you as brushing your teeth in the morning, be patient with those who are less at ease with it. An increasing number of students can be called *digital natives*—those who have used technology virtually their entire lives—and their experiences lead them to be considerably more tech savvy.

Journal Reflections

Could I Live without Technology?

1. What do you use technology for most? Texting? E-mail? Surfing the web? Tasks at work? Classwork?

2. How much time do you spend using technology? How does it affect your social relationships?

3. What technological device could you live without? What devices could you *not* live without?

4. How much and what kinds of technology would you like to have in your courses? Why?

In fact, a *digital divide* separates students who have considerable and easy access to computers and technology from students for whom access to computers is difficult. The digital divide is especially pronounced between older and less affluent students and younger, more affluent students.

Technology and Your Academic Life

Even if you don't feel particularly proficient with technology in general, it already plays a big role in your life. Computers run your car's engine, make your digital camera work, allow you to record iPod tunes, and make sure the bus you're waiting for runs on time.

Technology has revolutionized academic life as well. You will encounter technology in a variety of different ways in your online classes:

▶ **Course websites.** Most online college courses have a website associated with them. The website may reside in a nationally developed course management software system (such as Blackboard, Moodle, or eCollege) with which your college may have a licensing agreement. In other cases, colleges develop their own course management systems.

Whatever course learning management system is used, the website will probably contain basic information about the course, such as a copy of the syllabus, or important emergency updates, such as class cancellations or changes in paper due dates.

Depending on the instructor, the website may be much more elaborate and play a more central role in the class. For instance, class websites that require a username and password for access may contain exercises and quizzes to be completed (and scored) online. All your grades for the class may be stored on the website, accessible to you at any time of the day or night.

In classes that require essay writing, you will submit all of your papers electronically. Your instructor may ask you to upload them to the class website. If you upload your papers to the class website, your instructor can read them online, post comments on your submissions, and return them to you through the website. You may hold virtual discussions on the site, or you may even be required to take your major tests and final exams on the website.

▶ **Textbook companion websites.** Most textbooks have a website that is tied to the book. The website typically includes chapter summaries, interactive reviews, flash cards, and practice tests. These resources, which are usually described in the preface to most textbooks, can be extremely valuable study tools.

▶ **Podcasts.** In online classes, instructors sometimes produce an audio or video recording, called a **podcast**, of lectures or other instructional material relevant to the class. You can either access podcasts on the web or download them to a mobile device (such as an iPod) that permits you to listen to and view them outside of class whenever you want.

▶ **Blogs.** Some instructors maintain blogs of their own. A **blog** is a kind of web-based public diary in which a writer offers ideas, thoughts, short essays, and commentary. If your instructor has a blog and tells you to read it, get in the habit of checking it routinely. It not only will contain information relevant to the course that you'll need to know, but also may reveal personal insights that can help you know your instructor better.

▶ **Lecture capture technology.** In online classes with **lecture capture technology**, instructors upload an audio or video recording of lectures, along with a feed of the PowerPoint slides or other material that is being presented.

Lecture capture offers several advantages. For example, when studying for a test, you can easily review material with which you may be having trouble. And because the lecture capture is indexed to words on the PowerPoint slides, you can review key concepts, skipping to the material that is most important or hardest for you to understand and learn.

However, it's important to not always expect your online instructors to use lecture capture technology, as many may not incorporate it in their instruction.

podcast
An audio or video recording that can be accessed on the Internet and viewed on a computer or downloaded to a mobile device.

blog
A web-based public diary in which a writer provides commentary, ideas, thoughts, and short essays.

lecture capture technology
Technology in which instructors upload in-class lectures, slides, and videos to a website, which students can later access to review the material presented in class.

From the perspective of . . .

A STUDENT What technology do you find intimidating in your online classes? What steps can you take to overcome your anxiety?

Getting the Most Out of Instructors' Online PowerPoint Materials

An increasing number of online instructors are using more visual or interactive programs such as PowerPoint to present course material more dynamically than typed Word documents do.

This newer technology calls for fresh strategies for absorbing the information. Here are some tips:

- **Don't copy everything that is on every slide.** Instructors can present far more information on their slides than they will assess. Concentrate on taking down the key points.

- **Remember that key points on slides are . . . key points.** The key points (typically indicated by bullets) often relate to central concepts. Use these points to help organize your studying for tests, and don't be surprised if test questions directly assess the bulleted items on slides.

- **Remember that the presentation slides your instructor posts online do not replace your own notes on the course materials.** If you miss a reading assignment, or dislike taking notes, don't assume that the slides your instructor posts online are sufficient.

Using the Web

The web has revolutionized communication. And we haven't seen anything yet: Visionaries say it won't be too long before it will allow our refrigerators to order milk when supplies are running low or permit our physicians to constantly monitor our vital organs.

The **web** (or, as it was originally called, the *World Wide Web*) provides a graphical means of locating and accessing information on the Internet. Using the web has become the standard way to find and use such information. The web provides a way to transmit typewritten text, visual material, and auditory information—graphics, photos, music, sound bites, video clips, and much more.

The Internet provides the backbone of virtual communication. Among its most common uses are the following:

- ▶ **E-mail. E-mail**, short for "electronic mail," offers a way for people to send and receive messages with incredible speed. For online college programs, e-mail is the most common form of communication between students and faculty.

- ▶ **Text messaging (or texting). Text messaging (texting)** permits you to send short messages from mobile phones to other phones or e-mail accounts. They are typically limited to 160 characters or less. Using text messaging, you can communicate with others in real time. You can also sign up to receive automatic text messages, such as receiving information whenever there are breaking news events. Most student-to-student communication uses text messaging.

web
A highly graphical interface between users and the Internet that permits users to transmit and receive not only text but also pictorial, video, and audio information.

e-mail
Electronic mail, a system of communication that permits users to send and receive messages via the Internet.

► **Video messaging. Video message services** such as Skype or FaceTime allow users to communicate using video, voice, and instant messaging over the web. Skype alone has almost seven million users. Video messaging is generally free, and it can be used on desktop computers, laptops, and smartphones.

Using E-Mail Effectively

Although e-mail (as illustrated in **Figure 7.1**) has become a major means of written communication for many of us, you may be unaware of some of the basics of how it works. For example, every e-mail address contains three basic elements:

► **Mailbox name.** The mailbox name—the name assigned to your account on an e-mail system—is often some variant of your own name (e.g., conan_obrien), though it may also be totally fictitious (e.g., hepcat9).

► **@.** The "at" sign.

► **Domain name.** The domain name is the name of the organization that hosts the e-mail "post office" to which the user subscribes—often an institution (e.g., **umass.edu** or **mcgraw-hill.com**), an Internet service provider (e.g., **aol.com** or **earthlink.net**), or a multifaceted system such as **yahoo.com**. *Host computers* are connected directly to the Internet. You can usually tell what kind of an organization hosts an e-mail account by the last part of the address (the *extension*): for example, *.edu* is an educational organization, *.com* is a commercial organization, *.org* is a nonprofit or charitable organization, *.mil* is the military, and *.gov* is a governmental organization (see **Table 7.1**).

Many e-mail providers (e.g., Gmail or Yahoo! Mail) have their own, unique e-mail systems on which e-mail can be retrieved anywhere you have access to the web. Others use particular software programs such as Microsoft's Outlook or

text messaging (texting)
This communication method permits you to send short messages from mobile phones to other phones or e-mail accounts.

video message service
Video messages that are sent between smartphones.

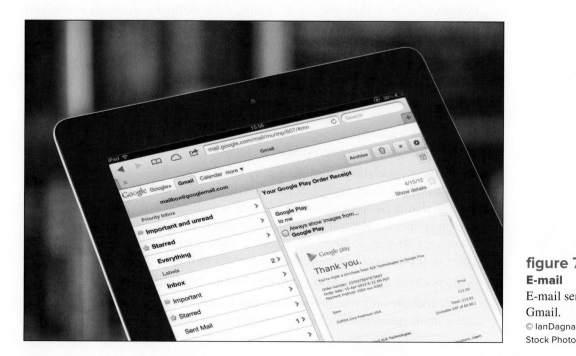

figure 7.1
E-mail
E-mail sent via Google's Gmail.
© IanDagnall Computing/Alamy Stock Photo

table 7.1   Domain Extensions

E-Mail Address	Extension	Type of Organization
jasper.johns@asu.edu	.EDU	Arizona State University—Educational
dowd@nytimes.com	.COM	*The New York Times*—Commercial
send.help@redcross.org	.ORG	American Red Cross—Charitable or nonprofit
general@army.mil	.MIL	United States Army—Military
head.counter@census.gov	.GOV	U.S. Census Bureau—Government

Outlook Express, to send and receive mail; you must have that software installed on your computer to retrieve your e-mail. Sometimes colleges have their own unique e-mail system that you can access through your college website.

Writing Effective E-mail Messages

Although you may communicate more frequently with your peers via texting, most online instructors are reluctant to give out their phone numbers, meaning you will primarily communicate with them via e-mail. Even if you are an experienced e-mail user, you can do several things to improve the effectiveness of the messages you send. Among the most important to keep in mind when writing formal e-mail messages are the following:

▶ **Use an informative subject line.** Don't say "IMPORTANT" or "meeting" or "question." None of those help recipients sort out your message from the dozens of others that may be clogging their in-boxes. Instead, something like "Reminder: supervisor applications due 5:00 pm 10/11" is considerably more useful. In addition, *always* use a subject line: Some recipients routinely delete messages without a subject line, fearing they contain viruses.

▶ **Make sure the recipient knows who you are.** If you are writing someone you know only casually, jog their memory with a bit of information about yourself. If you don't know them at all, identify yourself early in the message ("I am a college student who is interested in an internship . . .").

▶ **Keep messages short and focused.** E-mail messages are most effective when they are short and direct. If at all possible, keep your message short enough that it fits on one screen without scrolling down to see the rest. The reason is simple: Recipients sometimes don't read beyond the beginning of a message. If you do need to include a good deal of material, number each point or set them off by bullets so recipients will know to read down.

▶ **Always check spelling and grammar before sending an e-mail.**

▶ **Try to include only one major topic per e-mail.** It's often better to write separate e-mails rather than including a hodgepodge of unrelated points in an e-mail. This is especially true if you want a response to each of the different points.

- **Put requests near the beginning of the e-mail.** If you want the recipient to do something in response to your message, respectfully put the request at the very beginning of your message. Be explicit, while being polite.

- **Keep attachments to a minimum.** If possible, include all relevant information in the body of your e-mail, unless requested to do otherwise. Large attachments clog people's e-mail accounts and may be slow to download. In addition, recipients who don't know you personally may fear your attachment contains a virus and will not open it.

- **Avoid abbreviations and emoticons in formal e-mails.** When writing texts and e-mails to friends, abbreviations such as AFAIK ("as far as I know"), BTW ("by the way"), CYA ("see ya"), OIC ("oh, I see"), and WTG ("way to go") are fine. So are **emoticons (or smileys)**, which signal the emotion that you are trying to convey. However, they should be avoided in formal e-mails. Recipients may not be familiar with them, and they may make your e-mail seem overly casual.

- **Above all, always be respectful and courteous.** It always pays to be polite. In fact, as we discuss next, there are certain guiding principles that govern civility on the web and that you should always keep in mind when writing e-mail.

Netiquette: Showing Civility on the Web

Although e-mail and text communication are usually less formal than a letter, it is essential to maintain civility and demonstrate good etiquette, which in the technology world is known as *netiquette*. Here are some rules:

- **Don't write anything in an e-mail or text message that you'll regret seeing on the front page of your local newspaper.** Yes, e-mail and texts are usually private; but the private message you write can easily be forwarded by the recipient to another person or even scores of other people. Worse yet, it's fairly easy to hit "reply all" when you mean simply to "reply." In this case, you might think that you are responding to an individual, when in fact the e-mail will go to everyone who received the message, along with you.

- **Be careful of the tone you convey.** It is harder in e-mail and texts to express the same kind of personality, and often the same degree of subtlety, that our voice, our handwriting, or even our stationery can add to other forms of communication. This means that attempts at humor and especially sarcasm can backfire.

  If you're using humor, consider adding an emoticon to clarify the intent of your message if you are writing to someone you know well. Avoid emoticons in e-mails to people you don't know well. Better to err on the side of formality.

- **Never write anything in an e-mail or text that you wouldn't say in person.** If you wouldn't say something in a face-to-face conversation, don't say it electronically.

- **Don't use all capital letters.** Using all caps MAKES IT LOOK AS IF YOU'RE SHOUTING.

- **Never send an e-mail or text when you are angry.** No matter how annoyed you are about something someone has written in a message, don't respond in kind—or at least wait until you've cooled down. Take a deep breath, and wait for your anger to pass.

▶ **Be especially polite and professional when writing to instructors and on-the-job supervisors.** Instructors often get dozens, and sometimes hundreds, of e-mails from students each week, and they are especially sensitive to messages that are inappropriate. Follow these guidelines to be sure your e-mail will receive maximum attention:

- Always use the subject line in e-mail messages, identifying the class you are in and describing the general topic of the e-mail (e.g., "Psych 100, Lec 3, exam query").
- Address instructors politely (as in "Dear Professor xx," as opposed to, say, "Yo, Prof!" or "Hey!"). Unless your instructor has specifically told you otherwise, never use his or her first name.
- Avoid the high-priority flag.
- Be concise. Make your point quickly and try not to write more than a few paragraphs. Make one point per e-mail.
- Avoid emoticons, nonstandard abbreviations, and slang; you're writing an instructor, not a friend.
- Don't tell your instructor that you need to hear from him or her immediately. It's fine to convey that your concerns are urgent, but don't make demands. If there is a deadline involved—for instance, if you are facing a registration deadline—respectfully ask for a response before that date.
- At the end of every message, thank the instructor and be sure to sign your complete name.
- Finally, proofread what you've written and make sure your spell-check tool is on.

To consider e-mail and text message netiquette more closely, complete **Try It! 1**.

In-Person Netiquette: Using Technology Appropriately

In many situations, there are standards for appropriate use of technology. For example, your boss does not want you to answer a cell phone call while he or she is speaking.

Follow these guidelines to ensure you don't offend anyone with how you use technology:

▶ **Turn off your cell phone in formal settings.** If you're in a meeting, keep your cell phone off (or set in "vibrate" mode). Cell phones ringing at random times are distracting and annoying.

▶ **Don't send text messages or make calls while someone else is speaking.** It's obvious that you should be paying attention to what your boss or co-workers are saying, rather than what's going on in the rest of the world.

▶ **If you use your laptop to take notes, stay on task.** No matter how tempting it is to check your e-mail messages, text with a friend, check Facebook, or surf the web, avoid the temptation. Use your laptop to take notes, and nothing else.

Using E-Mail Netiquette

Read the e-mail below, written by a student to his instructor, and respond to the questions that follow.

| ⬤ ⬤ ⬤ | Class | ▭ |

| Send | Chat | Attach | Address | Fonts | Colors | Save As Draft |

To: Professor@ketchum.edu

Cc:

≡▾ **Subject:** Class

Yo, Professor!!!

    I'm in your class, and I couldn't come yesterday because I had something I had to do. Did I miss anything important? Can u send me any assignments u gave out AS SOON AS POSSIBLE so I can work on it?

      I'm attaching the worksheet that was do. Hope it doesn't fill up your mailbox too much   :-) !!
        BTW, when is ur next test?
          BJ

© McGraw-Hill Education

---

1. What rules of "netiquette" does the e-mail violate?

2. If you were the instructor to whom the e-mail message was sent, how do you think you would react to receiving it? What questions would you have about the message?

3. Based on the e-mail, what opinion might you have of the student who wrote it?

4. Rewrite the e-mail so that it is consistent with good netiquette.

Protecting Yourself: Spam, Cybersecurity, and Online Safety

The downside of e-mail is *spam,* the virtual equivalent of junk mail. Spam may range from get-rich-quick schemes to advertisements for body enhancements or pornography. Spam is more than a nuisance; it takes up valuable transmission resources ("bandwidth"), disk space, and computer time.

    Some e-mail systems apply a filter that uses a few simple rules to separate e-mail you actually want to read from spam. Unfortunately, these systems are not perfect: They sometimes let junk through and can even at times dispose of messages you want. The only absolutely reliable way to deal with spam is to delete it yourself as quickly as possible.

Spam filters are one aspect of broader efforts to maintain security on computers. **Cybersecurity** refers to measures taken to protect computers and computer systems against unauthorized access or attack. Every computer connected to the web is subject to multiple attacks from *hackers,* criminals (and sometimes foreign governments) who illegally attempt to gain access to and tamper with information on your computer. In fact, the average computer connected to the web is attacked by hackers every 39 seconds, 24 hours a day.

Here are a few tips for dealing with spam:

► Consider using two e-mail addresses—one for personal messages and one for college and professional messages.

► When you choose a password, make it long (8 or more characters) and complex (include letters, numbers, punctuation, and symbols).

► Don't use the same password on every program.

► *Never* give anyone your password, and change your password frequently.

► Install anti-virus programs on your personal computer. It is essential to protect yourself from hackers by installing an anti-virus program such as McAfee or Norton Security.

► *Never* respond to an e-mail that asks for personal or financial information, even if it appears to be legitimate. Such requests may originate in *crimeware,* programs that steal personal financial information. For instance, in a practice called *phishing,* spam or pop-up messages are used to trick you into disclosing bank account or credit card numbers, passwords, or other personal information.

   In a phishing scam, the e-mail appears to be from a legitimate source and asks you to update or validate information by providing account information. In reality, such messages are from con artists seeking to steal your identity. E-mails that contain promises of riches for little effort, offer deals that seem too good to be true, or threaten that accounts will be closed unless you provide information immediately are likely bogus.

► *Do not click* on any links in the e-mail message until you're sure it's real. Not only can such links lead to the disclosure of personal information about you, but they may lead to the secret installation of software that can spy on you.

► *Never* open an attachment from someone you don't know. Computer viruses, which can ruin everything on your hard drive, are often spread through e-mail attachments.

► Finally, if your e-mail program has a spam filter, periodically check your spam folder to make sure no legitimate e-mails may have been directed there by mistake.

Keeping Safe

There's an even darker side to the web than financial criminals looking to steal from you. Specifically, you need to be wary of sexual predators who use the web to identify potential victims. To help protect yourself, use these guidelines:

1. Don't give out personal information to strangers, such as your name, phone number, address, hometown, or future schedule—anything that can be used to identify you.

2. Never send photos of yourself or friends or family to someone you don't know.

3. Don't reply to e-mails that are offensive, weird, or distressing in any way.

cybersecurity
Measures taken to protect computers and computer systems against unauthorized access or attack.

4. If you plan to meet someone you've known only from the web, for example, from a dating site, be cautious. Meet them in a visible, public location. Even then, meet someone only in a visible, public location in which many people will be present. *Don't* have someone you don't know pick you up at your home. Tell a friend or family member whom you are meeting and where you are going, and stay sober.

5. If you do have problems with someone over e-mail, immediately contact your college or local police.

Social Networking Websites

Most college students use social networking websites such as **Facebook.com** or Twitter to stay in touch with their friends, acquaintances, and even total strangers. The number of users is huge: Facebook has more than 845 million active users and Twitter 140 million.

Facebook provides users with the ability to post information to friends who have access to their online profiles. Users can post updates, post photos, exchange messages, list their personal interests, and share other information. Because it can be accessed on any computer or mobile device connected to the web, Facebook allows users to stay in constant touch with others.

Twitter allows users to send and receive short messages of up to 140 characters, called *tweets*. People can send short updates about what they are doing, offer opinions about events, or tell people where they are at a given moment. The tweets are sent to followers who have signed up to receive a person's tweets.

Although social networking websites offer many possibilities for interacting with friends, making new acquaintances, and sharing information, they need to be used appropriately. Remember that *what's posted on the web stays on the web*— potentially forever. Even if you delete information from a social networking site, it may still reside on someone else's computer.

Consequently, don't post information about yourself or photos that you wouldn't want your instructors, parents, or future employers seeing. For instance, faculty at colleges can—and sometimes do—read students' postings.

Furthermore, employers increasingly are using information posted on social networking sites in their hiring decisions. You might also want to consider maintaining two social media accounts: one for public consumption (that employers may read) and a personal account for close friends and family.

In short, be thoughtful of what you post about yourself. And be sure the privacy settings on your social network accounts are set in a way that protects your privacy.

At the same time, be an informed consumer of material you encounter on social networking websites. Some of the profiles contain bogus material or are entirely false. Individuals sometimes disguise their identities or make up false ones. It's important to verify whom you are communicating with before exchanging personal information.

≫LO7-2 Distance Learning: Classes without Walls

There may be many reasons why you decided to enroll in a **distance learning** course. You may have realized that your schedule changed too much from one day to the next to fit in a course that meets at a regularly scheduled time. You may have been interested in an unusual course topic that your hometown college doesn't offer. Or maybe you wanted to take a class during the summer, but you live too far from your college's campus.

distance learning
The teaching of courses at another institution, with student participation via video technology or the web.

Distance learning is a form of education in which students participate via the web or other kinds of technology. Although most distance learning courses are taught via the web, some may use teleconferencing, fax, and/or express mail.

The key feature of distance learning courses is the nature of interaction between instructor and students, as online classes are most often virtual.

Some schools use webcasts of lectures with virtual discussion rooms or employ lectures on videotape or CDs, but you may never even know what your instructor or classmates look like or hear their voices.

Most distance learning courses involve multiple students and an instructor assigned to the course. As a distance learner, you may read lecture notes posted on the web, search and browse websites, write papers, and post replies, along with other students, to discussion topics posted by your instructor on a *message board* or a *discussion board.* You will see your instructor's and classmates' responses through comments they post on the web. You may be expected to read a textbook entirely on your own, and you may take online quizzes and exams.

blended (or hybrid) courses

Courses in which instruction is a combination of the traditional face-to-face classroom interaction and a significant amount of online learning.

You may already be familiar with the kinds of technologies used in distance learning courses. In **blended (or hybrid) courses**, instruction is a combination of the traditional face-to-face classroom interaction and a significant amount of online learning. Students in blended courses generally spend more time working alone or in collaboration with others online. They also may collaborate with fellow students outside of class on the web.

In contrast to blended courses, *all* instruction takes place electronically in distance learning classes that are fully online. As a distance learner in a fully online course, you will never meet your instructor and fellow students in person. However, you will get to know them through virtual interactions online.

On the other hand, in *self-paced distance learning courses,* students move ahead at their own pace. There is no "live" instructor or other students with whom to interact; all instruction occurs in prerecorded formats. Grading is entirely computer-scored. Because your progress is entirely self-paced, you need to manage your time carefully. It's a lot easier to stay caught up on assignments than to try to catch up on them.

Successful distance learning depends on being proactive in identifying possible challenges you may encounter with taking an online class. Complete **Try It! 2** to assess possible obstacles in distance learning.

Distance learning classes have both advantages and disadvantages. On the plus side, distance learning courses offer the following:

▶ **You can take a web-based distance learning course anywhere that you have access to the web.** You can be at home, at the office, or on vacation on the beach and still participate.

▶ **Distance learning classes are often more flexible than traditional classes.** You can participate in a course any time of the day or night, and you typically don't have to be in class at a specific time. This is particularly helpful for those with time-consuming family obligations such as child care.

▶ **Distance learning classes are often self-paced.** You may be able to spread out your work over the course of a week, or you may do the work in a concentrated manner on one day.

▶ **You may have more contact with your instructor than you do with a traditional class.** Even though you may not have face-to-face contact, you may have greater access to your instructor, via e-mail and the web, than in traditional classes. You can leave messages for your instructor any time of the night or day; most instructors of distance learning classes respond in a timely manner.

Confronting the Obstacles to Distance Learning

How you participate in classes, interact with your classmates, communicate with your teachers, and complete your assignments may make distance learning more or less challenging. Read the following statements and indicate whether you agree or disagree with them to better understand what obstacles you may encounter as a distance learner.

	Agree	Disagree
1. I need the stimulation of other students to learn well.		
2. I need to see my teacher's face, expressions, and body language to interpret what is being said.		
3. I participate a lot in class discussions.		
4. I prefer to hear information presented orally rather than reading it in a book or article.		
5. I'm not very good at keeping up with reading assignments.		
6. I'm easily distracted.		
7. I'm not very well organized.		
8. Keeping track of time and holding to schedules is NOT a strength of mine.		
9. I need a lot of "hand-holding" while I work on long assignments.		
10. I need a close social network to share my feelings, ideas, and complaints with.		
11. I'm not very good at writing.		
12. Basically, I'm not very patient.		

The more you agree with these statements, the more challenges you may face as a distance learner. Interpret your results according to this informal scale:

Disagreed with 10–12 statements = Strong ability to adapt to distance learning

Disagreed with 7–9 statements = Good ability to adapt to distance learning

Agreed with 6–9 statements = May be a little challenging to adapt to distance learning

Agreed with 10–12 statements = May be a struggle to adapt to distance learning

▶ **Shy students may find it easier to "speak up" in a distance learning class.** You can think through your responses to make sure you are communicating just what you wish to say. You don't have to worry about speaking in front of other people. For many people, distance learning is liberating.

▶ **You can become a better writer.** Because distance learning usually involves more writing than traditional courses, you receive more practice writing—and more feedback for it—than in traditional classes.

On the other hand, distance learning has disadvantages that you should keep in mind:

► **You are a prisoner of technology.** If you lose access to a computer and the web, you won't be able to participate in the class until the problem is fixed.

► **You won't have direct, face-to-face contact with your instructor or other students.** Distance learning can be isolating, and students sometimes feel alone and lost in cyberspace.

► **You won't get immediate feedback.** In your distance learning class, it may be hours, or sometimes days, before you receive feedback on what you have posted to a message board, depending on how well the pace of other students matches your own.

► **Distance learning classes require significant discipline, personal responsibility, and time management skills.** You must carve out the time yourself. Although instructors provide a schedule of when things are due, you have to work out the timing of getting them done.

You must be focused and committed to keeping up with the course. You need to be prepared to work hard on your own for a substantial number of hours each week.

Despite these potential challenges to distance learning courses, they are becoming increasingly popular. In fact, increasing numbers of colleges are offering *MOOCs,* or *Massive Open Online Courses,* which are free and in some cases attract tens of thousands of students. Many companies encourage employees with crowded schedules to take distance learning as a way of providing continuing education.

As a distance learner, follow these steps, which are summarized in the P.O.W.E.R. Plan here.

P.O.W.E.R. Plan

 ## Identifying Distance Learning Course Possibilities

How did you find a distance learning course? Did you research which online colleges offered programs that interested you? Did you investigate if your local college offered distance learning classes?

Most likely, you went on the web. By searching the web, you can find distance learning courses ranging from automotive engineering to zoology. Don't be deterred by the physical location of the institution that offers the course. It doesn't matter where the college is located because as you may have experienced, you'll never have to go to the campus itself.

But before you sign up for a potential course that you would like to count toward your degree, *make sure that your own college will give you credit for it.* Check with your advisor and registrar's office to be certain.

You should also find out what the requirements of a course are before you actually sign up for it. Check the syllabus carefully and see how it meshes with your schedule. If it is a summer course and you are going to be away from your computer for a week, you may not be able to make up the work you miss.

Finally, try to talk with someone who has taken the course before. Was the instructor responsive, providing feedback rapidly? If necessary, could you speak with the instructor by phone or via video technology such as Skype? Was the course load reasonable? (**Try It! 3** will help you to work through the process.)

Get Some Distance on the Problem

See if you can find distance learning courses of interest to you that are offered by another college. You might try the following resources to start your search:

- *The Chronicle of Higher Education* 's Distance Education offers daily updates. (**chronicle.com**).
- Harvard Extension School's Distance Learning website offers a number of links and information on pursuing courses at Harvard (**www.extension.harvard.edu/distance-education**).

Try to find five courses you would be interested in and list them. After you have completed your list, answer the questions below.

1. How diverse were the courses you were able to find?

2. Were particular subject areas better represented than others?

3. Why do you think this might be?

 Organize   # Obtaining Access to Technology

Although you don't need to be a computer expert, you will need some minimal e-mail and web skills as a distance learner. If you don't have sufficient technological expertise, consider beefing up your computer skills by taking a computer course or workshop in your spare time.

You'll also need access to a computer connected to the Internet. It doesn't have to be your own computer, but you will certainly need regular and convenient access to one. Make sure that the computer you plan to use has sufficient internal resources to quickly connect to the Internet; a very slow connection is frustrating.

Be sure to make all your arrangements for computer access prior to the start of a course. It can take several weeks to set up Internet service on a home computer if you don't have it already.

In addition, you should familiarize yourself with the course learning management system (LMS) before the course starts. The **learning management system (LMS)** is the software that delivers the distance learning course to your computer. It typically provides the course content such as online lectures or material to read, as well as a course syllabus, calendar, tests, and a way to track your grades.

The most common LMSs are Blackboard, Canvas, Moodle, Desire2Learn, and Angel. In some cases, a college will brand its LMS with its own name.

Although all LMSs are designed to work well with a variety of browsers, there are certain browsers that may work better with them than others. The common browsers are Mozilla Firefox, Google Chrome, and Safari. Be sure to use the browser that is recommended to be best for the LMS you will be using.

learning management system (LMS)
The software that delivers a distance learning course and typically provides the course content, calendars, and tests, and tracks grades.

 ## Participating in a Distance Learning Class

Successfully participating in a distance learning course involves several skills that are distinct from those needed for traditional classes. To get the most out of a distance learning course, you'll need to do the following:

▶ **Manage your time carefully.** You won't have the luxury of a regular schedule of class lectures, so you'll have to manage your time carefully. No one is going to remind you that you need to sit down at a computer and work. You will need every bit of self-discipline to be successful in a distance learning course.

▶ **Check in frequently.** Instructors may make crucial changes in the course requirements. Make sure to check for any changes in due dates or class expectations.

▶ **Find a cyberbuddy.** At the start of the semester, try to make personal contact with at least one other student in the class. You can do this by e-mailing, phoning, or instant messaging. You can share study strategies and notes. Connecting with another student can help you avoid feelings of isolation that may interfere with your success.

▶ **Make copies of everything.** Don't assume everything will go well in cyberspace. Have a backup stored on a flashdrive or on another computer.

▶ **Have a technology backup plan.** Computers crash, your connection to the Internet may go down, or an e-mailed assignment may be mysteriously delayed or sent back to you. Don't wait until the last minute to work on and submit assignments, and have a plan in place if your primary computer is unavailable.

You might consider using a cloud storage system such as Dropbox or Google Drive. Even if your own computer crashes, you'll be able to access your computer files from any computer.

 ## Considering Your Online Performance

Unlike many courses, in which almost all the feedback comes from the instructor, much of the feedback in your distance learning course may come from your fellow students. Consider what you can learn from their comments, while keeping in mind that they are, like you, students themselves.

At the same time you'll be receiving feedback, you will likely be providing feedback to your classmates. Consider the nature of feedback you provide, and be sure that you use the basic principles of classroom civility.

 ## Reflecting on What and How You Have Learned

As you reflect on your distance learning experience, go beyond the technology and think about what, and how much, you have learned. Ask yourself whether you learned as much as you would have in a traditional class.

Also think about how your distance learning experience could have been more effective for you. And think about whether you were so absorbed by the technology that you lost sight of the real goal of the course: learning new material.

Most educational experts believe that distance learning will play an increasingly important role in higher education. Furthermore, because it offers an efficient way of educating people in far-flung locales, it is a natural means of promoting lifelong learning experiences.

» LO 7-3 Fact Finding: Developing Information Competency

One of the greatest advances brought about by technology involves the area of research. More than ever, people require **information competency**, the ability to determine what information is necessary, and then to locate, evaluate, and effectively use that information. The sheer abundance of material available today makes information competency a critical skill.

We'll consider the ways in which you can use the two primary storehouses of information available today to boost your own level of information competency. One you can walk or drive to—your local library. The other—the web—doesn't have a physical location. Both are indispensable in anyone's quest for information.

<aside>
information competency
The ability to determine what information is necessary, and then to locate, evaluate, and effectively use that information.
</aside>

Libraries

No matter how imposing or humble their physical appearance, whether they contain only a few hundred volumes or hundreds of thousands of them, libraries are a good place to focus your efforts as you seek out and gather information. Although every library is different, all share two key elements: the material they hold—their basic collections—and tools to help you locate the material you need.

What Can Be Found in a Library's Basic Collection?

Libraries obviously contain books, but they typically have a lot more than that, including some or all of the following:

▶ **Periodicals.** *Periodicals* include specialized journals for professionals in a field, magazines, and newspapers. Many periodicals can now be found online.

▶ **Indexes and online databases.** An index provides a listing of periodical articles by title, author, and subject. Some indexes also provide a short summary, or *abstract,* of the contents of each article.

Most indexes come in electronic form known as an **online database**, an organized body of information on related topics. For example, the National Center for Biotechnology Information (NCBI) maintains *Medline,* an online public database that provides information on medical research. The advantage of online databases over traditional, print-based indexes is that the database sometimes provides the full text of material it identifies in a search.

<aside>
online database
An index in electronic form composed of an organized body of information on related topics.
</aside>

> "Knowledge is of two kinds: we know a subject ourselves, or we know where we can find information upon it."
> **Samuel Johnson**

▶ **Encyclopedias.** Some encyclopedias, such as the *Encyclopaedia Britannica* or *World Book Encyclopedia,* attempt to cover the entire range of knowledge, and they may take up many volumes. Others are more specialized, covering only a particular field, such as the *Encyclopedia of Human Behavior* or the *Encyclopedia of Religion.* Most are available online, though some are still printed as multivolume sets of books. Encyclopedias provide a good general view of a topic, but they lack depth: Use them at the earliest stage of your hunt for information for an overview of key issues, and move from there to more specific and current sources.

- ▶ **Government documents.** Census records, laws, and tax codes are some of the millions of government documents that are stored in libraries.

- ▶ **Musical scores.** The music to *Rent,* the Brahms *Alto Rhapsody,* and The Beatles' greatest hits are among the musical scores you can find in libraries.

- ▶ **Reserve collections.** Reserve collections hold items that instructors assign for a class. Although they are typically found, and accessed, online, sometimes they are in the form of material that may be physically removed from the library for a limited period of time. Reserve collections may contain not only books and articles, but also videos, CDs, laptops, and multimedia equipment.

Locating Information in a Library

The place to begin searching for information in a library is the library catalog. Catalogs list all materials that are held in the library and provide their location. Most library catalogs are computerized, though a few still use name cards filed in drawers or microform (microfiche or microfilm). You are usually able to access computerized catalogs from home or residence hall rooms, as well as from computers housed in the library itself.

Library catalogs traditionally allow searches by title, author name, and subject; electronic catalogs also typically allow searching by keyword. Individual catalog entries generally include additional information about the material, such as the publisher, date of publication, number of pages, and similar information.

Say, for example, you're writing a paper on Ernest Hemingway. To find books he *wrote* in an electronic catalog, you would enter his name in the "author" field. You may be presented with the listing shown in **Figure 7.2**.

Of course, you could also search on "Hemingway" as the subject, which would yield a list of books *about* him and his work; if you entered his name in a "keyword" search, the catalog would return a more comprehensive list of books both by *and* about him.

The key piece of information in a catalog entry is the book's **call number**, a code that tells you exactly where to find it. Most college libraries use the Library

call number
A unique classification number assigned to every book (or other resource) in a library. Call numbers are used for ease of location.

figure 7.2
Online Catalog Entry
Online catalog entry for a book called *The Old Man and the Sea.* Note especially the call number and due date: These will tell you where the book is to be found and whether it is on the shelves or is checked out.
© McGraw-Hill Education

of Congress classification system, which assigns to each book a unique combination of letters and numbers.

Because the record illustrated in **Figure 7.2** is from an electronic search, it contains further helpful information. The word "Available" under "Due Date" tells you that one copy of the book has not been checked out by another patron and should be sitting on the shelf. You'll need to familiarize yourself with your local library's particular system to know precisely how you can make most efficient use of the catalog. Chances are there's a handout or a posted set of instructions nearby.

Once you have identified the material you need and where it is located, you'll need to go find it. In all but the biggest libraries, you can simply go into the **stacks**, the place containing shelves where the books and other materials are kept, and—using the call number—hunt for it. In libraries with closed stacks, you must fill out a form with the call numbers of the books you want. A library aide will find the material and deliver it to a central location.

What if you go to the location in the stacks where the material is supposed to be and you can't find it? The material may be checked out, in use by someone else at that time, incorrectly shelved, or simply lost. Whatever the reason, *don't give up.* If the material is checked out to another user, ask a librarian if you can **recall** the material, a process by which the library contacts the person who has the book and asks him or her to return it.

If the librarian informs you that the material is not checked out, wait a few days and see if it appears on the shelf. Someone may have been using it while you were looking for it. If it was misshelved, the librarian may be able to find it. If the material is truly lost, you may be able to get it from another library through **interlibrary loan**, a system by which libraries share resources.

Finally, even if you do find exactly what you were looking for, take a moment to scan the shelves. Because books and other materials are generally grouped by topic, you may find other useful titles in the same place. One of the pleasures of libraries is the possibility of finding an unexpected treasure—material that your catalog search did not initially identify but that may provide you with exactly what you need.

stacks
The shelves on which books and other materials are stored in a library.

recall
A way to request library materials from another person who has them.

interlibrary loan
A system by which libraries share resources, making them available to patrons of different libraries.

Finding Information on the Web

The web is vast—sometimes frustratingly so. In fact, no one knows how much material exists on the web. Not only is more information added to the web every day, but the information also resides on thousands of individual computers. Anyone with minimal web savvy and access to a *server* (a computer with a permanent Internet connection) can set up a personal website.

The fact that anyone can put information on the web is both the biggest asset and the greatest disadvantage of using the web as an information source. Because minimal computer skill is the only expertise a person needs to set up a web page, there may be as much misinformation on the website as there is information. Consequently, keep the usual consumer

© S. Olsson/PhotoAlto RF

rule in mind: Buyer beware. Unless the website has been established and is maintained by a reliable organization, the information it contains may not be accurate.

browser

A program that provides a way of navigating around the information on the web.

▶ **Browsers.** To use the web, your computer has to have a browser. A **browser**, as its name implies, is a program that provides a way of looking at the information on the web. Among the major browsers are Microsoft's Internet Explorer, Google Chrome, and Firefox's Mozilla.

Using a browser is a bit like taking a taxi: Once you get in, you get to where you want to go by providing an address. The address, also known as a URL (Uniform Resource Locator), identifies a unique location on the web, a *website* or a *web page* (one of the parts of a site).

Web addresses are combinations of letters and symbols. They typically start off with **"www.[domain_name].[xxx]"** —the address of the hosting website (e.g., **www.iastate.edu**, the home page for Iowa State University). If you're looking for a subsite or a particular page on the site, the address becomes increasingly specific: **www.iastate.edu/visitors/** will take you to a "visitors" site—a collection of pages—hosted by **iastate.edu**. A *page* on that site—for example, **http://www.museums.iastate.edu/BAM.html**, which connects you with the Iowa State Museums—ends with a specific name, usually followed by ".htm," ".html," or ".shtml." Because most addresses begin with "http://," this part of the address is sometimes dropped in references to a site.

You can often get a decent idea of what kind of site you're going to by taking a careful look at the web address: You can tell that **www.connect.mhedu cation.com**, for example, is a site that has something to do with "connect" and is hosted by a commercial entity (which you might or might not recognize as McGraw-Hill Higher Education). (Hmm, might be worth checking out . . .)

web page

A location (or site) on the web housing information from a single source and that (typically) links to other pages.

▶ **Web pages.** Web pages are the heart of the web. A **web page** is a document that presents you with information. The information may appear as text on the screen, to be read like a book (or, more accurately, like an ancient scroll). It might include a video clip, an audio clip, a photo, a portrait, a graph, or a figure. It might offer a news service photo of the president of the United States or a backyard snapshot of someone's family reunion.

link

A means of "jumping" automatically from one web page to another.

▶ **Links.** Websites typically provide you with **links**—embedded addresses to other sites or documents that, at a click, cause your browser automatically to "jump" there. Just as an encyclopedia article on forests might say at the end, "See also Trees," web pages often refer to other sites on the web— only it's easier than with a book. You just have to click on the link with your mouse and—*poof!*—you're there.

search engine

A computerized index to information on the web.

▶ **Search engines.** A **search engine** is simply a computerized index to information on the web. When you know what information you want to find but don't have an address for it, a search engine can often steer you toward relevant sites.

From the perspective of . . .

A LAW ENFORCEMENT PROFESSIONAL Technology is changing the approach to many long-established career fields. What technology changes could potentially impact your chosen profession?

The various parts of the web are similar to the components of traditional libraries, as illustrated in **Figure 7.3**. A web browser is equivalent to a library card; it gives you access to vast quantities of material. Websites are like the books of a library; web pages are the book pages, where the content resides. Links are analogous to "see also" portions of books that suggest related information. And search engines are like a library's card catalog, directing you to specific locations.

Locating Information on the Web

There is no central catalog of the contents of the web; instead, there are a number of different search engines. Furthermore, depending on the search engine you use and the type of search you do, you'll identify different information.

Search engines themselves are located on the web, so you have to know their addresses. After you reach the "home" address of a search engine, you enter your search terms. The search engine then provides a list of websites that may contain information relevant to your search.

Although most people are familiar with the most popular search engine, Google, there are actually many search engines. Others include (in order of popularity) Bing, Yahoo!, Ask, AOL, Wow, and WebCrawler. Although they all are useful for searches on the web, they do so using somewhat different strategies.

Some search engines, such as Yahoo!, specialize in organizing information by subject, making it easy to search for information on, say, different dog breeds, the Islamic religion, or car repair. Using Yahoo! for its subject directories is like searching for information using the subject entries in a library catalog.

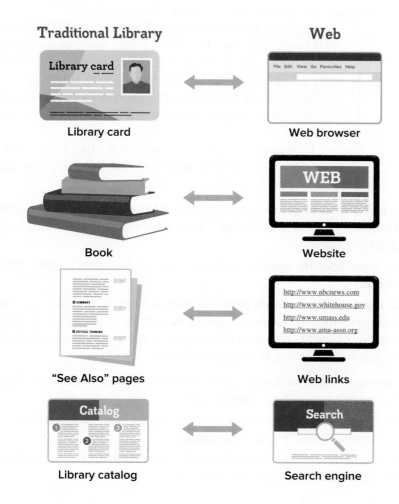

Traditional Library

Library card

Book

"See Also" pages

Library catalog

Web

Web browser

Website

Web links

Search engine

figure 7.3
Comparison of Library and Web
The various parts of the web are similar to the components of a traditional library.

Other search engines, such as Google, catalog many more pages than Yahoo! but don't group them by subject. Due to the breadth of their coverage, they might be more useful when you are looking for obscure pieces of information or for numerous sources for different perspectives on a topic. Using Google or AltaVista is like performing a keyword search in a library catalog.

Finally, a third type of search engine is exemplified by Ask.com. Known as metasearch tools, these sites send your search commands to other search engines, compiling the results into a single, unified list.

There's no single search engine that works best. Most people develop their own preferences based on their experience. The best advice: Try out several of them and see which works best for you. To get started, work through **Try It! 4**, "Work the Web: Information, Please!"

Becoming a Savvy Surfer

The process you use to search the web couldn't be easier—or more difficult. The vast amounts of material online and the relative ease of navigation afforded by the web make finding information quite simple. What is hard is finding appropriate information.

Consider a search in which you enter the question,"How do I use the web?" into the home page of Google. That search will identify over 3.5 *billion* websites related to the topic.

Using the list of sites generated by the search is simple. With the mouse, click on the site address of the relevant document, and the home page of the site will (eventually) appear on your computer screen. You can then take notes on the material, in the same way you'd take notes on material in a book.

> "Don't let that little glowing screen become an adversary. If you plan correctly, the computer can become your most useful tool at college—next to your brain."
>
> **Greg Gottesman, author**

Many of the million sites Google returned, however, may well be of little use. It's easy in such a search to end up in a virtual dead end, in which the information you have found is only minimally related to the topic you're researching. If you do find yourself at a site that's of no use to you, simply hit the "back" button on your browser until you return to where you started.

How can you limit your search in the first place, so that you find sites more directly relevant? The following tips can help you to get the most from a search:[1]

1. **Before you even begin to type anything into your computer, ask yourself the question you want answered.** Then identify the two or three important words in that question.

2. **Go to your favorite search engine.** Google is the most popular today, but preferences vary.

3. **Type three or four words into the search engine,** making sure they are spelled correctly. Then search. Note: You can do a few things here to limit the number of results returned, thus making your search more efficient. Most search engines allow you to use the following:

   - *Quotation marks,* to denote a phrase—words that should appear together, in a specific order (e.g., "animal rights").
   - *Plus signs,* used before terms that must appear in all results returned (+ "animal rights" + experimentation).
   - *Minus signs,* used before terms you do not want to appear in results (+ "animal rights" + experimentation – fur).

Work the Web: Information, Please!

Try to find the answer to the first question below on Google (**www.google.com**), Yahoo! (**www.yahoo.com**), *and* Bing (**www.bing.com**). Then use whichever search engine you prefer to find answers to the remaining questions.

1. What was the French Revolution and when did it occur?

2. Who is Keyser Soze?

3. What are the words of Dr. Martin Luther King Jr.'s "I Have a Dream" speech?

4. Are diesel engines more efficient than gasoline engines?

5. What is the ecu?

How easy was it for you to find the answers to the questions? Which search engine(s) did you prefer, and why?

- *Boolean operators*—words like AND, OR, AND NOT, and NEAR (e.g., "animal rights" AND experimentation NOT fur).

Check the "Help" section of your preferred search engine for more precise information on limiting your searches.

4. **Open a new window,** type in a different set of search terms, and search again.

5. **Identify the common links between the two searches.** Read the very brief summaries provided.

6. **Open a word processing window.** Copy and paste the site's address into that window and follow it with an annotation of your own.

7. **See if you have found the answer you were looking for.** If not, reformulate your question to come up with new key words. If you have found the answer, you're done!

8. **Avoid the temptation to rely on Wikipedia pages.** Very often, a search will yield a Wikipedia entry. *Wikipedia* is a free online encyclopedia created through the joint efforts of dozens, hundreds, or even thousands of people. Anyone can create or edit an article, and it is assumed that the power of multiple contributors can ensure the accuracy of the article.

The reality is that Wikipedia entries vary considerably in accuracy. Although some involve the collective knowledge of so many people that they are largely accurate, in some cases the material is suspect. Consequently, use information in Wikipedia entries as a starting place, not an endpoint. In some cases, in fact, instructors will not allow the use of material obtained solely from Wikipedia in their students' papers.

9. **Resist the temptation to simply cut and paste the material you've found into a new document.** It's too easy to succumb to plagiarism if you simply copy material. Instead, take notes on the material using the critical thinking and notetaking skills you've developed.

Then save your notes. You can save your notes on a computer's hard drive, on a flash drive, or in the cloud (if you use Dropbox or Google Docs). You can also print out hard copies of what you create virtually.

However you do it, *make sure you save material frequently and make backup copies.* Nothing is more frustrating than laboring over a document for hours and having it disappear into cyberspace.

Evaluating the Information You Find on the Web

In most instances, you'll find more information than you need, and you'll have to evaluate the information you have found. Some of the important questions you must address before you can feel confident about what you've found include the following:

▶ **How authoritative is the information?** It is absolutely essential to consider the source of the material. Approach every piece of information with a critical eye, trying to determine what the author's biases might be. The best approach is to use multiple sources of information. If one source diverges radically from the others, you may reasonably question the reliability of that source.

Another approach is to consider the publisher of the material or sponsoring institution. For instance, sites established by well-known publishers and organizations are more likely to contain accurate information than those created by unknown (and sometimes anonymous) authors. Remember, the web is completely unregulated: *Anyone* can put *anything* on the web.

▶ **How current is the information?** No matter what the subject, information is changing at a rapid rate. Consider whether what you've found is the most recent and up-to-date material. Compare older sources to newer ones to identify changes in the ways in which the topic is considered.

▶ **How well are claims documented?** Are there references and citations to support the information? Are specific studies identified?

A Final Word

The Information Age presents us with great promise and opportunity. Through the use of media such as e-mail and the Internet, we have at our fingertips the ability to communicate with others around the world. We can break the bounds of our physical location and reach across geography to learn about others. The computer keyboard truly can be said to contain keys to the entire earth and its peoples.

Using the Web at Work

The skills you learn at finding and sorting information on the web will have many uses in your working life. Nearly every modern office is equipped with Internet-ready computers. Your employer will probably expect you to be able to find specific pieces of information—addresses, dates, phone numbers, and so forth—using the web, regardless of your specific profession. Further, in many industries, web skills are crucial. Real estate agents, for example, need to be able to use the web to assess markets and post offerings; accountants need to be able to research costs; salespeople need to be able to get background on present and potential clients.

Even if you don't work in an office setting, you will find great use for the web. Whatever professional problem you are facing—from an engine you can't fix to a patient who won't cooperate—there are others who have faced it before, and probably more than one of these people have shared their experiences online. Your evaluation skills will be crucial in applying what you find on the web to your job, but it's likely that there is helpful, reliable information online to be found.

Speaking *of* Success

Courtesy of Jalye Caratachea

NAME: **Jalye Caratachea**

EDUCATION: **Northwestern College—Associate Degree in Applied Science/Criminal Justice**

POSITION: **Patrol Officer, East Hazel Crest Police Department; East Hazel Crest, Illinois**

Jalye Caratachea had been years out of school, was married, and was raising a family. But that didn't stop her from pursuing her goal of entering the profession of law enforcement. Overcoming her fears of returning to school, Caratachea dove into her studies, earning a degree, and eventually getting her dream job—police officer.

"I really wanted to pursue my education," Caratachea says. "I wanted to get a job that I enjoyed. So, I found the time to go back to school."

A President's List student while at Northwestern College, Caratachea credits her courses as preparing her well for the profession of police work.

"I particularly enjoyed the criminal justice courses that were actually taught by former police officers," she explains. "The officers brought real-life experience to the online discussions, making them very interesting and keeping me engaged."

A psychology course also proved useful.

"One of the things I remember from my psychology course was an essay on how men and women differ when it comes to anger," Caratachea says. "Sometimes when I have to go on a call that involves a domestic dispute, I recall that class and remember that it takes longer for men to calm down than women." She also learned about issues of mental health, knowledge of which is helpful in understanding the people with whom she comes in contact.

"When I'm at work, my goal is to generate voluntary compliance," she goes on. "As an officer, I use what's called verbal judo. I deflect and redirect using phrases like, 'I understand, but . . .' or 'I appreciate that, but . . . .' I have to understand that I must treat people like I would like to be treated under the same circumstances, but at the same time getting them to do what I want."

Being a police officer requires a dedication to be professional at all times and to try to look at all situations objectively, according to Caratachea.

"When dealing with certain police matters, I really have to remember that I need to put my personal feelings aside and try to deal with the issue at hand," she says. "I am there to do a job and usually I come in contact with people when they are at their worst.

"Basically, the approach I take is to do things lawfully, have empathy, but not take things personally," she adds.

[RETHINK]

1. What do you think Caratachea may mean when she says she has made choices involving her family that people she meets at work haven't made?

2. Caratachea says that she learned in her psychology class that men and women differ in how they experience anger. What do you think some of those differences might be, and why?

Looking Back

LO 7-1 Explain how technology impacts you and your education.

▶ Course websites, textbook websites, podcasts, blogs, wikis, classroom presentation programs, individual response technology (IRT), and lecture capture technology are among the major educational uses of technology.

▶ The web includes e-mail, text messaging, video messaging, and search engines.

▶ E-mail and text messaging permit instant communication with others. Although college students tend to communicate more using text messaging, most student–instructor communication is conducted via e-mail.

LO 7-2 Describe strategies for effective distance learning.

▶ Distance learning is a form of education that does not require the physical presence of a student in a classroom. It is usually conducted over the web.

▶ Distance learning requires some adjustments for students, but it is increasingly popular.

LO 7-3 Discuss approaches for developing information competency.

▶ There are two main sources of information today: libraries and the web.

▶ Information in libraries is available in print form, electronic form, and microform.

▶ Library resources can be found through the use of the library catalog, which may be print-based but is increasingly likely to be computerized.

▶ The web is another major source of information. Web users access web pages (or sites) by using a browser, locate information by using search engines, and move from site to site by following links on each web page.

▶ Using the web effectively to find information can be tricky. It has many dead ends, false trails, and distractions, and the accuracy of the information presented as fact can be difficult to assess.

▶ Information on the web must be carefully evaluated by considering how reliable the source is, how current the information is, how well the source's claims are documented, and how complete the information is.

[KEY TERMS AND CONCEPTS]

Blended (or hybrid) courses (p. 174)
Blog (p. 165)
Browser (p. 182)
Call number (p. 180)
Cybersecurity (p. 172)
Distance learning (p. 173)
E-mail (p. 166)
Emoticons (or smileys) (p. 169)

Information competency (p. 179)
Interlibrary loan (p. 181)
Learning management system (LMS) (p. 177)
Lecture capture technology (p. 165)
Link (p. 182)
Online database (p. 179)
Podcast (p. 165)

Recall (p. 181)
Search engine (p. 182)
Stacks (p. 181)
Text messaging (texting) (p. 166)
Video message service (p. 167)
Web (p. 166)
Web page (p. 182)

[RESOURCES]

ON THE WEB

Many sites on the web provide the opportunity to extend your learning about the material in this chapter. Although the web addresses were accurate at the time the book was printed, check the Connect Library or ask your instructor for any changes that may have occurred.

▶ Pretty much anything you want to know about high tech, from the definition of a smartphone to an explanation of Utopic Unicorn, can be found at Webopedia (**http://www.webopedia.com/**). It also includes a list of the latest terms.

▶ The WWW Virtual Library (**www.vlib.org/**) is one of the oldest catalogs of the web, providing useful links to thousands of subjects.

▶ Yahoo! (**www.yahoo.com**) is a very popular Internet search engine and subject directory. Unlike Google, as a subject directory, Yahoo! allows browsing through prearranged categories (e.g., education, health, social science, and more). It also offers easy access to news, weather, maps, the Yellow Pages, and much more.

ON CAMPUS

If your college has a physical campus, you may consider visiting your college's computer center if you are having difficulty connecting to or surfing the web. Most campuses have consultants who can help you with the technical aspects of computer usage.

If you need access to computers, most college campuses also have computer labs. Typically, these labs provide computers with web access, as well as printers. It's important to check their hours, as they usually are not open 24/7.

Additionally, librarians at your college campus or at your local library are the people whom you should ask for help in locating information. In recent years, librarians—most of whom hold advanced degrees—have undergone a significant change in what they do, and most are equally at home using traditional print material and searching electronic information storehouses.

IN PRINT

A good introductory guide to computers is Ron White's *How Computers Work* (Que, 2014, 10th ed.). A very comprehensive and in-depth look at online research can be found in *Librarian's Guide to Online Searching* (Libraries Unlimited, 2015, 4th ed.), by Suzanne S. Bell. Finally, Leslie Bowman's *Online Learning: A User-Friendly Approach for High School and College Students* (R&L Education, 2010) offers clear instruction on becoming an effective online learner.

ENDNOTES

1. L. Liebovich, "Choosing Quick Hits over the Card Catalog," *New York Times*, August 10, 2000, pp. 1, 6. Based on material from Eliot Soloway, University of Michigan, School of Education.

The Case of . . .

The Empty Page

It had already been a long day for Joelle.

She'd worked two hours of overtime at her job supervising a call center. She'd driven home and immediately sat down at her computer to start work on her paper for her marketing class the next day. It was already 11:00 p.m. by the time she finished her research on the web. Then she began writing, opening a new file in her word processing program.

Joelle worked hard, drinking coffee to help her concentrate on the paper—and to keep her eyes open. When she was about three-quarters of the way done, her computer screen suddenly froze. Joelle pushed every button she could think of, but finally had to switch her computer off and then switch it back on. She opened the file for her paper . . . and saw an empty page.

To her horror, Joelle realized that her paper had been lost. She looked at the clock—it was almost 3:00 a.m. Did she really need to start her paper *all over again* ?

1. How well did Joelle use her time to work on her paper? What advice would you give her about the preparation stage of working on a paper?

2. Clearly, Joelle should have saved her work frequently while she was working. What else should she have done while working on her paper to help her recover from such a catastrophe?

3. Do you think Joelle's instructor would be sensitive to her problem? Do you think he or she would be willing to give her an extension? What could Joelle do to make her case that she had nearly finished the paper?

4. What should Joelle do next to begin reconstructing her paper and recovering as much of her work as possible?

Making Decisions and Problem Solving

Learning Outcomes

By the time you finish this chapter, you will be able to

» LO 8-1   Identify strategies for improving the quality of your decisions.

» LO 8-2   Implement plans to use for effective problem solving.

» LO 8-3   Recognize and avoid problems that affect critical thinking.

Ron Taubman had a tough decision coming up.

In three weeks, he would earn his electrician's degree. It had taken a great deal of effort and the sacrifice of a lot of free time, but he was almost there. It was what to do next, though, that was giving Ron problems.

All through college he had worked for a local contractor, picking up construction jobs when the contractor needed an extra pair of hands. Now that Ron was graduating with his electrician's degree, the contractor had offered to make him a permanent member of his construction crew. In short, he was being offered more work at a better salary.

Ron knew it was a great offer—but it was not Ron's only option. A friend he had met during an internship wanted to start his own electrician business, and he wanted Ron to be his partner. Working together, Ron's friend said, they could build the business quickly, and they would earn more and have more flexibility than if they worked for someone else.

As graduation approached, Ron knew he had to make up his mind. But he kept going around in circles. Was security more important than flexibility? How much was running his own business worth to him?

Ron knew he had to make up his mind. But how?

Looking Ahead

Like Ron, all of us face important decisions in our lives at one time or another. How can we make the right decisions? The best way is to employ some basic techniques that can help improve the quality of our decision making.

This chapter will give you a sense of what decision making is and is not, and it discusses a structured process that can help make your decisions the right ones. We'll also consider the related issue of problem solving. You will confront a variety of problems as you proceed through college and your career. We look at a number of proven techniques that will help you solve them.

Neither making decisions nor solving problems is easy. Sometimes the best decision or solution to a problem is one that we don't see at first; we all have mental blind spots. The best problem solvers and decision makers have learned how to use critical thinking to see around these blind spots. To help you improve your critical thinking skills, we'll examine some common problems that can affect our thinking and discuss several biases that can make us jump too quickly to conclusions.

»LO 8-1 Making Good Decisions: A Framework

Decision making is the process of deciding among various alternatives. Whether you are trying to decide between a Ford and a Honda; between an apartment that is close to your job and one that is close to family; or simply between a hamburger and a pizza—every one of these choices requires a decision. Some decisions are easily made and have few consequences, but others, such as whether to take one job or another, can involve the deepest examination of our beliefs and values.

Whatever you're deciding, you need to think critically in order to make a reasoned decision. You need to actively apply your past knowledge, synthesize and evaluate alternatives, and reason and reflect on a course of action. The greater your depth of thinking about the components of the decision, the more likely it is that you'll come up with the best choice.

decision making
The process of deciding among various alternatives.

P Prepare

Identify your goals

O Organize

Consider and assess
the alternatives

W Work

Make and carry out
the decision

E Evaluate

Consider the outcomes

R Rethink

Reconsider your goals
and options

P.O.W.E.R. Plan

To make a good decision, map out a strategy for making the choice that is best for you. Every decision can benefit from your systematically thinking through the options involved, based on the P.O.W.E.R. Plan illustrated here.

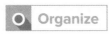 Prepare
Identifying Your Goals

Every decision starts with the end you have in mind: the goals you wish to accomplish by making the decision.

For example, suppose you are trying to decide how to spend a little extra money: on a gym membership or on a computer programming webinar. To decide, you need to consider both your short- and your long-term goals. For instance, the gym membership may raise your level of fitness and help you lose weight, something you'd promised yourself you would do. The webinar will be interesting, but the skills you'll learn may not be applicable to your current job. In terms of short-term goals, then, the gym membership may be the better choice. On the other hand, while the programming class may not provide as clear-cut an immediate payoff, it may help you meet your longer-term goal of entering the technology industry.

In short, every decision should start with a consideration of what our short- and long-term goals are. Identifying the goals that underlie decisions ensures that we make decisions in the context of our entire lives and not just to provide short-term answers to immediate problems.

O Organize
Considering and Assessing the Alternatives

Every decision is based on weighing various alternatives. Determining what those alternatives are, and their possible consequences, is often the most difficult part of decision making.

> "Nothing is more difficult, and therefore more precious, than to be able to decide."
>
> **Napoleon I, *Maxims*, 1804–1815**

Develop a List of Alternatives

It's important not only to think thoroughly about the obvious alternatives but also to consider those that are less obvious. For many decisions, there are choices beyond the "this or that" alternatives that can dominate our thinking. How can you be sure that you've considered all the possible alternatives? Using the technique of freewriting can help.

In **freewriting**, one writes continuously for a fixed period of time, perhaps 5 or 10 minutes. During this period, the idea is to write as many different ideas as possible, without stopping. It makes no difference whether the alternatives are good or bad or even whether they make sense. All that matters is that you let yourself brainstorm about the topic for a while and get it down on paper.

With freewriting, evaluating the worth of the ideas you've generated comes later. After you have produced as many possibilities as you can, then you go back and sift out the reasonable ones from those that are truly unlikely or just plain wacky. It's OK if you have to delete quite a few alternatives from your list; the process is likely to have liberated some truly reasonable alternatives that you might not otherwise have come up with. (Try the technique in the "Use Freewriting" exercise—see **Try It! 1**.)

freewriting
A technique involving continuous, nonstop writing, without self-criticism, for a fixed period of time.

Use Freewriting

Use freewriting to think of as many answers as you can to each of the following questions. The ground rules are that you should spend three minutes on each question, generating as many ideas as possible—regardless of whether they are feasible. To give yourself maximum freedom, write each answer on a separate page.

1. How can you make room in your schedule to take one more online course next term than you're taking this term?

2. How can someone get from the 3rd floor to the 20th floor of a building?

3. What should you do if you suspect that one of your co-workers is a space alien?

4. What would happen if the average life span were extended to 125 years?

After generating ideas, go back and evaluate them. How many were actually feasible or realistic? Do you think freewriting led to the production of more or fewer ideas than you would have come up with if you hadn't used the process? Did the quality of ideas change?

Assess Alternatives

Once you have generated as extensive a list of alternatives as possible, assess them. You need to follow three key steps when assessing each alternative:

1. *Determine the possible outcomes for each alternative.* Some outcomes are positive, some negative. Consider as many as you can think of. For example, if you are considering ways of solving transportation problems, one alternative might be to purchase a car. That alternative produces several potential outcomes. For example, you know that it will be easier to get wherever you want to go, and you might even have a better social life—clearly positive outcomes. But it is also true that buying and owning a car will be expensive, or it may be difficult to find convenient parking—both significant negative outcomes.

2. *Determine the probability that those outcomes will take place.* Some outcomes are far more likely than others. To take this into account, make a rough estimate of the likelihood that an outcome will come to pass, ranging from 100 percent (it is certain that it will occur) to 0 percent (it is certain that it will never occur). Obviously, the probabilities are just guesses, but going through the exercise of estimating them will make the outcomes more real and will permit you to compare the various alternatives against one another more easily.

3. *Compare the alternatives, taking into account the potential outcomes of each.* Systematically compare each of the alternatives. Then ask yourself the key question: Which alternative, on balance, provides the most positive (and most likely) outcomes?

We've all been there: facing a mind-boggling array of similar choices. However, by systematically assessing the alternatives, we can make informed decisions that will satisfy us.
© LADO/Shutterstock.com

Obviously, not every decision requires such an elaborate process. In fact, most won't. But when it comes to major decisions, those that could have a large impact upon you and your life, it's worthwhile to follow a systematic process.

Take a look at **Career Connections** for another process that you can follow to help you make a career decision.

Making and Carrying Out the Decision

Working through the previous steps will lead you to the point of decision: choosing one of the alternatives you've identified. Having carried out the steps will make the actual decision easier, but not necessarily easy.

Choosing among Alternatives

The reason that important decisions are difficult is that the alternatives you have to choose from carry both benefits and costs. Choosing one alternative means that you have to accept the costs of that choice and give up the benefits of the other alternatives.

What if, after going through the steps of the process laid out here, you still can't make up your mind? Try these strategies:

▶ **Give the decision time.** Sometimes waiting helps. Time can give you a chance to think of additional alternatives. Sometimes the situation will change, or you'll have a change in viewpoint.

If all else fails, toss a coin to decide what alternative to follow. Tossing a coin at least brings you to a decision. Then, if you find you're unhappy with the result, you'll have gained important information about how you really feel regarding a particular choice.
© SuperStock/AGE Fotostock

▶ **Make a mental movie, acting out the various alternatives.** Many of us have difficulty seeing ourselves in the future and envisioning how various options would play out. One way to get around this difficulty is to cast yourself into a series of "mental movies" that have different endings depending on the decision you make. Working through the different scripts in your head makes potential outcomes far more real and less abstract than they would be if you simply left them as items on a list of various options.

▶ **Toss a coin.** This isn't as crazy as it sounds. If each alternative seems equally positive or negative to you, pull out a coin—make option A "heads" and B "tails." Then flip it. The real power of the coin-toss strategy is that it might help you discover your true feelings. It may happen while the coin is in the air, or it may be that when you see the result of the coin toss, you won't like the outcome and will say to yourself, "No way." In such a case, you've just found out how you really feel.

▶ **Ask for advice.** Although Western society teaches the virtues of rugged individualism, asking others for their advice is often an excellent strategy. A friend, an instructor, a parent, or a counselor can provide helpful recommendations—sometimes because they've had to make similar decisions themselves. You don't have to take their advice, but it can help to listen to what they have to say.

Weighing Job Possibilities

One of the most difficult decisions you'll ever make is choosing between job offers. Although it's a tough position to be in, keep in mind that it is a *good* position, too—you are lucky to have multiple options.

Here's one method that can help you decide on the right job:

- Generate a selection of choices to consider. Include not only the job options you have, but also alternative ideas such as pursuing other jobs, earning a degree, starting your own business, and so forth. Even if you doubt you'll select one of these other options, considering them will help you assess what you truly want to do.

- Determine life-satisfaction considerations that are important to you. Generate a list of criteria to use in weighing the possibilities. For instance, you might want to consider the following:

  Benefits (vacation, health insurance, etc.)

  Income

  Spouse's opinion

  Friends' opinions

  Interest in the activity

  Prestige

  Job security

  Time off

  Benefit to society

  Geographic location

  Practicality/attainability

  Everyday working conditions

- Determine how well a particular option fulfills each of the life-satisfaction factors you consider important. By systematically considering how a potential path fulfills each of the criteria you use, you'll be able to compare different options. One easy way to do this is to create a chart like the one in **Table 8.1** (which shows an example of how two job options for a massage therapist might fulfill the various criteria).

- Compare different choices. Using the chart, evaluate your possibilities. Keep in mind that this is just a rough guide and that it's only as accurate as (a) the effort you put into completing it and (b) your understanding of a given choice. Use the results in conjunction with other things you find out about the jobs—and yourself.

table 8.1 Making Career Decisions

Life-Satisfaction Considerations	Possible Choice #1 *Massage therapist at Vida Spa*	Possible Choice #2 *Sports massage therapist at State University*	Possible Choice #3	Possible Choice #4
Benefits		√		
Income	√	√		
Spouse's opinion		√		
Friends' opinions		√		
Interest in the activity	√	√		
Prestige				
Job security/job openings		√		
Time off	√			
Benefit to society	√	√		
Practicality/attainability	√	√		
Everyday working conditions	√			
Other				
Other				
Other				
Other				
Other				

- ▶ **Avoid overanalysis and overthinking decisions.** Life is full of ambiguous problems. If you wait until you are absolutely, 100% certain you have made the right decision, you may never act. Remember that almost all decisions can be reversed.

- ▶ **Go with your gut feeling.** Call it what you like—gut feeling, intuition, hunch, superstition—but sometimes we need to go with our hearts and not our minds. If you've thought rationally about a decision and have been unable to determine the best course of action but have a gut feeling that one choice is better than another, follow your feelings.

  Following a gut feeling does not mean that you don't need to consider the pros and cons of a decision rationally and carefully. In fact, generally our "intuitions" are best when informed by the thoughtfulness of a more rational process.

© Viktor Gladkov/Shutterstock.com

From the perspective of . . .

A STUDENT Balancing education and life can be fraught with many alternatives and choices. How do you prioritize options when making a decision?

Carrying Out the Decision

Ultimately, decisions must move from thought to action—they have to be carried out. Consequently, the final stage in making a decision is to act upon it. You need to turn your decision into behavior.

E Evaluate | Considering the Outcomes

Did you make the right decision?

Even if you've spent time and mental effort in thinking through a decision, you still need to consider the results. Even well-considered decisions can end up being wrong, either because you neglected to consider something or because something has changed: either you or the situation.

> "In any moment of decision, the best thing you can do is the right thing, the next best thing is the wrong thing, and the worst thing you can do is nothing."
> **President Theodore Roosevelt**

Remember, it's never too late to change your mind. In fact, even major life decisions are often reversible. That's why it's so important to evaluate your choices. If you chose the wrong alternative, reverse course and reconsider your options.

It's not a bad thing to change your mind. In fact, admitting that a decision was a mistake is often the wisest and most courageous course of action. You don't want to be so rigidly committed to a decision that you're unable to evaluate the consequences objectively. Give yourself permission to be wrong.

Journal Reflections

My Decision Crossroads

Have you ever made a decision that proved to be of great importance in terms of the direction your life would take? For example, perhaps you broke off a romantic relationship, or decided to quit a job to go back to school, or took a stand on a controversial political issue. Reflect on that decision by answering these questions.

1. What was an important decision that you made that had significant effects on your life?

2. What have been the main benefits and disadvantages that you derived from the decision?

3. Every decision to do something is also a decision not to do other things. What did your decision keep you from doing?

4. Considering both the benefits and the disadvantages of the decision, would you say that you made a good decision?

5. Thinking critically about the approach you used to make the decision, what alternative approaches might you have used to make it? Could these alternatives have produced a different decision? How?

 R **Rethink**

Reconsidering Your Goals and Options

We can get to most places by multiple routes. There's the fastest and most direct route, which will get us to our destination in the least amount of time. Then there's the longer, more scenic route, where the trip itself provides pleasure. You can "take the long way home," as the song goes.

Is one route better than the other? Often not. Both take us to our destination. However, the experience of reaching our goal will have been very different.

Decisions about how to achieve a goal are similar to traveling down different routes. There's often no single decision that is best, just as there's often no single road to a particular place. Consequently, it's important to periodically reconsider the major decisions that we've made about our lives.

Ask yourself these questions:

▶ Are my decisions still producing the desired consequences?

▶ Are my decisions still appropriate, given my circumstances and changes in my life?

▶ Are my decisions consistent with what I want to get out of life?

Periodically taking stock like this is the best way to make sure that your decisions are taking you where you want to go. Taking stock also helps you be more effective in making future decisions.

»LO 8-2 Problem Solving: Applying Critical Thinking to Find Solutions

Two trains are approaching one another, each moving at 60 miles an hour. If the trains continue moving at the same speed, how long will it be before . . .

problem solving
The process of generating alternatives to work on.

If this is what comes to mind when you think of problem solving, think again. **Problem solving** encompasses more than the abstract, often unrealistic situations portrayed in math texts. It involves everyday, commonplace situations: How do we divide the restaurant bill so that each person pays a fair share? How do I keep my 1-year-old from tumbling down the stairs when there seems to be no way to fasten a gate at the top? How can I stop a faucet from dripping? How do I manage to study for a test and do the laundry the same evening?

The central task of problem solving is *generating* alternatives. In problem solving, we need to define the problem and generate as many solutions as we can.

What's the Problem?

The first step in solving any problem is to be as clear as you can about what the problem is. This may sound easy, but often it isn't. In fact, it may take some time to figure out just what is at stake.

The reason is that some problems are big and hard to define, while others are quite precise, such as mathematical equations or the solution to a jigsaw puzzle. Determining how to stop terrorism or finding peace in the Middle East are big, ill-defined problems. Simply determining what information is required to solve such problems can be a major undertaking.

To determine what the problem is and set yourself on a course for finding a solution, ask yourself these questions:

▶ What is the initial set of facts?

▶ What is it that I need to solve?

▶ Which parts of the problem appear to be most critical to finding a solution?

▶ Is there some information that can be ignored?

"Problems are only opportunities in work clothes."

Henry J. Kaiser (1882–1967), entrepreneur, *Maxim*

The more systematically you approach a problem, the better. For instance, you can apply the five P.O.W.E.R. steps to problems, in a way similar to how they can be used to make decisions. When you consider a problem systematically and think through your options, your choices will become clearer to you.

As you clarify what the problem is, you may find that you have encountered similar problems before. Your experience with them may suggest the means to the solution of the current problem. For example, consider the problem of the trains rushing toward each other. If you have worked on this kind of problem before, you might know a fairly simple equation you can write to determine how long it will take before they meet. If someone asks you about the problem she has in keeping her toddler from tumbling down the stairs, you might offer your experience in keeping your own children from visiting an off-limits area of your house.

On the other hand, to solve many of the problems we face in our daily lives, we have to do more than reach into our memories of prior situations. Instead, we need to devise novel approaches. How do you do this? There are several strategies you might use.

Strategies for Solving Life's Messier Problems

▶ **Break the problem down into smaller, more manageable pieces.** Divide a problem into a series of subgoals. As you reach each subgoal, you get closer to your overall goal of solving the problem. For example, if your goal is to find a job in Montreal, a subgoal might be to learn French. By reaching this subgoal, you move closer to reaching your ultimate goal—a job in a country that interests you.

▶ **Work backward.** Sometimes you know the answer to the problem but not how to get there. Then it's best to work backward. A **working backward** strategy starts at the desired solution or goal and works backward, moving away from the goal. For example, if your in-laws show up unexpectedly and you are faced with the problem of preparing a quick dinner, you might imagine the end result—the meal on the table—and then work backward to consider how to prepare it.

▶ **Use a graph, chart, or drawing to redefine the problem.** Transforming words into pictures often can help us devise solutions that otherwise would elude us. One good example is this problem:

> *A hiker climbs a mountain on Saturday, leaving at sunrise and arriving at the top near sunset. He spends the night at the top. The next day, Sunday, he leaves at daybreak and heads down the mountain, following the same path that he climbed the day before. The question is this: Will there be any time during the second day when the hiker will be at exactly the same point on the mountain as he was at exactly the same time on the first day?*

Trying to solve the problem through the use of math or words is quite difficult. However, there's a simpler way: drawing the two paths. As you can see from **Figure 8.1**, the drawing helps provide a solution.

▶ **Consider the opposite.** Problems can sometimes be solved by considering the opposite of the problem you're seeking to solve. For example, to define "good mental health" you might try to define "bad mental health."

▶ **Use analogies.** Some problems can be solved through the use of an **analogy**, which is a comparison between concepts or objects that are alike in some respects but dissimilar in most others. For instance, if you liken a disastrous family vacation to a voyage on the *Titanic*, you're using an analogy.

Analogies may help us gain additional insight into the problem at hand, and they may provide an alternative framework for interpreting the information that is provided. For instance, the manufacturers of Pringles

working backward
The strategy of starting at the desired solution or goal and working toward the starting point of the problem.

analogy
A comparison between concepts or objects that are alike in some respects, but dissimilar in most others.

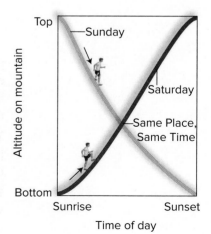

figure 8.1
Up and Down the Mountain: The Paths to a Solution

Exercise Your Problem-Solving Skills

Try to solve these problems.[1] To help you devise solutions, a hint regarding the best strategy to use is included after each problem.

1. One cold, dark, and rainy night, a college student has a flat tire on a deserted stretch of country road. He pulls onto the shoulder to change it. After removing the four lug nuts and placing them into the hub cap, he removes the flat tire and takes his spare out of the trunk. As he is moving the spare tire into position, his hand slips and he upsets the hub cap with the lug nuts, which tumble off into the night where he can't find them. What should he do? (*Hint:* Instead of asking how he might find the lug nuts, reframe the problem and ask where else he might find lug nuts.)

2. Cheryl, who is a construction worker, is paving a walk, and she needs to add water quickly to the concrete she has just poured. She reaches for her pail to get water from a spigot in the front of the house, but suddenly realizes the pail has a large rust hole in it and cannot be used. As the concrete dries prematurely, she fumbles through her toolbox for tools and materials with which to repair the pail. She finds many tools, but nothing that would serve to patch the pail. The house is locked and no one is home. What should she do? (*Hint:* When is a pail not a pail?)

3. What day follows the day before yesterday if two days from now will be Sunday? (*Hint:* Break it up or draw a diagram.)

4. Carrie has four chains, each three links long. She wants to join the four chains into a single, closed chain. Having a link opened costs 2 cents and having a link closed costs 3 cents. How can Carrie have the chains joined for 15 cents? (*Hint:* Can only end links be opened?)

5. What is two-thirds of one-half? (*Hint:* Reverse course.)

6. Juan has three separate large boxes. Inside each large box are two separate medium-sized boxes, and inside each of the medium boxes are four small boxes. How many boxes does Juan have altogether? (*Hint:* Draw it.)

After working to solve these problems, consider these questions: Which problems were the easiest to solve, and which were more difficult? Why? Were the hints helpful? Do you think there was more than one solution to any of the problems? Did your initial assumptions about the problem help or hinder your efforts to solve it? (*Note:* Answers to the problems are found in the Answers to Try it! 2 Problems section of this chapter.)

potato chips found that they could cut packaging costs if they slightly moistened the chips before packaging them—an idea that came when researchers noticed that dry tree leaves, which normally crumble easily, could be packed together tightly when they were wet.

▶ **Take another's perspective.** By viewing a problem from another person's point of view, it is often possible to obtain a new perspective on the problem that will make the problem easier to solve.

▶ **Forget about it.** Just as with decision making, sometimes it's best simply to walk away from a problem for a while. Just a few hours or days away from a problem may give us enough of a break to jar some hidden solutions from the recesses of our minds. The idea of "sleeping on it" also sometimes works; we may wake up refreshed and filled with new ideas.

Test these problem-solving strategies in **Try It! 2**.

Assessing Your Potential Solutions

If a problem clearly has only one answer, such as a math problem, this step in problem solving is relatively easy. You should be able to work the problem and figure out whether you've been successful.

In contrast, messier problems have several possible solutions, some of which may be more involved and costly than others. In these cases, it's necessary to compare alternative solutions and choose the best one. For example, suppose you want to surprise your best friend on her birthday. She is working in Omaha, about 90 miles from you, and you need to find a way to get there. Perhaps you could rent a car, take a bus, or find some other way. Money is an issue. You will want to figure out how much each alternative costs before choosing one as your solution to the problem. Since every penny you spend getting there is a penny less that you will have to celebrate, you will want to weigh the options carefully.

Finally, spend a bit of time seeing whether there is a way to refine the solution. Is the solution you've devised adequate? Does it address all aspects of the problem? Are there alternative approaches that might be superior? Answering these questions, and refining your solution to address them, can give you confidence that the solution you've come up with is the best. For example, if you're trying to get to Omaha, you might decide to use the ride board at your school to try to find a ride with someone going to Omaha that day. Maybe your friend's family is going to be driving in and could pick you up or could even lend you a car for the trip.

Remember that not every problem has a clear-cut solution. Sometimes we need to be satisfied with a degree of uncertainty and ambiguity. For some of us, such a lack of clarity is difficult, making us uneasy, and it may push us to choose a solution—any solution—that seems to solve the problem. Others of us feel more comfortable with ambiguity, but this may lead us to let problems ride, without resolving the situation.

Either way, it's important to consider what your own problem-solving style is when you seek to identify solutions. And keep in mind that often there is no perfect solution to a problem—only some solutions that are better than others.

From the perspective of . . .

A PHARMACY TECHNICIAN The ability to ask questions is a trait that will continue to matter in your career. What are some of the potential consequences of not asking questions in a field that presents possible health risks?

Reflect on the Process of Problem Solving

It's natural to step back and bask in the satisfaction of solving a tough problem. That's fine—but take a moment to consider your success. Each time we solve a problem we end up a couple steps ahead, but only if we've thought about the process we went through to solve it.

Go back and consider what it took to solve the problem. Can the means you used to come up with your solution be applied to more complex kinds of problems? If you arrived at a solution by drawing a chart, would this work on similar problems in the future? Taking a moment to rethink your solution can provide you with an opportunity to become an expert problem solver and, more generally, to improve your critical thinking skills. Don't let the opportunity slip away.

» LO 8-3 Don't Fool Yourself: Avoiding Everyday Problems in Critical Thinking

Being able to think clearly and without bias is the basis for critical thinking. As you have probably noticed already, the quality of the thinking you do regarding problems and decisions plays a crucial role in determining how successful you are.

Unfortunately, it is sometimes the alternative you *didn't* think of that can end up being the most satisfactory decision or solution. Furthermore, we are susceptible to **cognitive biases**, limitations, blind spots, and outright mistakes in our thinking that lead us to illogical or erroneous decisions. Cognitive biases occur because we apply habitual patterns of thought that may not be applicable to a problem at hand, due to failures of memory, or to outright miscalculations.

The good news is that we learn to think critically and avoid blind spots that hinder us in our decision making and problem solving. We can start by considering the common obstacles to critical thinking.

Here are some of the decision-making and problem-solving pitfalls to look out for. Avoiding them will improve your critical thinking greatly.

▶ **Don't assume that giving something a name explains it.** The mere fact that we can give an idea or problem a name doesn't mean we can explain it. Yet we often confuse the two.

For instance, consider the following sequences of questions and answers:

Q. *Why do I have so much trouble falling asleep?*

A. *Because you have insomnia.*

Q. *Why is he so unsociable?*

A. *Because he's an introvert.*

Q. *Why did the defendant shoot those people?*

A. *Because he's insane.*

Q. *How do you know he's insane?*

A. *Because only someone who was insane would shoot people in that way.*[2]

It's clear that none of these answers is satisfactory. All use circular reasoning, in which the alleged explanation for the behavior is simply the use of a label.

▶ **Don't accept vague generalities dressed up as definitive statements.** Read the following personality analysis and think about how well it applies to you:

You have a need for other people to like and admire you and a tendency to be critical of yourself. You also have a great deal of unused

cognitive bias
A limitation, blind spot, or mistake in thinking that leads to illogical or erroneous decisions.

potential that you have not turned to your advantage, and although you have some personality weaknesses, you are generally able to compensate for them. Nonetheless, relating to members of the opposite sex has presented problems to you, and while you appear to be disciplined and self-controlled to others, you tend to be anxious and insecure inside.

If you believe that these statements provide an amazingly accurate description of your unique qualities, you're not alone: Most college students believe that the descriptions are tailored specifically to them.[3] But how is that possible? It isn't. The reality is that the statements are so vague that they are virtually meaningless. The acceptance of vague but seemingly useful and significant statements about oneself and others has been called the *Barnum effect,* after showman and circus master P. T. Barnum, who coined the phrase "There's a sucker born every minute."

▶ **Don't confuse opinion with fact.** Opinions are not fact. Although we may be aware of this simple formula, almost all of us can be fooled into thinking that someone's opinion is the same as a fact.

A fact is information that is proven to be true. In contrast, an opinion represents judgments, reasoning, beliefs, inferences, or conclusions. If we accept some bit of information as a fact, we can use it to build our opinions. But if we are presented with an opinion, we need to determine the facts on which it is built to judge its reliability.

The difference between fact and opinion can sometimes be subtle. For instance, compare these two statements:

1. Every college student needs to take a writing course during the first term of college.

2. Many college students need to take a writing course during the first term of college.

The first statement is most likely an opinion because it is so absolute and unqualified. Words such as "every," "all," and "always" are often evidence of opinion. On the other hand, the second statement is more likely a fact since it contains the qualifier "many." In general, statements that are qualified in some way are more likely to be facts.

Complete **Try It! 3** to see the difficulties sometimes involved in distinguishing between fact and opinion.

▶ **Avoid jumping to conclusions.** Read this riddle and try to answer it:

A father and his son were driving along the interstate highway when the father lost control of the car, swerved off the road, and crashed into a utility pole. The father died instantly, and his son was critically injured. An ambulance rushed the boy to a nearby hospital. A prominent surgeon was summoned to provide immediate treatment. When the surgeon arrived and entered the operating room to examine the boy, a loud gasp was heard.

"I can't operate on this boy," the surgeon said. "He is my son."

How can this be?

If you find this puzzling, you've based your reasoning on an assumption: that the surgeon is a male. But suppose you had assumed that the surgeon was a female. Suddenly, the riddle becomes a lot easier. It's far easier to guess that the surgeon is the son's *mother* if we don't leap to embrace a faulty assumption.

Distinguish Fact from Opinion

Read the following statements and try to determine which are facts (put "F" on the line that follows the item) and which are opinions (put "O" on the line that follows the item).

1. College students should get at least 7 hours of sleep every night. _____
2. The average college student sleeps less than 7 hours a night. _____
3. Nike offers better styling and comfort than any other brand of shoe. _____
4. Two out of five sports figures surveyed preferred Nike over Converse shoes. _____
5. The U.S. government spends too much money on guns and missiles and not enough money on education. _____
6. Government figures show spending is much higher for guns and missiles than for education. _____
7. In general, U.S. high school students receive less classroom instruction in foreign languages than their counterparts in Europe and Asia. _____
8. No student in the United States should graduate without having studied a language other than English for at least 4 years. _____
9. Michael Jordan is the most outstanding, most exciting, and certainly most successful basketball player who ever stepped onto a court. _____

Items 1, 3, 5, 8, and 9 are opinions; the rest are facts. What are the main differences between opinion and fact?

Why is it so easy to jump to conclusions? One reason is that we sometimes aren't aware of the assumptions that underlie our thinking. Another is our reliance on "common sense."

▶ **Be skeptical of "common sense."** Much of what we call common sense makes contradictory claims. For example, if you believe in the notion "Absence makes the heart grow fonder," you may assume that your girlfriend, now working at a job in another city, will arrive home at Christmas even more in love with you than before. But what about "Out of sight, out of mind," which suggests a less positive outcome? Common sense often presents us with contradictory advice, making it a less-than-useful guide to decision making and problem solving.

▶ **Avoid the confirmation bias.** The *confirmation bias* occurs when we favor the first conclusion we come to and then ignore contradictory information that supports alternative solutions. Even when we find evidence that contradicts a solution we have chosen, we are apt to stick with our original conclusion.

The confirmation bias occurs for several reasons. For one thing, because rethinking a problem that appears to be solved already takes extra effort, we are apt to stick with our first solution. For another, we give greater weight to subsequent information that supports our initial position than to information that is not supportive of it.

▶ **Don't assume that just because two events occur together, one causes the other.** Just because two events appear to be associated with each other, we cannot conclude that one event has caused the other to occur. For example, suppose you read that a study showed that 89 percent of juvenile delinquents use marijuana. Does this mean that smoking marijuana *causes* juvenile delinquency?

What's the Real Explanation?

Even though two events are related to each other, it doesn't mean that one causes the other. Instead, there is often some other factor that is the actual cause of the relationship.

To see this for yourself, consider each of the following (actual!) findings. What might be a plausible explanation for each one?

1. Ice cream sales and the timing of shark attacks are highly related. Why?

2. The number of cavities children have and the size of their vocabulary are closely related. Why?

3. Skirt hemlines tend to rise as stock prices rise. Why?

4. Women with breast implants have a higher rate of suicide than those without breast implants. Why?

(continued)

No, it doesn't. It is pretty safe to say that 100 percent of juvenile delinquents grew up drinking milk. Would you feel comfortable saying that milk causes delinquency? With the association between marijuana use and delinquent behavior, it is very likely that there's some third factor—such as the influence of peers—that causes people both to (a) try drugs and (b) engage in delinquent behavior. The bottom line: We do not know the cause of the delinquency just because delinquents often smoke marijuana.

In short, we need to be careful in assuming causality. Even if two events or other kinds of variables occur together, it does not mean that one causes the other. To see this for yourself, take a look at the statements in **Try It! 4**, "What's the Real Explanation?"

5. People who own washing machines are more likely to die in car accidents than those who don't. Why?

6. Men who carry their cell phones in their front pants pockets have a lower sperm count than those who don't carry them in their front pants pockets. Why?

Once you've completed this Try It!, look at the possible explanations listed below. Keep in mind that these are simply theories; we don't know for sure if they're correct.

1. The actual cause is probably the temperature, which causes both sales of ice cream and ocean swimming to increase.
2. Both the number of cavities children have and the size of their vocabularies are related to their age.
3. Skirt hemlines go up, as does the stock market, when people are feeling less conservative and more optimistic.
4. Having breast implants and committing suicide both may be a result of unhappiness or a poor self-image.
5. People who own washing machines are more likely to own cars, and therefore they stand a higher risk of dying in a car crash.
6. Men with high-stress jobs may be more likely to have cell phones, and it is the stress that produces the low sperm count—not the placement of a phone in their pocket.

Using Critical Thinking in Your Classes

Nowhere is critical thinking more important to use—and demonstrate to your instructors—than when you're in your online classes. Here are some strategies to foster your skills as a critical thinker:

- **E-mail questions.** Most instructors welcome questions. Even if an instructor doesn't have time to provide a comprehensive e-mail response, the very act of formulating a question will help you think more critically about the course material.

- **Accept that some questions have no right or wrong answers.** Understanding that some questions have no simple answer is a sign of mental sophistication. Sometimes the best an instructor can do is present competing theories. Although you may want to know which theory is right, accept that sometimes no one knows the answer to that question—that's why they're theories, not facts!

- **Keep an open mind.** Your instructor and classmates have their own perspectives and opinions. Even if you disagree with them, try to figure out why they hold their views. It will help you see the multiple sides of different issues.

- **Don't deny your emotional reactions—manage them.** There may be times that an instructor or classmate posts something that is bothersome or even makes you angry. That's OK. But be sure to manage your emotions so that they don't overwhelm your rational self. And use your emotional reactions to gain self-understanding into what's important to you.

- **Don't be afraid of looking unintelligent.** No one wants to look foolish, especially in an online discussion with your classmates. But don't let self-defeating feelings prevent you from expressing your concerns. Take intellectual risks!

Speaking *of* Success

NAME: **Eliud Saavedra Jr.**

EDUCATION: **Associate's Degree, Architectural Drafting, Westwood College, Chicago, IL; Bachelor's Degree, Interior Design, Westwood College, Chicago, IL**

POSITION: **CAD (Computer Aided Drafting) Technician, KJWW Engineering Consultants**

Not satisfied with working as a mechanic after graduating from high school, Eliud Saavedra set his sights on not just finding a better-paying job but pursuing a college degree that would lead to better things.

"My financial situation wasn't very good, but I knew that if I got myself through college, it was going to pay off some day," he says. "Now I have a very good job."

Saavedra attended college as a full-time student and worked more than 40 hours a week to pay his tuition. He received an Associate's Degree from Westwood College in Chicago and was soon placed by the college in a job. But he wanted more—and after six years, Saavedra enrolled once again at Westwood and pursued a second degree.

"I took several courses at Westwood that prepared me well for my current job," he says. "I became passionate about learning a computer-aided drafting program, and got so good at it that I was assisting friends and family members with their studies. I put in a lot of time outside of class, as well, learning the drafting program and understanding how it works. Learning that program provided me with a strong foundation for the work I'm doing today.

Today, working at one of the leading engineering firms in the Midwest, Saavedra is involved in designing operating and MRI rooms for hospitals.

"I'm currently in the mechanical department, working with engineers putting together systems for ventilation, plumbing, and piping, but I'm soon going to be moving over to the electrical department and will be involved with designing lighting," he says.

For the future, Saavedra sees himself continuing to add to his skills and becoming more specialized in his field.

"Down the road, I do see myself as a full-blown electrical engineer and lighting designer, and one day achieving certification as a lighting consultant," he says.

[**RETHINK**]

- What sacrifices do you think Saavedra had to make in order to get a college education?

- What benefits do you think Saavedra could have obtained from helping his friends and family members?

Looking Back

LO 8-1 Identify strategies for improving the quality of your decisions.

▶ A structured process of decision making can clarify the issues involved, expand our options, and improve the quality of our choices.

▶ Good decision making begins with understanding your short- and long-term goals.

▶ Decision making is improved if you have a large number of alternatives.

▶ For difficult decisions, strategies include giving the decision time, acting out alternatives, tossing a coin to test your feelings, understanding that indecision is often a decision itself, and acting on gut feelings.

LO 8-2 Implement plans to use for effective problem solving.

▶ Problem solving entails the generation of alternatives to consider.

▶ We need to first understand and define the problem and to determine the important elements in coming to a solution to a problem.

▶ Approaches to generating solutions include breaking problems into pieces, working backward, using pictures, considering the opposite, using analogies, taking another's perspective, and "forgetting" the problem.

▶ Problem solving ultimately requires the evaluation and refinement of the solutions that have been generated.

LO 8-3 Recognize and avoid problems that affect critical thinking.

▶ Labeling, using vague generalities, accepting opinion as fact, jumping to conclusions, mistaking common sense, the confirmation bias, and assuming correlation all pose threats to critical thinking.

▶ Awareness of the biases that may affect our thinking can help us avoid them.

[KEY TERMS AND CONCEPTS]

Analogy (p. 201)

Cognitive bias (p. 204)

Decision making (p. 193)

Freewriting (p. 194)

Problem solving (p. 200)

Working backward (p. 201)

[RESOURCES]

ON THE WEB

The following sites on the web provide the opportunity to extend your learning about the material in this chapter. (Although the web addresses were accurate at the time this material was published, check the *P.O.W.E.R. Learning* Connect Library or contact your instructor for any changes that may have occurred.)

▶ Santa Clara University's site on ethical decision making covers topics such as fairness, common good, and rights. It also includes numerous links and a smartphone app. (**www.scu.edu/ethics/practicing/decision/**)

- "Basic Guidelines to Problem Solving and Decision Making" (**www.managementhelp. org/prsn_prd/prob_slv.htm**) by Carter McNamara provides basic guidelines to problem solving and decision making in seven steps. This site is rich in links to comprehensive approaches to decision making, critical and creative thinking, time management, and organization.

- Cuesta College offers a concise approach to critical thinking and problem solving at this site: **http://www.cuesta.edu/student/servs_classes/ssc/study_guides/critical_thinking/index.html**.

ON CAMPUS

If your college has a physical campus, and you are having a personal problem that is difficult to solve, don't hesitate to turn to staff at a counseling center or mental health center. Trained counselors and therapists can help you sort through the different options in an objective manner. They may identify possibilities for solutions that you didn't even know existed. Even if the person with whom you speak initially is not the right one, he or she can direct you to someone who can help.

IN PRINT

Steve Padget's *Creativity and Critical Thinking* (Routledge, 2012) provides an overview of how to use critical thinking in an educational context.

    Critical Thinking, by Brooke Moore and Richard Parker (McGraw-Hill, 2014, 11th ed.), teaches readers how to effectively consider alternate points of view while making personal choices.

    For a general overview of critical thinking skills, read Richard Paul and Linda Elder's *Critical Thinking: Tools for Taking Charge of Your Learning and Your Life* (Pearson, 2013, 2nd ed.).

ENDNOTES

1. Adapted from D. F. Halpern, *Thought and Knowledge: An Introduction to Critical Thinking*, 3rd ed. (Mahwah, NJ: Erlbaum, 1996); J. D. Bransford and B. S. Stein, *The Ideal Problem Solver*, 2nd ed. (New York: W. H. Freeman, 1993).
2. B. Forer, "The Fallacy of Personal Validation: A Classroom Demonstration of Gullibility," *Journal of Abnormal and Social Psychology* 44 (1949), pp. 118–23.
3. D. Byrne and L. Kelley, *An Introduction to Personality* 3rd ed. (Englewood Cliffs, NJ: Prentice Hall, 1981), p. 304.

[ANSWERS TO TRY IT! 2 PROBLEMS]

1. Remove one lug nut from each of the other three tires on the car and use these three to attach the spare tire. This will hold until four more lug nuts can be purchased.
2. Dump the tools out of the toolbox and use it as a pail.

3. Thursday.
4. Open all three links on one chain (cost = 6 cents) and use them to fasten the other three chains together (cost = 9 cents; total cost = 15 cents).

5. It is the same as one-half of two-thirds, or one-third.
6. 33 boxes (3 large, 6 medium, 24 small).

The Case of . . .
Left Holding the Lease

Erica had a problem.

She and her friend Karen had found a two-bedroom apartment to share for the upcoming year. The apartment was on the expensive side, but they had decided that it was worth it because it was in a great location. She and Karen had jointly paid the security deposit on the apartment. However, because Karen hadn't been around when it came time to sign the lease, only Erica had signed it. Consequently, Erica was legally responsible for fulfilling the terms of the lease.

Now, only two weeks before they were scheduled to move in, Karen told Erica that she had realized she couldn't afford the rent and that she had decided she had to live with her parents. Erica was simultaneously furious with Karen and panicky at the thought of having to pay the rent by herself.

How was she going to deal with the problem?

1. Is the problem a purely financial and legal one, or are there personal and social considerations that should be taken into account in solving the problem?

2. Is the problem solely Erica's problem, or should Karen take responsibility for solving it as well?

3. What alternatives does Erica have for dealing with the situation?

4. How should Erica go about evaluating the outcomes for each alternative?

5. Based on your analysis of the problem, what advice would you give Erica for dealing with the situation?

9

Learning Outcomes

By the time you finish this chapter, you will be able to

》 LO 9-1 Discuss why the increasing racial, ethnic, and cultural diversity of society is important to you.

》 LO 9-2 Utilize strategies to become more at ease with differences and diversity.

》 LO 9-3 Build lasting relationships and learn to deal with conflict.

Diversity and Relationships

© Dave and Les Jacobs/Blend Images RF

He was born in the Kapi'olani Maternity and Gynecological Hospital in Honolulu, Hawaii. His mother was an American of primarily English descent from Wichita, Kansas. His father was born in Africa, in Nyang'oma Kogelo, Nyanza Province, Kenya. His parents met while taking a Russian language class. He spent most of his childhood in Hawaii, except for a few years in Indonesia.

In describing his childhood, he later said, "The opportunity that Hawaii offered—to experience a variety of cultures in a climate of mutual respect—became an integral part of my world view, and a basis for the values that I hold most dear."

He is Barack Obama, who grew up to be President of the United States.

Looking Ahead

Whether you have skin that is black or white or brown, are Jewish or Muslim or Protestant or Greek Orthodox or Hindu, were born in Cuba or Vietnam or Boise, are able-bodied or physically challenged, college presents a world of new opportunities. Your online classes enable you to interact with people of very different backgrounds from your own. If you take the opportunity to form relationships with a variety of individuals, you will increase your understanding of the human experience and enrich your life. This will also benefit you greatly in your career because whatever your field, you will inevitably find yourself in situations where success will depend on your ability to collaborate effectively with people different from yourself.

In this chapter, we consider how social diversity and relationships affect your life experience. We examine the increasing diversity of American society and consider the meanings and social effects of race, ethnicity, and culture. We look at practical strategies for acknowledging—and shedding—prejudice and stereotypes and being receptive to others on their own merits.

We next discuss relationships from a broader perspective, exploring ways that you can build lasting friendships with others. Finally, the chapter discusses the conflicts that can arise between people and what you can do to resolve them.

» LO 9-1 Living in a World of Diversity

No matter where we live, our contacts with others who are racially, ethnically, and physically different from us are increasing. The web is bringing people from across the globe into our homes, as close to us as the computer sitting on our desk. Businesses now operate globally, so co-workers are likely to come from many different countries and cultures. Being comfortable with people whose backgrounds and beliefs may differ from our own is not only a social necessity but also virtually a requirement for career success.

By the mid-21st century, the percentage of people in the United States of African, Latin American, Asian, and Arabic ancestry will be greater than the percentage of those of Western European ancestry—a profound statistical, and social, shift.

Furthermore, it's not just racial and ethnic characteristics that constitute diversity. As you can see in the Diversity Wheel in **Figure 9.1**, diversity comprises characteristics such as gender, sexual orientation, age, and mental and physical characteristics. Layer on top of that factors such as education, religion, and income level, and the complexity of others—and ourselves—becomes apparent. In addition, people often have multiple diversities: One can be, for instance, a

figure 9.1
Diversity Wheel
Diversity is composed of many different characteristics, as exemplified by the Diversity Wheel.

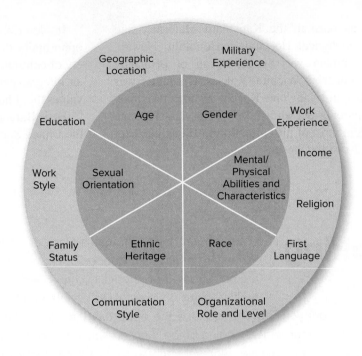

hearing-impaired lesbian African American woman, evoking responses from others that reflect any, all, or none of these identities. (You can examine the diversity of your own campus by completing **Try It! 1**.)

Race, Ethnicity, and Culture

Are you African American or Black? Caucasian or white or Euro-American? Hispanic or Latino? American Indian or Native American? Gay or lesbian? Physically challenged? A combination of various identities?

The language we use to describe our ethnic and racial group membership, and those of other people, is in constant flux. And what we call people matters. The subtleties of language affect how people think about members of particular groups, and how they think about themselves.

One of the difficulties in understanding diversity is that many of the terms we use are ill-defined and often overlapping. The term **race** is generally used to refer to obvious physical differences that set one group apart from others. According to such a definition, whites, Blacks, and Asian Americans are typically thought of as belonging to different races, determined largely by biological factors.

Ethnicity refers to shared national origins or cultural patterns. In the United States, for example, Puerto Ricans, Irish Americans, and Italian Americans are categorized as ethnic groups. However, ethnicity—like race—is very much in the eye of the beholder. For instance, a Cuban American woman who is a third-generation citizen of the United States may feel few ties or associations to Cuba. Yet whites may view her as "Hispanic," and Blacks may view her as "white."

Finally, **culture** comprises the learned behaviors, beliefs, and attitudes that are characteristic of an individual society or population. But it's more than that: Culture also encompasses the products that people create, such as architecture, music, art, and literature. Culture is created and shaped by people, but at the same time it creates and shapes people's behavior.

race
Traditionally, biologically determined physical characteristics that set one group apart from others.

ethnicity
Shared national origins or cultural patterns.

culture
The learned behaviors, beliefs, and attitudes that are characteristic of an individual society or population, and the products that people create.

Determine the Diversity of Your Community

Try to assess the degree of diversity that exists in your community. *Community* can be a loosely defined term, but for this Try It! think of it as the group of people you encounter and interact with on a regular basis. When thinking of diversity, remember to include the many different ways in which people can be different from one another, including race, ethnicity, culture, sexual orientation, physical challenges, and so on.

Overall, how diverse would you say your community is?

Are there organizations in your community that promote diversity? Are there organizations that work to raise the visibility and understanding of particular groups within your community?

Is your online college community more or less diverse than your community at large? Why do you think this might be?

How does the diversity in your community compare to the following statistics on diversity in the United States as of the 2010 census: white, 72 percent; Hispanic or Latino, 16 percent; Black or African American, 13 percent; Asian, 5 percent; two or more races, 3 percent; American Indian and Alaska Native, .9 percent; Native Hawaiian and other Pacific Islander, .2 percent; other race, 6 percent? (Note: Percentages add up to more than 100 percent because Hispanics may be of any race and are therefore counted under more than one category.)

Race, ethnicity, and culture shape each of us to an enormous degree. They profoundly influence our view of others, as well as who we are. They affect how others treat us, and how we treat them in turn. They determine whether we look people in the eye when we meet them, how early we arrive when we're invited to dinner at a friend's house, and even, sometimes, how well we do in school or on the job.

Because many of us grew up in neighborhoods that are not ethnically diverse, we may have little or even no experience interacting with people who are different from us. Even in your online college courses, your exposure to people who have different backgrounds may be limited.

At some time, though, that will change. As the United States becomes increasingly diverse, it's a matter not of "if" but of "when" you will be exposed to people who have profoundly different backgrounds from your own. Whether in the workplace or in the neighborhood in which you reside, living in a diverse environment will be part of your life.

Workplace colleagues are increasingly diverse.
© Monkey businessimages/iStock/ Getty Images Plus/Getty Images RF

Building Cultural Competence

We're not born knowing how to drive a car or cook. We have to learn how to do these things. The same is true of developing a basic understanding of other races, ethnic groups, and cultures. Called **cultural competence**, this knowledge of

cultural competence
Knowledge and understanding about other races, ethnic groups, cultures, and minority groups.

P Prepare

Accept diversity as a valued part of your life

O Organize

Explore your own prejudices and stereotypes

W Work

Develop cultural competence

E Evaluate

Check your progress in attaining cultural competence

R Rethink

Understand how your own racial, ethnic, and cultural background affects others

P.O.W.E.R. Plan

others' customs, perspectives, background, and history can teach us a great deal about others, as well as ourselves. Cultural competence also provides a basis for civic engagement, permitting us to act with civility toward others and to make the most of our contributions to society.

Building cultural competence proceeds in several steps, outlined in the P.O.W.E.R. Plan.

P Prepare

Accepting Diversity as a Valued Part of Your Life

In the title of her book on social diversity, psychologist Beverly Tatum asks, "*Why Are All the Black Kids Sitting Together in the Cafeteria?*[1] She might just as well have asked a similar question about the white kids, the Asian American kids, and so forth. It often appears as if the world comes already divided into separate racial, ethnic, and cultural groups.

It's more than appearances: We form relationships more easily with others who are similar to us than with those who are different. It's easier to interact with others who look the same as we do, who come from similar backgrounds, and who share our race, ethnicity, and culture because we can take for granted certain shared cultural assumptions and views of the world.

But that doesn't mean that "easy" and "comfortable" translate into "good" or "right." We can learn a great deal more, and grow and be challenged, if we seek out people who are different from us. If you look beyond surface differences and find out what motivates other people, you can become aware of new ways of thinking about family, relationships, earning a living, and the value of education. It can be liberating to realize that others may hold very different perspectives from your own and that there are many ways to lead your life.

Letting diversity into your own life also has very practical implications: As we discuss in **Career Connections**, learning to accept and work with people who are different from you is a crucial skill that will help you in whatever job you hold.

© PictureNet Corporation/Alamy Stock Photo RF

From the perspective of . . .

A STUDENT Having a diverse group of classmates in your online classes can help you see the world in a broader way. Have you ever had a classmate relate an experience in an online post that impacted your thought process?

O Organize

Exploring Your Own Prejudices and Stereotypes

Arab. Gay. African American. Hispanic. Female. Disabled. Overweight.

Quick: What comes into your mind when you think about each of these labels? If you're like most people, you don't draw a blank. Instead, a collection of images and feelings comes into your mind, based on what you know, have been told, or assume about the group.

Journal Reflections

Thinking about Race, Ethnicity, and Culture

1. Were race and ethnicity discussed in your family as you were growing up? In what ways?

2. Do you demonstrate—through your behavior, attitudes, and/or beliefs—your own ethnic background? How?

3. Are there cultural differences between you and members of other races or ethnicities? What are they?

4. Are you proud of your ethnicity? Why?

5. Think what it would be like to be a member of a racial group or ethnicity other than your own. In what ways would your childhood and adolescence have been different? How would you view the world differently?

The fact that we don't draw a blank when thinking about each of these terms means that we already have a set of attitudes and beliefs about them and the groups they represent. Acknowledging and then examining these preexisting assumptions is a first step toward developing cultural competence: We need to explore our own prejudices and stereotypes.

Prejudice refers to evaluations or judgments of members of a group that are based primarily on their membership in the group, rather than on their individual characteristics. For example, the auto mechanic who doesn't expect a woman to understand auto repair or the job supervisor who finds it unthinkable that a father might want to take a leave for child care are engaging in gender prejudice. *Gender prejudice* is evaluating individuals on the basis of their being a male or female and not on their own specific characteristics or abilities. Similarly, prejudice can be directed toward individuals because of their race, ethnic origin, sexual orientation, age, physical disability, or even physical attractiveness.

Prejudice leads to discrimination. *Discrimination* is behavior directed toward individuals on the basis of their membership in a particular group. Discrimination can result in exclusion from jobs and educational opportunities. It also may result in members of particular groups receiving lower salaries and benefits.

prejudice
Evaluations or judgments of members of a group that are based primarily on membership in the group and not on the particular characteristics of individuals.

Diversity in the Workplace

Diversity, and issues relating to it, are a part of today's workplace. For example, in one California computer assembly company with several thousand employees, 40 different languages and dialects are spoken among people representing 30 nationalities.[2] Furthermore, employers must deal with issues ranging from whether time off for religious holidays should count as vacation time to whether the partner of a gay or lesbian worker should be covered by the worker's medical insurance.

The gulf in the workplace between people with different cultural backgrounds may be wide. For instance, an immigrant from Japan might consider it the height of immodesty to outline his or her accomplishments in a job interview. The explanation? In Japan, the general cultural expectation is that people should stress their incompetence; to do otherwise would be considered highly immodest.

The increasing diversity of the workplace means that increasing your cultural competence will serve you well. It will help you perform on work teams that are composed of people of different races and ethnic backgrounds. It will allow you to supervise people whose native language and customs are different from yours. And it will help you to develop the skills to work for a boss from another country and cultural background.

Equally important, gaining cultural competence will help you respond to the legal issues that surround diversity. It is illegal for employers to discriminate on the basis of race, ethnic background, age, gender, or physical disability. Cultural competence will help you not only to deal with the letter of the law, but also to understand why embracing diversity is so important to getting along with others in the workplace.

stereotypes

Beliefs and expectations about members of a group that are held simply because of their membership in the group.

Prejudice and discrimination are maintained by **stereotypes**—beliefs and expectations about members of a group. For example, do you think that women don't do as well as men in math? Do you agree that "white men can't jump"? Do you think that people on welfare are lazy?

If you answered yes to any of these questions, you hold stereotypes about the group being referred to. It is the degree of generalization involved that makes stereotypes inaccurate. Some women don't do well in math. But the fact is, many women do perfectly fine in math, and many men don't. Stereotypes ignore this diversity.

To develop cultural competence, it's important to identify our prejudices and stereotypes and to fight them. Sometimes they are quite subtle and difficult to detect. For instance, a wealth of data taken from observation of elementary school classrooms shows that teachers are often more responsive to boys than to girls. The teachers don't know they're doing it; it's a subtle, but very real, bias.

Why does this happen? In part it's because we're exposed to stereotypes from a very young age. Parents and relatives teach them to us, sometimes unwittingly, sometimes deliberately. The media illustrate them constantly and often in very subtle ways. For instance, African Americans and Latinos are often portrayed as unemployed or as criminals, women are less likely than men to be shown as employed, and gay men are frequently depicted as effeminate.

But it's not only stereotypes that lead us to view members of other groups differently from those of our own. For many people, their own membership in a cultural or racial or ethnic group is a source of pride and self-worth. There's nothing wrong with this. However, these feelings can lead to a less desirable outcome: the belief that their own group is superior to others. As a result, people inflate the positive

"Prejudice is the child of ignorance."
William Hazlitt, essayist

Check Your Stereotype Quotient

Do you hold stereotypes about other people? How pervasive do you think they are? Respond to the following informal questionnaire to get a sense of your susceptibility to stereotyping.

1. When you see five African American students sitting together in a cafeteria, do you think that they are exhibiting racism? Do you think the same thing when you see five white students sitting together in a cafeteria?

2. When you are speaking with a person who has a speech-related disorder such as stuttering, are you likely to conclude that the person is less intelligent than a fluent speaker?

3. When an elderly woman can't remember something, do you assume her forgetfulness is because she is old or perhaps has Alzheimer's disease?

4. When an attractive blonde female co-worker states an opinion, are you surprised if the opinion is intelligent and well expressed?

5. If a person with a mobility disorder turns down your offer for assistance, are you offended and resentful?

6. If you found out that a star professional football player is gay, would you be surprised?

What do you think your answers tell you about yourself and your views of others?

aspects of their own group and belittle groups to which they do not belong. The bottom line is continuing prejudice.

To overcome stereotypes and to develop cultural competence, we must first explore and identify our prejudices. To begin that process, complete **Try It! 2**, "Check Your Stereotype Quotient."

>> LO9-2   W Work

Developing Cultural Competence

Although it's neither easy nor simple to increase your understanding of and sensitivity to other cultures, it can be done. Several strategies are effective:

▶ **Study other cultures and customs.** Take an online anthropology course, study religion, or learn history. If you understand the purposes behind different cultural customs, attitudes, and beliefs, you will be able to understand the richness and meaning of other people's cultural heritage.

▶ **Travel.** There is no better way to learn about people from other cultures than to see those cultures firsthand. Vacations offer you the time to travel, and relatively inexpensive direct flights can take you to Europe, Asia, and other places around the globe. Sometimes, in fact, it's cheaper to take a transoceanic flight than to travel to closer locations in the United States.

Travel provides us with an opportunity to become immersed in very different cultures and to see the world—and ourselves—through different eyes.
© Design Pics Inc/Alamy Stock Photo RF

If you can't afford airfare, take a car or bus ride to Mexico or Canada. In many parts of Canada, French is spoken and the culture is decidedly different from that in the United States (or the rest of Canada, for that matter).

Travel needn't be international, however. If you are from the northern states, head south. If you are from California, consider heading east. If you live in a large metropolitan area, travel to a different area from ones you're familiar with. No matter where you go, simply finding yourself in a new context can aid your efforts to learn about other cultures.

▶ **Participate in community service.** By becoming involved in community service, such as tutoring middle-school students, volunteering to work with the homeless, or working on an environmental cleanup, you get the opportunity to interact with people who may be very different from those you're accustomed to.

▶ **Don't ignore people's backgrounds.** None of us is color-blind. Or blind to ethnicity. Or to culture. It's impossible to be completely unaffected by people's racial, ethnic, and cultural backgrounds. So why pretend to be? Cultural heritage is an important part of other people's identity, and to pretend that their background doesn't exist and has no impact on them is unrealistic at best, and insulting at worst. It's important, though, to distinguish between accepting the fact that other people's backgrounds affect them and pigeonholing people and expecting them to behave in particular ways.

▶ **Don't make assumptions about who people are.** Don't assume that someone is heterosexual just because most people are heterosexual. Don't assume that someone with an Italian-sounding last name is Italian. Don't assume that a Black person has two Black parents.

▶ **Accept differences.** Different does not mean better. Different does not mean worse. Different just means not looking, acting, or believing exactly the same as you. We shouldn't attach any kind of value to being different; it's neither better nor worse than being similar.

In fact, even people who seem obviously different on the surface probably share many similarities with you. Like you, they have commitments to family or loved ones; they have fears and anxieties like yours; and they have aspirations and dreams, just as you do.

The important point about differences is that we need to accept and embrace them. Think about some differences you may have with people who are similar to you. Perhaps you really can't stand baseball, yet one of your childhood friends has followed the game since he was five and loves it. Chances are you both accept that you have different tastes and see this difference as part of who each of you is.

 **Evaluate**

Checking Your Progress in Attaining Cultural Competence

Because cultural groups are constantly changing, developing cultural competence is an ongoing process. To evaluate where you stand, ask yourself the following questions. Be honest!

▶ Do I make judgments about others based on external features, such as skin color, ethnic background, cultural customs, gender, weight, or physical appearance?

▶ Who are my friends? Do they represent diversity or are they generally similar to me?

▶ Do I openly express positive values relating to diversity? Do I sit back passively when others express stereotypes and prejudices, or do I actively question their remarks?

▶ Am I educating myself about the history and varying experiences of different racial, ethnic, and cultural groups?

▶ Do I give special treatment to members of particular groups, or am I even-handed in my relationships?

▶ Do I recognize that, despite surface differences, all people have the same basic needs?

▶ Do I feel so much pride in my own racial, ethnic, and cultural heritage that it leads me to look less favorably upon members of other groups?

▶ Do I seek to understand events and situations through the perspectives of others and not just my own?

 Rethink

Understanding How Your Own Racial, Ethnic, and Cultural Background Affects Others

If you are a member of a group that traditionally has been the target of prejudice and discrimination, you probably don't need to be told that your race, ethnicity, and cultural background affect the way that others treat you. But even if you are a member of a traditionally dominant group in society, the way in which others respond to you is, in part, a result of others' assumptions about the group of which you are a part.

Diversity in Your Online Class

The increasing diversity of students in online classes presents both opportunities and challenges. The opportunity comes from the possibility of learning on a firsthand basis about others and their experiences. The challenge comes when people who may be very different from us call into question some of our most fundamental beliefs and convictions.

Here are some ways that you can be better equipped to navigate challenges with diversity in your online classes:

- **Present your opinions in a respectful manner online.** Don't get annoyed or angry when others disagree with your point of view. Be tolerant of others' perspectives and their thinking.

- **Don't assume you can understand what it's like to be a member of another race, ethnicity, cultural group, or gender.** Discuss your own experiences, and don't assume you know what others have experienced.

- **Don't treat people as representatives of the groups to which they belong.** Don't ask someone in the discussion board how members of his or her racial, ethnic, or cultural group think, feel, or behave with respect to a particular issue. No single individual can speak for an entire group. Furthermore, group members are likely to display little uniformity on most issues and in most behaviors. Consequently, this type of question is ultimately impossible to answer.

- **Seek out students who are different from you.** If you are assigned to provide feedback on one of your classmate's discussion board posts, comment on someone's post who's different from you. You may learn more from those who are dissimilar than from those who are like you.

- **Don't be afraid to offer your opinion out of concerns for "political correctness."** If you offer an opinion in a respectful, thoughtful, and tolerant manner, you should feel free to share your opinion. Even if your views are minority opinions, they deserve to be considered.

In short, both how we view others and how we ourselves are viewed are affected by the groups to which we—and others—belong. But keep this in mind: No matter how different other students, co-workers, or community members are from you in terms of their race, ethnicity, and cultural background, they undoubtedly share many of the same concerns you do. Like all of us, they question themselves, wonder whether they will be successful, and fret about making ends meet. Bridging the surface difference between you and others can result in the development of close, lasting social ties—a topic we consider next.

Building Lasting Relationships

"I have met the most amazing individuals and made the most incredible friends in such a short amount of time."

Student, Wittenberg University, in M. Sponholz and J. Sponholz, *The Princeton Review College Companion* (New York: Random House, 1996), p. 24.

Few of us lead our lives in isolation. There's a reason for this: Relationships with others are a critical aspect of our sense of well-being. The support of friends and relatives helps us feel good about ourselves. In fact, studies have found that our physical and psychological health may suffer without friendships. The social support of others acts as a guard against stress and illness. And if we do get sick, we recover more quickly if we have a supportive network of friends.

Our relationships with others also help us understand who we are. To understand our own abilities and achievements, we compare them with those of others who are similar to ourselves. Our attitudes, beliefs, and values are influenced—and shaped—by others. We are who we are largely because of the people with whom we come in contact.

Making Friends

Although some of us naturally make friends with ease, for others making friends is more difficult. But building relationships is not a mystery. Here are several ways to go about it:

▶ **Invest time in others.** There's no better way to demonstrate that you are interested in being friends than investing time. Relationships need to be nourished by the commitment of time. You can't expect friendships to flourish unless you spend time with people.

▶ **Reveal yourself.** Good friends understand each other. The best way to make that happen is to let others get to know you. Be open and honest about the things you like and dislike. Talk about where you come from and what your family is like. By honestly communicating your beliefs and attitudes, you give others the chance to learn those things you have in common.

▶ **Show concern and caring.** This is really the substance of friendship and the basis for the trust that develops between friends. Don't be afraid to show your interest in the fortunes of others and to share the sadness when they suffer some setback or loss.

▶ **Be open to friendships with people who are very different from you.** Don't assume the only "appropriate" friends are your peers who are similar to you. Open yourself to friends who are older, who are younger, who work in different fields, and who are different from you in fundamental ways.

▶ **Recognize that not everyone makes a good friend.** People who put you down, consistently make you feel bad, or behave in ways that violate your own personal standards are not friends. Choose your friends based on the good feelings you have when you are with them and the concern and care they show for you. Friendship is a two-way street.

The R-Word: Relationships

Relationships move beyond friendship. They occur when two people feel emotionally attached, fulfill each other's needs, and generally feel interdependent. When a true relationship exists, several components are present:

▶ **Trust.** Relationships must be built on a foundation of trust. We need to be able to count on others and feel that they will be open with us.

▶ **Honesty.** No relationship can survive if the partners are not honest with each other. Each partner must share a commitment to the truth. Your life does not have to be a completely open book—it's the rare individual who has no secrets whatsoever—but it is important to be honest about your fundamental beliefs, values, and attitudes. Those in good relationships accept each other, blemishes and all. A relationship based on untruths or even half-truths lacks depth and meaning.

▶ **Mutual support.** Healthy relationships are characterized by mutual support. A partner's well-being should have an impact on you, and your well-being should affect your partner. In good relationships, the partners seek out what is best for both, and they act as advocates for and defend each other.

▶ **Loyalty.** The mark of a good relationship is loyalty. Loyalty implies that relationship partners are supportive of each other, even in times of adversity and difficulty.

▶ **Acceptance.** In good relationships small annoyances don't get in the way of the deeper connection between you and another person. We don't have to like everything others do to maintain relationships with them. We don't even have to appreciate or approve of every aspect of their personality. What is crucial is the willingness to accept others as they are, without constantly yearning for changes.

▶ **Willingness to embrace change.** Change is part of everyone's life. As people grow and develop, they change. So do relationships.

We need to accept change as a fundamental part of relationships and build upon that change. In fact, we need to welcome change. Although change brings challenges with it, it also helps us understand ourselves and our own place in the world more accurately.

It is only natural that some relationships will fade over time. People do outgrow each other. That's inevitable. What's important is not to live in fear that your relationship is so fragile that you have to avoid or ignore changes in who you and a partner are. Instead, both partners in a relationship should do their best to accept transformations in the relationship as a part of life.

Loneliness

Loneliness is a subjective state: We can be totally alone and not feel lonely, or we can be in the midst of a crowd and feel lonely. Loneliness occurs when we don't experience the level of connection with others that we desire. There are also different types of loneliness. Some of us feel lonely if we lack a deep emotional attachment to a single person, which can occur even if we have many friends. Others feel loneliness because they believe they don't have enough friends.

The reality is that there is no standard that indicates the "right" number of relationships. There's no standard against which to measure yourself and the number, and kind, of relationships that you have. It's something you need to decide.

Remember, also, that loneliness is not inevitable. There are several strategies you can use to deal with the feeling. You can become involved in a new activity, volunteering for a service organization or joining a recreational sports league. If you don't work, consider taking a job if it fits with your academic responsibilities. Not only will you have some more income, you'll have the chance to socialize with co-workers and perhaps form bonds of friendship with them, as well. You should also take advantage of the social opportunities you do have. Even if you don't think of yourself as a "people person," accept invitations from people you know to parties and other gatherings. You never know when you might meet someone you truly connect with.

What you *don't* say matters. Close, lasting relationships are often built on good listening skills.
© John Giustina/The Image Bank/Getty Images

Loneliness
A subjective state in which people do not experience the level of connection with others that they desire.

What if your feelings of loneliness are extreme and you experience a sense of complete isolation and alienation from others? If the feeling persists, it's wise to talk to a health service provider, college counseling center (if your college has a physical campus), or trusted family member. Although everyone feels isolated at times, such feelings shouldn't be extreme. Counselors can help you deal with them.

» LO 9-3 Communicating in Relationships

Communicating well in personal relationships is a blend of talking and listening. Not only does it help to do both well, but it is also important to know when it's time to listen and when it's time to speak up. Listening is an often overlooked skill in personal relationships. We may be so busy trying to communicate our feelings and interests that we overlook the need of the other person to be heard. As friendships develop into personal relationships, simply talking isn't enough. How you express yourself, especially in moments of difficulty, can be very important to getting your message across.

Being a Good Listener: The Power of Supportive Silence

When it comes to building relationships, how you listen is sometimes more important than what you say. The silence involved in listening is a powerful force, one that can bind us more closely to others.

You may already have discussed the art and science of listening as it applies to college success. The same principles that promote learning about academic topics also promote learning about our friends. You can't call yourself a good friend without knowing what others are like and what they are thinking. Good listening is one of the ways to enhance your understanding of others.

When we are heard, we appreciate it because we get the message that our listeners care about us, not just about themselves. Similarly, when we listen, we show that we have respect for those who are speaking, are interested in their ideas and beliefs, and are willing to take the time to pay attention to them.

There are several ways you can improve your ability to listen:

> "The reason why we have two ears and only one mouth is that we may listen the more and talk the less."
>
> **Zeno of Citium, philosopher**

1. **Stop talking!** Are you the kind of person who revels in telling stories about what happened to you? Do you wait eagerly for others to finish what they are saying so that you can jump in with a response? Do you accidentally cut other people off or finish their sentences while they are speaking?

   No one likes to be interrupted, even in casual conversation. In more personal relationships, it is a sign of not respecting what the other person has to say and is hurtful.

2. **Demonstrate that you are listening.** Linguists call them "conversational markers"—those nonverbal indications that we're listening. They consist of head nods, uh-huhs, OKs, and other signs that we're keeping up with the conversation. Eye contact is important too. Listening this way shows that we're paying attention and are interested in what the other person is saying.

In addition, don't multitask. If you're having a serious conversation, turn off your cell phone. If it does ring, don't look at caller ID. Even glancing at your phone for a moment shows you're not paying full attention.

3. **Use reflective feedback.** Carl Rogers, a respected therapist, developed a very useful way to lend support to someone and draw him or her out. In **reflective feedback**, a listener rephrases what a speaker has said, trying to echo the speaker's meaning. For example, a listener might say, "as I understand what you're saying . . . ," or "you seem to feel that . . . ," or "in other words, you believe that. . . ."

In each case, the summary statement doesn't just "play back" the speaker's statements literally. Instead, it is a rephrasing that captures the essence of the message in different words.

Reflective feedback has two big benefits. First, it provides speakers with a clear indication that you are listening and taking what they're saying seriously. Second, and equally important, it helps ensure that you have an accurate understanding of what the speaker is saying.

4. **Ask questions.** Asking questions shows that you are paying attention to a speaker's comments. Questions permit you to clarify what the speaker has said, and he or she can move the conversation forward. Further, people feel valued when others ask them about themselves.

5. **Admit when you're distracted.** We've all had those moments: Something is bothering you and you can't get it out of your mind, or you've simply got to finish something and don't really have time to chat. If at the same time someone wants to engage you in conversation, your distraction will undoubtedly show, making the other person feel you are not interested in her or him.

The way to deal with this situation is to admit that you're distracted. Simply saying, "I'd love to talk, but I've got to finish reading a chapter," is enough to explain the situation to your brother who wants to talk about his date.

It's Not Just Talk: Avoiding and Handling Conflicts in Relationships

Listening communicates a great deal in personal relationships, but as discussed previously, it is also important to put yourself forward. Generally, close relationships are built on good communication, so day to day there may be no problem in this regard. But when misunderstandings or conflicts occur—as they definitely will from time to time—communication can fall apart. In these situations your ability to communicate in words is tested, and more sensitive listening and more careful ways of saying what you think and feel are needed.

The Subject Is "I," and Not "You"

Suppose a close friend says something with which you disagree: "All you guys are the same—you expect to get everything your way!" You might respond by directing anger at the other person, directly or indirectly accusing the person of some imperfection. "You're always looking for something to complain about!" Such responses (and, as you will notice, the initial statement) typically include the word *you*. For instance, consider these possible responses to indicate disagreement: "*You* really don't understand"; "*You're* being stubborn"; and "How can *you* say that?"

These types of statements cast blame, make accusations, express criticism, and make assumptions about what's inside the other person's head. And they lead to defensive replies that will probably do little to move the conversation forward: "I am *not*!"; "I do so understand"; "I'm not being stubborn"; and "I can say that because that's the way I feel."

A far more reasonable tactic is to use "I" statements. **"I" statements** cast responses in terms of yourself and your individual interpretation. Instead of saying, for example, "You really don't understand," a more appropriate response would be, "I think we're misunderstanding each other." "You're not listening to me" could be rephrased as "I feel like I may not be getting my point across." And "Why don't you call when you're going to be late?" becomes "I worry that something has happened to you when you don't call if you are going to be late." In each case, "I" statements permit you to state your reaction in terms of your perception or understanding, rather than as a critical judgment about the other person. (Practice using "I" statements in **Try It! 3**.)

From the perspective of . . .

A HUMAN RESOURCES SPECIALIST Relationships are a key part of a successful professional environment. What might you need to know about fostering positive relationships in your professional life?

Resolving Conflict: A Win–Win Proposition

© Burke/Triolo Productions/
Brand X Pictures/Corbis RF

Even with careful attention to putting our own feelings forward instead of making accusations, whenever two people share their thoughts, concerns, fears, and honest reactions with each other, the chances are that sooner or later some sort of conflict will arise.

Conflict is not necessarily bad.

Often, people are upset simply by the fact that they are having a conflict. It is as though they believe conflicts don't occur in "good" relationships. In fact, however, conflict is helpful in some very important ways. It can force us to say what is really on our minds. It can allow us to clear up misconceptions and miscommunications before they begin to undermine the relationship. It can even give us practice at resolving conflicts with others with whom we might not share such good relations.

Outside the context of close relationships, conflict is not necessarily a bad thing, either. In the working world, conflict is often inevitable. Yet as in relationships, conflicts on the job can be beneficial. Misconceptions can be cleared up and new processes devised when co-workers engage in honest, productive discussion.

Like anything else, though, there are good ways to resolve conflict and there are bad ways. Good ways move people forward, defining the problem and promoting creative problem solving. Bad ways make the situation worse, driving people apart rather than bringing them together.

Try It! P O W E R

Switch "You" to "I"

Turn the following "you" statements into less aggressive "I" statements. For example, a possible "I" statement alternative to "You just don't get it, do you?" would be "I don't feel I'm making my feelings clear."

1. You just don't get it, do you?

2. You never listen to what I say.

3. You don't see where I'm coming from.

4. You don't really believe that, do you?

5. You never try to see my point of view.

6. Please stop interrupting me and listen to what I'm saying for a change.

7. Stop changing the subject!

8. You're not making sense.

9. You keep distorting what I say until I don't even know what point I'm trying to make.

10. You use too many "you" statements. Use more "I" statements when you're talking to others.

The following are some fundamental principles of conflict resolution that you can use when conflict occurs in personal and professional relationships:

▶ **Stop, look, and listen.** In the heat of an argument, all sorts of things that otherwise would go unsaid get said. If you find yourself making rash or hurtful statements, stop, look at yourself, and listen to what you and the other person are saying.

Stopping works like a circuit breaker that prevents a short circuit from causing a deadly fire. You've probably heard about counting to 10 to cool off when you're angry. Do it. Take a break and count to 10 . . . or 20 . . . or more. Whether you count to 10 or 100, stopping gives you time to think and not react rashly.

▶ **Defuse the argument.** Anger is not an emotion that encourages rational discourse. When you're angry and annoyed with someone, you're not in the best position to evaluate logically the merits of various arguments the person may offer. It may feel exhilarating to get our fury off our chests in the heat of an argument, but you can bet it isn't taking anyone any closer to resolving the problem.

Don't assume that you are 100 percent right and the other person is 100 percent wrong. Make your goal *solving the problem* rather than winning an argument.

▶ **Get personal.** Perhaps you've heard others suggest that you shouldn't get personal in an argument. In one sense that's true: Accusing people you're arguing with of having character flaws does nothing to resolve real issues.

At the same time, you should be willing to admit personal *responsibility* for at least part of the conflict. The conflict would not exist without you, so you need to accept that the argument has two sides and that you are not automatically blameless. This creates some solid ground from which you and the other person can begin to work on the problem.

▶ **Listen to the real message.** When people argue, what they say is often not the real message. There's typically an underlying communication—a subtext— that is the source of the conflict.

It's important, then, to dig beneath what you're hearing. If someone accuses you of being selfish, the real meaning hidden in the accusation may be that you don't give anyone else a chance to make decisions. Remember, arguments are usually about behavior, not underlying character and personality. What people *do* is not necessarily synonymous with who they *are*.

If you rephrase the person's statement in your own mind, it moves from an insult ("You're a bad person") to a request for a change of behavior ("Let me participate in decision making"). You're much more likely to respond reasonably when you don't feel that the essence of your being is under attack.

▶ **Show that you're listening.** It's not enough only to listen to the underlying message that someone is conveying. You also need to acknowledge the *explicit* message. For example, saying something like "OK. I can tell you are concerned about sharing the burden on our group project, and I think we should talk about it" acknowledges that you see the issue and admit that it is worthy of discussion. This is a far more successful strategy than firing back a counter-charge each time your co-worker makes a complaint.

▶ **If you are angry, acknowledge it.** Don't pretend that everything is fine if it isn't. Ultimately, relationships in which the partners bottle up their anger may suffer more than those in which the partners express their true feelings. If you're angry, say so, but do it in a way that is noncombative.

▶ **Ask for clarification.** As you're listening to another person's arguments, check out your understanding of what is being said. Don't assume that you know what's intended. Saying something like "Are you saying . . ." or "Do you mean that . . ." is a way of verifying that what you *think* someone means is really what is meant.

▶ **Make your requests explicit.** If you're upset that your spouse leaves clothes lying around your apartment, remarking that he or she is a "pig" shows more than that you are angry. It also shows that your intent is to hurt rather than to solve the problem.

It's far better to be explicit in your concerns. Say something like, "It would make me feel better if you would pick up your clothes from the floor." Couching your concern in this way changes the focus of the message from your spouse's personality to a specific behavior that can be changed.

▶ **Always remember that life is not a zero-sum game.** Many of us act as if life were a *zero-sum game*, a situation in which when one person wins, the other person automatically loses. It's what happens when you make a bet: If one person wins the bet, the other person loses.

Life is not like that. If one person wins an argument, it doesn't mean that others automatically have to lose it. And if someone loses an argument, it doesn't mean that others have automatically won. In fact, all too often conflict escalates so much that the argument turns into a lose–lose situation, where everyone ends up a loser.

However, life can be a win–win situation. The best resolution of conflict occurs when both parties walk away with something they want. Each may not have achieved *every* goal but will at least have enough to feel satisfied.

▶ **Finally, if a relationship involves emotional or physical abuse, you must seek help and end the relationship.** If a partner is emotionally or physically abusive to you, seek assistance from trained counselors. Don't wait. It is virtually impossible to deal with abuse on your own. Your college counseling center, mental health center, or medical center can offer you help. If you are physically threatened or injured, call 911.

When Relationships Are Over: Dealing with Endings

Not all relationships last a lifetime. Sometimes they just wind down, as the two people involved slowly lose interest in maintaining their partnership. At other times, they break apart, as disagreements build and there is not a strong enough bond to hold the two parties together. Or there may be an abrupt rupture if some event occurs that destroys one partner's feeling of trust.

Caring for others is rewarding but risky. When relationships don't work out, their endings can be painful, even devastating, for a time. Even when relationships evolve naturally and change is expected, the transformation in a relationship may not be easy. Parents die. Children grow up and move away from home. Siblings get new jobs on the other side of the country.

In the aftermath of a failed relationship, there are things you can do to ease the pain. The first is simple: Do *something*. Mow the lawn, clean out the closets, go for a run, see a movie. It won't completely get your mind off your loss, but it beats languishing at home, thinking about what you might have done differently or what could have been. Also, accept that you feel bad. If you're not experiencing unhappiness over the end of a relationship, it means that the relationship wasn't terribly meaningful in the first place. Understand that unhappiness normally accompanies the end of a relationship, and allow yourself your natural emotional response.

Finally, and perhaps most important, talk about your sadness. Seek out a friend or a relative. Discussing your feelings will help you deal with them better. If your sadness over a relationship feels totally overwhelming or continues for what you perceive to be too long a time, talk to a counselor or other professional. He or she can help you gain a better understanding of the situation and perhaps help you understand why you are taking it so hard.

Remember, there is one sure cure for the heartache of a lost relationship: time. The pain will eventually fade to a point where it is no longer difficult to manage. As the saying goes, time does heal virtually all wounds.

Speaking *of* Success

Courtesy of Nichole Whitney Philipp and Marsella Studio.

NAME: **Nichole Whitney Philipp**

SCHOOL: **Delaware County Community College, Media, Pennsylvania**

MAJOR: **Chemical engineering**

For Nichole Philipp, there was never any question that she would go to a two-year community college. Her father and sister both had attended Delaware County Community College because the degree programs were ideal. But it also was best suited to her academic needs.

In her two years at Delaware County, Philipp maintained a 4.0 cumulative average, and she was one of 50 community college students in the nation to be named a New Century Scholar. But college wasn't without its challenges.

"Reading and math were very difficult for me in elementary and high school," said Philipp. "Having learned how to weld when I was 7, and having worked on cars most of my life, I knew I wanted to pursue engineering. I thought that a community college would not only offer me the opportunity, but also provide me with more options to pursue my degree."

Pursuing a degree in engineering was challenging, particularly as the only female enrolled in her engineering class.

"Being the only woman was difficult at first, trying to earn the respect of your classmates and having to prove yourself. But I was determined to succeed, and once I started to do well and facilitated a few online discussions, everyone came around."

In an effort to commit herself to school, Philipp said she treated going to school as if it were a job.

"I would wake up at 8:00 in the morning, determined to finish the coursework for all of my online classes by 4:00 in the afternoon," Philipp explained. "I found that people who are serious about their college education really need to work three hours for every single class that they're in."

Strong planning and time management skills were keys to Philipp's academic success.

"I would sit down at the beginning of the week and would plan my studies, laying them out, hour by hour," she explained. "You need to learn good time management and to set goals. I think it's important to really think about the fact that no one is forcing you to go to college, and it's up to you how you perform," Philipp said.

[RETHINK]

- What kinds of stereotypes did Philipp likely face as she pursued her engineering degree?

- Do you think Philipp's being named a New Century Scholar helped her earn the respect of her classmates?

Looking
Back

LO 9-1 Discuss why the increasing racial, ethnic, and cultural diversity of society is important to you.

▶ The diversity of the United States—and of U.S. colleges—is increasing rapidly, and the world is becoming smaller as television, radio, the Internet, the web, and international commerce bring people and cultures closer together.

▶ Being aware of diversity can allow you to accept the challenge and opportunity of living and working with others who are very different from you.

LO 9-2 Utilize strategies to become more at ease with differences and diversity.

▶ Cultural competence begins with accepting diversity by seeking out others who are different from you, as well as exploring your own prejudices and stereotypes.

▶ You can learn about other cultures by traveling to other countries and geographic areas. It also helps to accept differences simply as differences.

LO 9-3 Build lasting relationships and learn to deal with conflict.

▶ Relationships not only provide social support and companionship, but also help people understand themselves.

▶ The central components of good relationships are trust, honesty, mutual support, loyalty, acceptance, and a willingness to embrace change.

▶ Listening is an important skill for relationship building, demonstrating that the listener really cares about the other person.

▶ Conflict is inevitable in relationships, and sometimes it is useful because it permits us to clear up misconceptions and miscommunications before they escalate.

▶ Although the end of a relationship can be very painful, the pain does subside over time.

[KEY TERMS AND CONCEPTS]

Cultural competence (p. 217)

Culture (p. 216)

Ethnicity (p. 216)

"I" statements (p. 229)

Loneliness (p. 226)

Prejudice (p. 219)

Race (p. 216)

Reflective feedback (p. 228)

Stereotypes (p. 220)

[RESOURCES]

ON THE WEB

The following sites on the web provide the opportunity to extend your learning about the material in this chapter. (Although the web addresses were accurate at the time this material was published, check the *P.O.W.E.R. Learning* Connect Library or contact your instructor for any changes that may have occurred.)

▶ "Communication Improvement" (**www.colorado.edu/conflict/peace/treatment/ commimp.htm**) is a post by the Conflict Research Consortium at the University of

Colorado. It includes a lengthy section on improving communication, with added links to improving listening skills and conflict resolution.

▶ The site "Language and Culture: An Introduction to Human Communication" provides a comprehensive look at language and culture covering all aspects of communication, from speech to body language, as used by cultures around the world. (**http://anthro.palomar.edu/language/default.htm**).

▶ "Race Relations" (**racerelations.about.com**), a comprehensive site on **About.com**, discusses topics ranging from affirmative action to white privilege. Hundreds of links are provided for more in-depth discussions and background on a variety of subjects, including race relations, hate crimes, gay/lesbian issues, and many other topics.

ON CAMPUS

Anyone who feels he or she is facing discrimination based on race, gender, ethnic status, sexual orientation, or national origin should contact a college official *immediately*. If your college has a physical campus, sometimes there is a specific office that handles such complaints. If you don't know which campus official to contact, speak to your academic advisor or someone in the dean's office, and you'll be directed to the appropriate person. The important thing is to act and not to suffer in silence. Discrimination is not only immoral, but also against the law.

IN PRINT

Beverly Tatum's *"Why Are All the Black Kids Sitting Together in the Cafeteria?" And Other Conversations about Race* (HarperCollins, 2003 rev. ed.) explores race, racism, and the everyday impact of prejudice.

In *Readings for Diversity and Social Justice* (Routledge, 2013, 3rd ed.), editors Maurianne Adams and Warren Blumenfeld compile a comprehensive collection of essays covering a wide variety of social issues.

Finally, Joseph Folger, Marshall Poole, and Randall Stutman's *Working through Conflict: Strategies for Relationships, Groups, and Organizations* (Allyn & Bacon, 2013) suggests a variety of practical approaches to resolving conflict.

ENDNOTES

1. B. D. Tatum, *"Why Are All the Black Kids Sitting Together in the Cafeteria?" And Other Conversations about Race* (New York: Basic Books, 1997).
2. M. S. Malone, "Translating Diversity into High-Tech Gains," *The New York Times*, July 18, 1993, p. B2.

The Case of . . .
Online Discussion Phobia

Jorge Azar had immigrated with his parents to the United States from the Dominican Republic when he was 11 years old. Although Jorge had become fluent in English, he still struggled with using proper grammar and verb tenses. Jorge had never felt self-conscious about it before. He'd lived most of his life in America in New York City, surrounded by different cultures, working jobs where no one cared about his writing abilities.

Now, though, Jorge had relocated with his wife out of New York. He'd enrolled in online college courses to earn his degree in software engineering. Jorge suddenly felt nervous to participate in the required online discussions. He was sure that no matter what he wrote, his fellow classmates would disregard it because of his poor grammar. Despite having graduated from high school with high marks, Jorge was struck dumb at the idea of responding to the online questions his instructors asked.

One day, Jorge couldn't avoid the problem anymore. In one of his programming classes, his instructor called him out on the online discussion board to explain a technical term. Jorge knew what the term meant and how to explain it . . . but he was afraid that if he posted his explanation, he'd receive criticism from his classmates. As the day ticked by and the instructor waited for Jorge's online post, Jorge started to wonder why he'd enrolled in college in the first place.

1. Can you identify with Jorge's situation? Are there aspects of yourself that you feel self-conscious about?

2. What assumptions does Jorge fear his classmates will make?

3. What assumptions about his classmates is Jorge making?

4. What advice would you give Jorge to help him feel more comfortable, in participating not just in online discussion boards, but in college in general?

5. Have you ever judged someone based not on what they wrote, but on how they wrote it? What did you learn from this incident, and how could you avoid it in the future?

Learning Outcomes

By the time you finish this chapter you will be able to

» LO **10-1** Explain what stress is and how to control it.

» LO **10-2** Discuss what is involved in keeping well.

» LO **10-3** Discuss strategies for managing your money.

Juggling: Stress, Money, Family, and Work

It had been a long day for Diana Michaels—and now, lying in bed, she couldn't fall asleep.

The many stresses and worries of her day kept repeating in her mind. The babysitter she relied on to watch her youngest children in the morning when she went to work had told her she wanted a raise. Diana, a single mother, wasn't sure she could afford to pay more and still pay all the other bills: utilities, rent, car insurance, tuition, and the rest. Her paycheck from her job as an administrative assistant at a hospital was already stretched thin. And given that she worked full time and was going to college, she didn't think she could find time to take on a new job or even additional shifts.

Diana reassured herself that she could figure out a way to save a little more money. She told herself that at the moment, what she really needed was sleep. She had to get up at 5:00 a.m. to exercise, then get her oldest child to school, then go to work. But all she could do was toss and turn, stressing about the many challenges she had to face in the morning.

Looking Ahead

Do you ever feel like Diana? Do you ever stay awake wondering how you'll meet the demands of family, bills, college, and work? Then you're no stranger to stress. It's something that all of us experience from time to time, but that college can often exacerbate. It isn't easy to be a student on top of being a parent, a spouse, an employee, and so forth. Almost one-third of first-year college students report feeling frequently overwhelmed with all they need to do.[1]

Coping with stress is one of the challenges that college students face. The many demands on your time can make you feel that you'll never finish what needs to get done. This pressure produces wear and tear on your body and mind, and it's easy to fall prey to ill health as a result.

However, stress and poor health are not inevitable outcomes. In fact, by following simple guidelines and deciding to make health a conscious priority, you can maintain good physical and mental health. It's not easy to balance the many responsibilities of study and work and family, but it is possible.

Perhaps the greatest source of stress for college students, if not for most people in general, is money. Even under the best of circumstances, our finances present us with many challenges. But money stress is not inevitable either. This chapter will show you how to manage your money. It begins by discussing the process of preparing a budget and identifying your financial goals—the basis for money management. The chapter goes on to examine ways you can keep track of your spending and estimate your financial needs and resources, and discusses ways to control your spending habits and save money.

»LO 10-1 Living with Stress

Stressed out? Tests, papers, job demands, family problems, volunteer activities. . . . It's no surprise that these can produce stress. But it may be a surprise to know that so can graduating from college, starting your dream job, falling in love, getting married, and even winning the lottery.

Virtually *anything*—good or bad—is capable of producing stress if it presents us with a challenge. **Stress** is the physical and emotional response we have to events that threaten or challenge us. It is rooted in the primitive "fight or flight" response wired into all animals—human and nonhuman. You see it in cats, for instance, when confronted by a dog or other threat: Their backs go up, their fur stands on end, their eyes widen, and, ultimately, they either take off or attack. The challenge stimulating this revved-up response is called a *stressor*. For humans, stressors can range from a first date to losing our wallet to experiencing a tornado or hurricane.

stress
The physical and emotional response to events that threaten or challenge us.

Because our everyday lives are filled with events that can be interpreted as threatening or challenging, stress is commonplace in most people's lives. There are three main types of stressors:

1. *Cataclysmic events* are events that occur suddenly and affect many people simultaneously. Tornadoes, hurricanes, and plane crashes are examples of cataclysmic events.

2. *Personal stressors* are major life events that produce a negative physical and psychological reaction. Failing a course, losing a job, and ending a relationship are all examples of personal stressors. Sometimes positive events—such as getting married or starting a new job—can act as personal stressors. Although the short-term impact of a personal stressor can be difficult, the long-term consequences may decline as people learn to adapt to the situation.

3. *Daily hassles* are the minor irritants of life that, singly, produce relatively little stress. Waiting in a traffic jam, receiving a bill riddled with mistakes, and being interrupted by noises of major construction while trying to study are examples of such minor irritants. However, daily hassles add up, and cumulatively, they can produce even more stress than a single larger-scale event. (**Figure 10.1** indicates the most common daily hassles in people's lives.)

What Is Happening When We Are Stressed?

Stress does more than make us feel anxious, upset, and fearful. Beneath those responses, we are experiencing many different physical reactions, each placing a high demand on our body's resources. Our hearts beat faster, our breathing becomes more rapid and shallow, and we produce more sweat. Our internal organs churn out a variety of hormones.

In the long run, these physical responses wear down our immune system, our body's defense against disease. We become more susceptible to a variety of diseases, ranging from the common cold and headaches to strokes and heart disease. In fact, surveys have found that the greater the number of stressful events a person experiences over the course of a year, the more likely it is that he or she will have a major illness (see **Try It! 1**, "Assess Your Susceptibility to Stress-Related Illness").

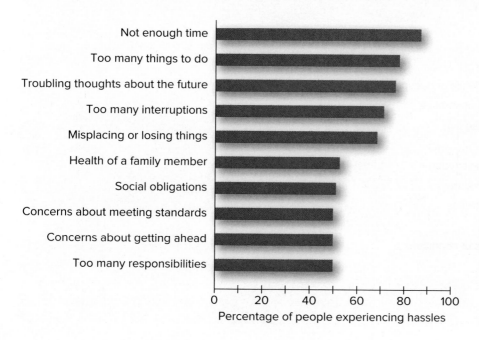

figure 10.1
Daily Hassles
Source: K. Chamberlain and S. Zika, "The Minor Events Approach to Stress: Support for Use of Daily Hassles," *British Journal of Psychology* 81 (1990), pp. 469–481.

Assess Your Susceptibility to Stress-Related Illness

Are you susceptible to a stress-related illness? The more stress in your life, the more likely it is that you will experience a major illness.

To determine the stress in your life, take the stressor value given beside each event you have experienced and multiply it by the number of occurrences over the past year (up to a maximum of four), and then add up these scores.

87 Spouse died

77 Married

77 Close family member died

76 Divorced

74 Marriage separation

68 Close friend died

68 Was pregnant or fathered a child

65 Major illness or injury

62 Got fired

60 Terminated a marriage or close relationship

58 Experienced sexual problems

58 Marriage was reconciled

57 Major shift in self-concept

56 Witnessed a major change in the health or behavior of a family member

54 Became engaged

53 Suffered a major change in finances

52 Took out a large mortgage or loan

52 Change in drug use

50 Experienced a major change in values

50 Change in number of arguments with your spouse

50 New member joined family

50 Started college

50 Started at a new school

50 Began a new type of work

49 Large change in independence and responsibility

47 Large change in work responsibilities

46 Major change in alcohol use

45 Changed personal habits

44 Difficulty with school administration

43 Attended school while working

43 Major change in social activities

42 In-law difficulties

42 Changes in working hours or conditions

42 Moved to a new house

41 Spouse started or stopped working outside the home

41 Changed majors

41 Change in dating life

40 Significant personal achievement

38 Boss problems

38 Changed number of school activities

37 Changed type of recreation

36 Major change in religious activities

34 Major change in sleeping habits

33 Took a trip or vacation

30 Major change in eating habits

26 Major change in the number of family events

22 Guilty of minor law violations

Scoring: If your total score is above 1,435, you are in a high-stress category and therefore more at risk for experiencing a stress-related illness.

But keep in mind the limitations of this questionnaire. There may be factors in your life that produce high stress that are not listed. In addition, a high score does not mean that you are sure to get sick. Many other factors determine ill health, and high stress is only one cause. Other positive factors in your life, such as getting enough sleep and exercise, may prevent illness.

Still, having an unusually high amount of stress in your life is a cause for concern. If you do score high, you may want to take steps to reduce it.

Handling Stress

Stress is an inevitable part of life. In fact, a life with no stress at all would be so boring, so uneventful, that you'd quickly miss the stress that had been removed.

That doesn't mean, though, that we have to sit back and accept stress when it does arise. **Coping** is the effort to control, reduce, or tolerate the threats that lead to stress. There are many tactics you can employ to cope with the stress in your life, regardless of its cause or intensity.

Being in good physical condition is one excellent way to prepare for future stress. Stress takes its toll on your body, so it makes sense that the stronger and fitter you are, the less negative impact stress will have on you. For example, a regular exercise program reduces heart rate, respiration rate, and blood pressure at times when the body is at rest—making us better able to withstand the negative consequences of stress.

If you drink a lot of coffee or soda, a change in your diet may be enough to bring about a reduction in stress. Coffee, soda, chocolate, and a surprising number of other foods contain caffeine, which can make you feel jittery and anxious even without stress; add a stressor, and the reaction can be very intense and unpleasant.

Eating right can alleviate another problem: obesity. Being overweight can bring on stress for several reasons. For one thing, the extra pounds drag down the functioning of the body. This can lead to fatigue and a reduced ability to bounce

coping
The effort to control, reduce, or learn to tolerate the threats that lead to stress.

back when we encounter challenges to our well-being. In addition, feeling heavy in a society that acclaims the virtues of slimness can be stressful in and of itself.

Of course, stress is not just a question of diet and exercise. To cope with stress, you need to understand what causes it. In some cases, it's obvious—a series of bad test grades in a course, a family problem that keeps getting worse, a job supervisor who seems to delight in making things difficult. In other cases, however, the causes of stress may be more subtle. Perhaps your relationship with your wife or husband is rocky, and you have a nagging feeling that something is wrong.

Whatever the source of stress, you need to pinpoint it. To organize your assault on stress, then, take a piece of paper and list the major circumstances that are causing you stress. Just listing them will help put you in control, and you'll be better able to figure out strategies for coping with them.

Developing Effective Coping Strategies

> "There is more to life than increasing its speed."
> **Mahatma Gandhi**

A wide variety of tactics can help you deal with stress once you've identified its sources. In addition to lifestyle changes outlined above, among the most effective approaches to coping are these:

- ▶ **Take charge of the situation.** Stress is most apt to arise when we are faced with situations over which we have little or no control. If you take charge of the situation, you'll reduce the experience of stress. For example, if several work assignments are given to you all on the same day, you might try recruiting a co-worker to help lighten your load.

- ▶ **Don't waste energy trying to change the unchangeable.** There are some situations that you simply can't control. You can't change the fact that you have come down with a case of the flu, and you can't change your performance on a test you took last week. Don't hit your head against a brick wall and try to modify things that can't be changed. Use your energy to improve the situation, not to rewrite history.

- ▶ **Look for the silver lining.** Stress arises when we perceive a situation as threatening. If we can change how we perceive that situation, we can change our reactions to it. For instance, if your information technology instructor requires you to create a difficult computer program in a very short time, the saving grace is that you may be able to use the skill to your advantage in getting a high-paying job down the road. (You can practice finding the silver lining in **Try It! 2.**)

- ▶ **Talk to friends and family. Social support**, or assistance and comfort supplied by others, can help us through stressful periods. Turning to our friends and family and simply talking about the stress we're under can help us tolerate it more effectively. Even anonymous telephone hotlines can provide us with social support. (The U.S. Department of Health and Human Services maintains a master toll-free number that can provide telephone numbers and addresses of many national helplines and support groups. You can reach it by calling 1-800-336-4797.)

- ▶ **Relax.** Because stress produces constant wear and tear on the body, it seems logical that practices that lead to the relaxation of the body might lead to a reduction in stress. And that's just what happens. Using any one of several techniques for producing physical relaxation can prevent stress. Among the best relaxation

social support
Assistance and comfort supplied by others in times of stress.

Look for the Silver Lining

Consider the following list of potentially stressful situations. Try to find something positive—a silver lining—in each of them. The first two are completed to get you started.

Situation	Silver Lining
1. Your car just broke down and repairing it is more than you can afford right now.	1. This is the perfect time to begin exercising by walking and using your bicycle.
2. Your boss just yelled at you and threatened to fire you.	2. Either this is a good time to open an honest discussion with your boss about your job situation, OR this is a good time to get a more fulfilling job.
3. You have two papers due on Monday and there's a great concert you want to go to on Saturday night.	3.
4. You just failed an important test.	4.
5. You're flat broke, you promised your friend you'd visit him, and you can't afford the tickets right now.	5.
6. Your last date went poorly and you think your girlfriend/boyfriend was hinting that it was time to break up.	6.
7. You just found out you missed the due date for your mortgage payment.	7.
8. You just got cut from a sports team or club activity you loved.	8.
9. Your best friend is starting to behave coldly and seems not to enjoy being with you as much as before.	9.
10. You just realized you don't really want to pursue the career you're training for in college.	10.

techniques is *meditation*. Though often associated with its roots in the ancient Eastern religion of Zen Buddhism, meditation, a technique for refocusing attention and producing bodily relaxation, is practiced in some form by members of virtually every major religion. Meditation reduces blood pressure, slows respiration, and in general reduces bodily tension. You can learn about practicing meditation online, at the library, or at a meditation center in your area.

► **Keep your commitments.** Suppose you've promised a friend that you'll help him move, and you've promised yourself that you'll spend more time with your children. You've also been selected by your online instructor to respond to each of your classmate's discussion board posts for the week, and you've made a commitment to volunteer at your daughter's bake sale. Now you are facing all the demands connected to these commitments and feeling stressed.

You may be tempted to cope with the feeling by breaking some or all of your commitments, thinking, "I just need to sit at home and relax in front of the television!" This is not coping. It is escaping, and it doesn't reduce stress. Ducking out of commitments, whether to yourself or to others, will make you feel guilty and anxious and will be another source of stress—one without the satisfaction of having accomplished what you set out to do. Find ways to keep your promises.

From the perspective of . . .

A STUDENT The educational process can be stressful. When you consider your future career path, what are the areas of stress you may need to address?

© Blend Images/Punchstock RF

Placing Stress in Perspective

It's easy to think of stress as an enemy. In fact, most approaches to coping are geared to overcoming the negative consequences of stress. But consider the following two principles, which in the end may help you more than any others in dealing with stress:

► **Don't sweat the small stuff . . . and it's all small stuff.** Stress expert Richard Carlson[2] emphasizes the importance of putting the circumstances we encounter into the proper perspective. He argues that we frequently let ourselves get upset about situations that are actually minor.

So what if someone cuts us off in traffic or unfairly criticizes us? It's hardly the end of the world. If an unpleasant event has no long-term consequences, it's often best to let it go. One of the best ways to reduce stress, consequently, is to maintain an appropriate perspective on the events of your life.

► **Make peace with stress.** Think of what it would be like to have no stress—none at all—in your life. Would you really be happier, better adjusted, and more successful? The answer is "probably not." A life that presented no challenges would probably be, in a word, boring. So think about stress as an exciting, though admittedly sometimes difficult, friend. Welcome it, at least in moderation, because its presence indicates that your life is stimulating, challenging, and exciting—and who would want it any other way?

Keeping Well

Eat right. Exercise. Get plenty of sleep.

Pretty simple, isn't it? We learn the fundamentals of fitness and health in the first years of elementary school.

Yet for millions of us, wellness is an elusive goal. We eat on the fly, stopping for a bite at the drive-in window of a fast-food restaurant. Most of us don't exercise enough, either because we feel we don't have enough time or because it's not much fun for us. And as for sleep, we're a nation in which getting by with as little sleep as possible is seen as a badge of honor.

For many college students, the bad habits are only made worse by the need to manage so many different sets of responsibilities. It is hard to concentrate on keeping well when you also need to keep your children cared for, your boss happy, your schoolwork complete, your household managed. Personal health can easily get lost in the shuffle of all these competing demands. At the end of the day, too many students feel as if they've run themselves ragged just trying to do the minimum to meet their many obligations.

> "The first wealth is health."
>
> **Ralph Waldo Emerson, author and poet**

Yet your health is too important to just ignore. There are strategies you can use to balance your commitments, and you can begin to eat more properly, exercise more effectively, and sleep better. Approaches to accomplishing these goals include the following:

Juggling Your Responsibilities

▶ **Identify your priorities.** Taking your child to the dentist or studying for a final exam are examples of tasks that absolutely have to be accomplished. Updating your blog or cleaning out your garage are things that can be left to another day. This distinction seems obvious, yet too often we allow lower-priority tasks to crowd out the high-priority ones. Identify what is most important for you to achieve, and use your time and energy to accomplish these high-priority goals.

▶ **Use proven time management techniques.** There are only 24 hours in a day. Often, though, it can seem there are 25 hours' worth of work to do—or more. To get a handle on your schedule, use the strategies outlined in Chapter 2. Creating daily to-do lists, calendars, and so forth will be a huge help in effectively meeting your many responsibilities.

▶ **Communicate with others about your obligations.** Remember that the people in your life—bosses, family members, instructors, friends—can't know you are managing a wide set of responsibilities unless you *tell them*. And while you can't expect special treatment just because you have a child at home or a second job to go to, you'll be surprised at how understanding others will be of such circumstances. Additionally, by communicating with those around you, you can work with them to find solutions when your life starts to feel overwhelming.

▶ **Multitask.** Don't draw strict limits regarding what you do and when. If you have a free 20 minutes at your job, use it to catch up on reading for classes. When your children are napping, see if there is work for your job you can accomplish at home. You don't want to fill every spare minute with work, but you want to take advantage of the gaps in your hectic day.

- **Don't put your own needs last.** It's easy to cut corners in your schedule by giving yourself the least attention—sleeping less, skipping leisure activities, eating on the go. But this sort of lifestyle is not sustainable. You need to treat yourself well if you are going to be an effective parent, student, and employee.

Eating Right

- **Eat a variety of "whole" foods, including fruits, vegetables, and grain products.** Strive to eat a range of different foods. If you make variety your goal, you will end up eating the right foods. You can learn more about maintaining variety in your diet by visiting the government website (**www.choosemyplate .gov**) that describes the food guide plate and allows you to construct a personalized eating plan.

- **Avoid processed foods.** Make an effort to choose "whole" foods, or foods in a state as close as possible to their natural state: Brown rice is better than white rice, and both are better than a preservative-filled, packaged "rice casserole" mix.

- **Avoid foods that are high in sugar and salt content.** Read labels on product packages carefully and beware of hidden sugars and salts. Many ingredients that end in -ose (such as dextrose, sucrose, maltose, and fructose) are actually sugars; salt can lurk within any number of compounds beginning with the word *sodium*.

  - **Seek a diet low in fat and cholesterol.** The fat that is to be especially avoided is saturated fat—the most difficult for your body to rid itself of.

  - **Remember: Less is more.** You don't need to walk away stuffed from every meal. Moderation is the key. To be sure you don't eat more than your body is telling you to eat, pay attention to internal hunger cues.

- **Schedule three regular meals a day.** Eating should be a priority—a definite part of your daily schedule. Avoid skipping any meals. Breakfast is particularly important; get up early enough to eat a full meal.

- **Be sensitive to the hidden contents of various foods.** Soda and chocolate can contain substantial quantities of caffeine, which can disrupt your sleep and, along with coffee, become addictive. Many cereals—even those labeled "low fat"—contain a considerable amount of sugar or salt. Pay attention to labels. And watch out for fast foods: Research finds that eating fast foods just a few times a week leads to significant weight gains over the long run.[3]

- **If you want to lose weight, follow a sensible diet.** There's really only one proven way to lose weight: Control your food portions, eat a well-balanced diet, and increase the amount of exercise you get. Fad, quick-fix diets are ineffective. (And, of course, consult a physician before making any major changes in your diet.)

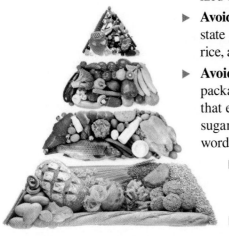

© Valentyn Volkov/Shutterstock.com

Making Exercise a Part of Your Life

Exercise produces a variety of benefits. Your body will run more efficiently, you'll have more energy, your heart and circulatory system will run more smoothly, and you'll be able to bounce back from stress and illness more quickly.

- **Choose a type of exercise that you like.** Exercising will be a chore you end up avoiding if you don't enjoy what you're doing.

- **Incorporate exercise into your life.** Take the stairs instead of elevators. When you're on campus, take the longer way to reach your destination. Leave your car at home and walk to campus or work. If you drive, take the farthest parking space from the building to which you're heading.

- **Make exercise a group activity.** Exercising with others brings you social support and turns exercise into a social activity. You'll be more likely to stick to a program if you have a regular "exercise date" with a friend.

- **Vary your routine.** You don't need to do the same kind of exercise day after day. Choose different sorts of activities that will involve different parts of your body and keep you from getting bored. For example, for cardiovascular fitness, you might alternate among running, swimming, biking, and using a cardio training machine.

One note of caution: Before you begin an exercise program, it is a good idea to have a physical checkup, even if you feel you're in the peak of health. This is especially true if you're starting an exercise program after years of inactivity. You also might consult a personal trainer at the gym to set up a program that gradually builds you up to more vigorous exercise.

Getting a Good Night's Sleep

Do you feel as if you don't get enough sleep? You probably don't. Most college students are sleep deprived, a condition that causes them to feel fatigued, short-tempered, and tense. Sleep deprivation makes staying alert in class nearly impossible (see the **Course Connections** feature).

Ultimately, insufficient sleep leads to declines in academic, work, and physical performance. You can't do your best at anything if you're exhausted—or even tired.

Often the solution to the problem is simply to allow yourself more time to sleep. Most people need around eight hours of sleep each night, though there are wide individual differences. In addition to sleeping more, there are some relatively simple changes you can make in your behavior that will help you sleep better. They include the following:

- **Exercise more.** Regular exercise will help you sleep more soundly at night, as well as help you cope with stress that might otherwise keep you awake.

- **Have a regular bedtime.** By going to bed at pretty much the same time each night, you give your body a regular rhythm and make sleep a habit.

- **Use your bed for sleeping and not as an all-purpose area.** Don't use your bed as a place to study, read, eat, or watch TV. Let your bed be a trigger for sleep.

- **Avoid caffeine after lunch.** The stimulant effects of caffeine (found in coffee, tea, and some soft drinks) may last as long as 8 to 12 hours after it's consumed.

When we have more responsibilities than time, sleep is often the first thing to suffer. Getting an appropriate amount of sleep can actually help you get more done in the time you do have.
© Rob Melnychuk/Getty Images RF

Staying Alert in Class

If you're having trouble staying alert and—even worse—staying awake while you study or complete homework assignments, the best solution is to get more sleep. Short of that, there are several strategies you can try to help stay awake:

- Throw yourself into the work. Pay close attention to the reading materials, take notes, ask questions about the content, and generally be fully engaged in your studies. You should do this anyway, but making a special effort when you're exhausted can get you through a period of fatigue.

- Sit up straight. Pinch yourself. Stretch your muscles in different parts of your body. Fidget. Any activity will help you thwart fatigue and feel more alert.

- Eat or drink something cold while you study. The mere activity of eating a snack or drinking can help you stay awake.

- Avoid heavy meals before studying or completing coursework. Your body's natural reaction to a full stomach is to call for a nap, the opposite of what you want to achieve.

- Stay cool. Take off your coat or jacket, turn on a fan, or sit by an open window.

- Take off *one* shoe. This creates a temperature difference, which can be helpful in keeping you awake.

▶ **Drink a glass of milk at bedtime.** Your mom was right: Drinking a glass of milk before you go to bed will help you get to sleep. The reason: Milk contains a natural chemical that makes you drowsy.

▶ **Avoid sleeping pills.** Steer clear of sleeping pills. Although they may be temporarily effective, in the long run they impair your ability to sleep because they disrupt your natural sleep cycles.

▶ **Don't try to force sleep on yourself.** Although this advice sounds odd, it turns out that one of the reasons we have trouble sleeping is that we try too hard. Consequently, when you go to bed, just relax, and don't even attempt to go to sleep. If you're awake after 10 minutes or so, get up and do something else. Only go back to bed when you feel tired. Do this as often as necessary. If you follow this regimen for several weeks—and don't take naps or rest during the day—eventually getting into your bed will trigger sleep.

≫ LO 10-3 Managing Your Money

If you have money problems—and there's virtually no one who doesn't have some concerns about finances—the solution is to develop a budget. A **budget** is a formal plan that accounts and plans for expenditures and income. Taking your goals into account, a budget helps determine how much money you should be spending each month, based on your income and your other financial resources. Budgets also help prepare for the unexpected, such as the loss of a job or an illness that would reduce your income, or for sudden, unanticipated expenses, such as a major car repair.

Although all budgets are based on an uncomplicated premise—expenditures should not exceed income—budgeting is not simple. There are several times during the year that require especially large expenditures, such as the start of a

budget
A formal plan that accounts for expenditures and income.

Budgeting on the Job

If you've ever held a job, the salary you received was determined, in part, by your employer's budget.

Although they may not always be accessible to every employee, budgets are part of the world of work. Regardless of who the employer is—be it a small dry cleaning business or the massive federal government—there is a budget outlining anticipated income and expenditures. Managers are expected to keep to the budget, and if their expenditures exceed what is budgeted, they are held accountable.

For this reason, the ability to create and live within a budget is an important skill to acquire. Not only will it help keep your own finances under control, but it will also prepare you to be financially responsible and savvy on the job—qualities that are highly valued by employers.

semester, when you must pay your tuition and purchase books. Furthermore, your income can be erratic; it can rise and fall depending on overtime, whether another member of your family starts or stops working, and so forth. But a budget will help you deal with the ups and downs in your finances. Learning budgeting skills can also help you at work, as discussed in this chapter's **Career Connections**.

Most of all, a budget provides security. It will let you take control of your money, permitting you to spend it as you need to without guilt, because you have planned for the expenditure. It also makes it easier to put money aside because you know that your current financial sacrifice will be rewarded later, when you can make a purchase that you've been planning for.

Budgeting is very personal: What is appropriate for one person doesn't work for another. For a few people, keeping track of their spending comes naturally; they enjoy accounting for every dollar that passes through their hands. For most people, though, developing a budget—and sticking to it—does not come easily.

However, if you follow several basic steps—illustrated in the P.O.W.E.R. Plan—the process of budgeting is straightforward.

> "There was a time when a fool and his money were soon parted, but now it happens to everybody."
>
> **Adlai Stevenson, politician**

P | **Prepare** | ## Identifying Your Financial Goals

Your first reaction when asked to identify your financial goals may be that the question is a no-brainer: You want to have more money to spend. But it's not that simple. You need to ask yourself *why* you want more money. What would you spend it on? What would bring you the most satisfaction? Purchasing an iPad? Paying off your debt? Saving money for a vacation? Starting a business? Paying for college rather than taking out loans?

You won't be able to develop a budget that will work for you until you determine your short- and long-term financial goals. To determine them, use **Try It! 3**, "Identify Your Financial Goals."

P Prepare
Identify financial goals

O Organize
Determine expenditures and income

W Work
Make a budget that adds up

E Evaluate
Review the budget

R Rethink
Rethink financial options

P.O.W.E.R. Plan

Identify Your Financial Goals

Determining your financial goals will help set you on the path to securing your financial future. Use this Try It! to get started.

Step 1. Use the planning tool below to identify and organize your financial goals.

Short-Term Goals

What would you like to have money for in the short term (over the next 3 months)? Consider these categories:

Personal necessities (such as food, lodging, clothes, household supplies, transportation, loan and credit card payments, medical and child care expenses):

Educational necessities (such as tuition, fees, books, school supplies, computer expenses):

Social needs (e.g., getting together with family, friends, and others; clubs and teams; charitable contributions):

Entertainment (e.g., movies and shows, trips, recreation and sports):

Other:

Mid-Range Goals

What would you like to have money for soon (3 months from now to a year from now), but not immediately? Use the same categories:

Personal necessities:

Educational necessities:

Social needs:

Entertainment:

Other:

Long-Range Goals

What would you like to have money for 1 to 3 years from now? Use the same categories:

Personal necessities:

Educational necessities:

Social needs:

Entertainment:

Other:

Step 2. Now put each of your lists in *priority* order.

Short-Term Priorities:

Mid-Range Priorities:

Long-Range Priorities:

What does the list tell you about what is important to you? Did you find any surprises? Would you classify yourself as a financial risk-taker or someone who values financial security?

 **Organize** ## Determining Your Expenditures and Income

Do you open your wallet for the $10 that was there yesterday and find only a dollar? Spending money without realizing it is a common affliction.

There's only one way to get a handle on where your money is going: Keep track of it. To get an overview of your expenditures, go through any records you've kept to identify where you've spent money for the last year—old checks, rent and utility receipts, and previous college bills can help you.

In addition, keep track of everything you spend for a week. *Everything.* When you spend 75 cents for a candy bar from a vending machine, write it down. When you buy lunch for $4.99 at a fast-food restaurant, write it down. When you buy a 45-cent stamp, write it down.

Record your expenditures in a small notebook or on your smartphone. It may be tedious, but you're doing it for only a week. And it will be eye-opening: People are usually surprised at how much they spend on little items without thinking about it.

From the perspective of . . .

A RECENT GRADUATE Have you considered how your new career may impact your personal budget? What preparations might you need to make to ensure that a higher monthly income results in a better standard of living?

© Jose Luis Pelaez, Inc./Blend Images/Corbis RF

Make a list of everything you think you'll need to spend over the next year. Some items are easy to think of, such as rent and tuition payments, because they occur regularly and the amount you pay is fixed. Others are harder to budget for because they can vary substantially. For example, the price of gasoline changes frequently. If you have a long commute to work, the changing price of gasoline can cause substantial variation in what you pay each month. (Use **Table 10.1** to estimate your expenditures for the coming year.).

When you are listing your upcoming expenditures, be sure to include an amount that you will routinely put aside into a savings account that pays you interest. It's important to get into the habit of saving money. Even if you start off small—putting aside just a few dollars a week—the practice of regularly putting aside some amount of your income is central to good financial management.

Determine Your Income Sources

You probably have a pretty good idea of how much money you have each month. But it's as important to list each source of income as it is to account for everything you spend.

Add up what you make from any jobs you hold. Also list any support you receive from family members, including occasional gifts you might get from relatives. Finally, include any financial aid (such as tuition reductions, loan payments, or scholarships) you receive from your college. Use **Table 10.2** to record this information. When you do, be sure to list the amounts you receive in terms of after-tax income.

W | Work | Making a Budget That Adds Up

If you've prepared and organized your budget, actually constructing your budget is as easy as adding 2 + 2. Well, not exactly; the numbers will be larger. But all you

	table 10.1 Estimated Expenditures, Next 12 Months			
Category	Now to 3 Months from Now	3–6 Months from Now	6–9 Months from Now	9–12 Months from Now
Personal Necessities				
Food				
Shelter (rent, utilities, etc.)				
Clothing				
Household supplies				
Transportation (car payments, gas, car repairs, bus tickets, etc.)				
Loan and credit card payments				
Medical expenses				
Child care expenses				
Other				
Educational Necessities				
Tuition and fees				
Books				
School supplies				
Computer expenses				
Other				
Social Needs				
Relationships				
Clubs and teams				
Charitable contributions				
Other				
Entertainment				
Movies and shows				
Trips				
Recreation and sports				
Other				
TOTAL				

table 10.2 Estimated Income, Next 12 Months

Category	Now to 3 Months from Now	3–6 Months from Now	6–9 Months from Now	9–12 Months from Now
Wages				
Family support				
Financial aid				
Tuition reductions				
Loan income				
Scholarship payments				
Other				
Interest and dividends				
Gifts				
Other				
TOTAL				

© pumkinpie/Alamy Stock Photo

need to do is add up your list of expenses, and then add up your sources of income. In a perfect world, the two numbers will be equal.

But most of the time, the world is not perfect: Most of us find that expenditures are larger than our income. After all, if we had plenty of excess cash, we probably wouldn't be bothering to make a budget in the first place.

If you find you spend more than you make, there are only two things to do: decrease your spending or increase your income. It's often easiest to decrease expenditures because your expenses tend to be more under your control. For instance, there are many things you can do to save money, including the following:

▶ **Control impulse buying.** If you shop for your groceries, always take a list with you, and don't shop when you're hungry.

▶ **Make and take your own lunch.** Brown-bag lunches can save you a substantial amount of money over purchasing your lunches, even if you go to a fast-food restaurant or snack bar.

▶ **Read the daily newspaper and magazines at the library or online.** Not only do college libraries subscribe to many daily newspapers and magazines, but major newspapers and magazines are also online.

▶ **Check bills for errors.** Computers make mistakes, and so do the people who enter the data into them. So make sure that your charges on any bill are accurate.

▶ **Cut up your credit cards and pay cash.** Using a credit card is seductive; when you take out your plastic, it's easy to feel as if you're not really spending money. If you use cash for purchases instead, you'll see the money going out.

▶ **Make major purchases only during sales.** Plan major purchases so they coincide with sales.

- **Share and trade.** Pool your resources with friends. Car pool, share resources such as computers, and trade clothes.
- **Live more simply.** Is cable TV an absolute necessity? Is it really necessary to eat out once a week? Do you buy clothes because you need them or because you want them? If you don't have an unlimited service plan, do you really need to send so many text messages? Could you move to a less expensive cellphone plan?

There are as many ways to save money as there are people looking to save it. But keep in mind that saving money should not necessarily be an end in itself. Don't spend hours thinking of ways to save a dime, and don't get upset about situations where you are forced to spend money. The goal is to bring your budget into balance, not to become a tightwad who keeps track of every penny and feels that spending money is a personal failure. To help you get started, get a sense of your current style of saving money in **Try It! 4**.

Finally, it's important to remember that budgets may be brought into balance not only by decreasing expenditures, but also by increasing income. The most direct way to increase income is to get a part-time job that will accommodate your academic responsibilities, or to work a few more hours at a job if you already have one.

E Evaluate | Reviewing Your Budget

Budgets are not meant to be set in stone. You should review where you stand financially each month. Only by monitoring how closely actual expenditures and income match your budget projections will you be able to maintain control of your finances.

You don't need to continually keep track of every penny you spend to evaluate your success in budgeting. As you gain more experience with your budget, you'll begin to get a better sense of your finances. You'll know when it may be possible to consider splurging on a gift for a friend and when you need to operate in penny-pinching mode.

The important thing is to keep your expenditures under control. Review, and if necessary revise, your budget to fit any changes in circumstances. Maybe you receive a raise at your job. Maybe the cost of gas goes down. Or maybe you face a reduction in income. Whatever the change in circumstances, evaluate how it affects your budget, and revise the budget accordingly.

R Rethink | Rethink Your Financial Options

If all goes well, the process of budgeting will put you in control of your financial life. Your expenditures will match your income, and you won't face major money worries.

In the real world, of course, events have a way of inflicting disaster on even the best-laid plans:

- You lose your job and can't afford to pay next month's rent.
- Your car breaks down and needs a $300 repair. You don't have $300.
- Your parents run into financial difficulties and you feel you need to help support them.
- Your dishwasher breaks, and repairing it will cost $1,500. If you pay for repairs, you can't afford a tuition payment.

All of us face financial difficulties at one time or another. Sometimes it happens suddenly and without warning. Other times people sink more gradually into

Determine Your Saving Style

Read each of the following statements and rate how well it describes you, using this scale:

1 = That's me

2 = Sometimes

3 = That's not me

	1	2	3
1. I count the change I'm given by cashiers in stores and restaurants.			
2. I always pick up all the change I receive from a transaction in a store, even if it's only a few cents.			
3. I don't buy something right away if I'm pretty sure it will go on sale soon.			
4. I feel a real sense of accomplishment if I buy something on sale.			
5. I always remember how much I paid for something.			
6. If something goes on sale soon after I've bought it, I feel cheated.			
7. I have money in at least one interest-bearing bank account.			
8. I rarely lend people money.			
9. If I lend money to someone repeatedly without getting it back, I stop lending it to that person.			
10. I share resources (e.g., CDs, books, magazines) with other people to save money.			
11. I'm good at putting money away for big items that I really want.			
12. I believe most generic or off-brand items are just as good as name brands.			

Add up your ratings. Interpret your total score according to this informal guide:

12–15: Very aggressive saving style

16–20: Careful saving style

21–27: Fairly loose saving style

28–32: Loose saving style

33–36: Nonexistent saving style

What are the advantages and disadvantages of your saving style? How do you think your saving style would affect your ability to keep to a budget? If you are dissatisfied with your saving style, how might you be able to change it?

financial problems, each month accumulating more debt until they reach a point at which they can't pay their bills.

However it happens, finding yourself with too little money to pay your bills requires action. You need to confront the situation and take steps to solve the problem. The worst thing to do is nothing. Hiding from those to whom you owe money makes the situation worse. Your creditors—the institutions and people to whom you owe money—will assume that you don't care, and they'll be spurred on to take harsher action.

These are the steps to take if you do find yourself with financial difficulties (also see **Table 10.3**).

▶ **Assess the problem.** Make a list of what you owe and to whom. Look at the bottom line and figure out a reasonable amount you can put toward each debt. Work out a specific plan that can lead you out of the situation.

   If you have multiple loans, there are two main approaches to paying off what you owe. The *avalanche model of debt reduction* suggests paying off loans with the highest interest rate first. That helps reduce the accumulation of interest charges. In contrast, the *snowball model of debt reduction* emphasizes paying off loans with the lowest balance first. By paying off the smaller debts, you'll have more money to pay off other loans. In addition, it gives you a psychological boost to rid yourself of at least some debt.

   Both methods work. What's important is making a choice and having a plan.

▶ **Contact each of your creditors.** Start with your bank, credit card companies, and landlord, and continue through each creditor. It's best to visit personally, but a phone call will do.

   When you speak with them, explain the situation. If the problem is due to illness or unemployment, let them know. If it's due to overspending, let them know that. Tell them what you plan to do to pay off your debt, and show them your plan. The fact that you have a plan demonstrates not only what you intend to do, but also that you are serious about your situation and capable of financial planning.

   If you've had a clean financial record in the past, your creditors may be willing to agree to your plan. Ultimately, it is cheaper for them to accept smaller payments over a longer time than to hire a collection agency.

▶ **See a credit counselor.** If you can't work out a repayment plan on your own, visit a credit counseling service. These are nonprofit organizations that help people who find themselves in financial trouble. (Make sure the individuals you seek out are legitimate; there are scams in which individuals pose as credit counselors. Your bank or a creditor can help you identify a reputable one, or call the National Foundation for Credit Counseling at 1-800-388-2227 or visit their website at **www.nfcc.org**.)

▶ **Stick to the plan.** Once you have a plan to get yourself out of debt, follow it. Unless you diligently make the payments you commit to, you'll find your debt spiraling out of control once again. It's essential, then, to regard your plan as a firm commitment and stick to it.

table 10.3	Steps in Dealing with Financial Difficulties
Assess the Problem	Make a list of what you owe and to whom. Figure out a reasonable amount you can put toward each debt. Work out a specific plan.
Contact Each of Your Creditors	Start with your bank, credit card companies, and landlord. Explain the situation. Show them your plan to pay off debt.
See a Credit Counselor	If you cannot work out a repayment plan on your own, visit a credit counseling service.
Stick to the Plan	Once you have a plan, make a commitment to stick to it. Your bank or creditor can help you identify a credit counselor.

Speaking *of* Success

NAME: **Michael A. Sparks**

SCHOOL: **Triangle Tech, Erie, Pennsylvania**

MAJOR: **Mechanical Computer-Aided Drafting, Associate's Degree**

"If someone says you can't do something, prove them wrong."

Taking his father's words of wisdom as a guide to life, and armed with a strong desire to succeed, Michael Sparks set out to meet a series of challenging health issues and pursue an education.

Finding that a traditional college wasn't meeting his needs, he enrolled at Triangle Tech and took on a demanding and intense program in mechanical computer-aided drafting.

"It was a 16-month-long course," Sparks said. "Four semesters of four months each. There was a lot of math from the basics through trigonometry and calculus, as well as computer classes.

"We had a class of the fundamentals of drafting where we started out drawing by hand on a piece of paper and then gradually moving on to computer programs such as AutoCad and Microstation XMV8," he added.

While math came easy, Sparks noted that his weak areas were writing and grammar, so at Triangle Tech he sought out help.

"Preparing papers was a big challenge since in high school I wasn't required to write very much," he said. "But at Triangle Tech we would have to write detailed explanations of how things we designed worked. I had difficulty with that, but there was a great teacher who worked with me, and I got to where I was writing perfect papers.

"I was able to develop better sentence structure," he added. "My sentences were always run-on, but with his help I was able to shorten them and make them clearer."

His efforts paid off: He received high honors at graduation, as well as the school's Outstanding Tech Award. But his greatest achievement to date has been his receipt of the Career College Association's Graduate Recognition for Excellence, Achievement, and Talent (G.R.E.A.T.) Award. "Basically the award is given to students who went above and beyond to be successful in their studies, pushing through obstacles that life throws in your way that may cause one to lose focus on goals," he said.

"None of these things would have been possible for me without the support that my family gave me," said Sparks. "I would not be the man I am today if it were not for them pushing me to go above and beyond in everything I have ever done."

[RETHINK]

- Do you agree with the advice that if someone says you can't do something, prove them wrong? Why or why not?

- Why is it important for students entering a field where math skills are central to also develop their writing skills?

Looking Back

LO 10-1 Explain what stress is and how to control it.

▶ Stress is a common experience, appearing in three main forms: cataclysmic events, personal stressors, and daily hassles. Not only is excessive stress unpleasant and upsetting, but it also has negative effects on the body and mind.

▶ Coping with stress involves becoming prepared for future stress through proper diet and exercise, identifying the causes of stress in one's life, taking control of stress, seeking social support, practicing relaxation techniques, training oneself to redefine and reinterpret stressful situations, and keeping one's promises.

▶ In extreme cases, stress can lead to posttraumatic stress syndrome and suicide.

LO 10-2 Discuss what is involved in keeping well.

▶ For all people, keeping fit and healthy is both essential and challenging. It is vital to learn to eat properly, especially by eating a variety of foods on a regular schedule and by restricting your intake of fat, cholesterol, and salt.

▶ Exercise is valuable because it improves health and well-being. Choosing exercises that we like, making everyday activities a part of exercise, and exercising with others can help form the habit of exercise.

▶ The third key element of good health is sleeping properly. Good exercise and eating habits can contribute to sound sleep, as can the development of regular sleeping habits and the use of sleep-assisting practices.

LO 10-3 Discuss strategies for managing your money.

▶ Concerns about money can be significantly reduced through the creation of a budget by which spending and income can be planned, accounted for, and aligned with your goals.

▶ Budgets provide security by helping you control your finances and avoid surprises.

▶ The process of budgeting involves identifying your financial goals, keeping track of current expenses and estimating future expenses, and making the necessary adjustments to keep income and spending in balance.

[KEY TERMS AND CONCEPTS]

Budget (p. 248)
Coping (p. 241)

Social support (p. 242)
Stress (p. 238)

[RESOURCES]

ON THE WEB

The following sites on the web provide the opportunity to extend your learning about stress, health, and wellness. (Although the web addresses were accurate at the time the book was printed, check the *P.O.W.E.R. Learning* website [**www.mhhe.com/power**] for any changes that may have occurred.)

- The Academy of Nutrition and Dietetics's website not only provides information for its professional members, but also includes updated consumer tips and articles (**www.eatright.org/Public/**). Features include strategies for smart grocery shopping, discussion of the latest fad diets, and guidelines for healthy eating.

- "Stress Management" (**http://stress.about.com//**), on **About.com**, offers in-depth and comprehensive information on coping with stress. Dozens of links cover teens through the elderly, self-assessment, psychotherapy, and relaxation techniques.

- "Finaid: The SmartStudent Guide to College Financial Aid" (**www.finaid.org**) provides a free, comprehensive, independent, and objective guide to student financial aid. It was created by Mark Kantrowitz, author of *The Prentice Hall Guide to Scholarships and Fellowships for Math and Science Students.* The site's "calculators" page (**www.finaid.org/calculators/**) offers lots of online calculators, including College Cost Projector, Savings Plan Designer, Expected Family Contribution and Financial Aid Calculator, Loan Payment Calculator, and Student Loan Advisor (undergraduate).

- "Money Management" (**http://www.ndm.edu/admissions/financial-aid/money-management/**), sponsored by Notre Dame of Maryland University, offers a variety of links covering everything from debt management to loan forgiveness programs.

AT SCHOOL

If your college has a physical campus, mental health counselors may be available who can help you deal with emotional problems. If you are depressed, have trouble sleeping, or suffer other problems, speaking with a counselor can be extremely helpful.

If you are receiving financial aid, there may be an on-campus office devoted to the complexities of scholarships, loan processing, and other forms of aid. The personnel in the office can be very helpful in maximizing your financial aid package as well as in solving financial problems related to your schooling.

IN PRINT

Coping with Stress in a Changing World (5th ed.), by Richard Bonna (McGraw-Hill, 2011), provides techniques for coping with stress and its effects on your health and in your life. *A Mindfulness-Based Stress Reduction Workbook,* by Bob Stahl et al. (New Harbinger Publications, 2010), offers insights and practical exercises.

YOU: The Owner's Manual, Updated and Expanded Edition: An Insider's Guide to the Body That Will Make You Healthier and Younger (Collins Living, 2008) is an engaging and comprehensive book that not only provides practical information on how the body works but also offers hundreds of pointers on how to live healthier, resist disease, and maintain a high quality of life.

Paying for College without Going Broke 2012, by Kalman Chany (Princeton Review, 2011), includes many practical tips for finding ways to finance a college education. *The Ultimate Scholarship Book 2012,* by Gen and Kelly Tanabe (Supercollege, 2011), offers a variety of ways to identify scholarships to pay for college.

Emily Sawtelle's *How to Make a Simple Budget and a Winning Financial Plan* (Saverie Books, 2012) offers helpful guidance on financial management.

ENDNOTES

1. L. J. Sax, A. W. Astin, W. S. Korn, and K. Mahoney, *The American Freshman: National Norms for Fall 1999* (Los Angeles: Higher Education Research Institute, UCLA, 1999).
2. R. Carlson, *Don't Sweat the Small Stuff . . . and It's All Small Stuff* (New York: Hyperion, 1997).
3. M. Pereira, A. I. Kartashov, C. B. Ebbeling, L. Van Horn, M. L. Slattery, D. R. Jacobs Jr., and D. S. Ludwig, "Fast-Food Habits, Weight Gain, and Insulin Resistance (The CARDIA Study): 15-Year Prospective Analysis," *The Lancet* 365 (2005, January 1), pp. 36–42.

The Case of ...
The Breaking Point

Staring at the balance in his checking account on his computer screen, Antonio Butler thought to himself, *It is all over.*

"It" was his college career. For three semesters, Antonio had worked two jobs to pay his way through school. He'd been careful with his money, only rarely indulging in major new purchases such as a new computer and a refurbished car stereo.

Now, though, financial events beyond his control had taken their toll. His brother had broken his leg on a construction site and couldn't return to work for months. While the details of his compensation were being worked out, Antonio had helped support his brother and his young niece.

Staring at his checking account, Antonio realized that supporting his brother had added up to a lot more than he thought. Now his tuition was due—and Antonio simply did not have the money. Antonio had never felt the sinking sensation he now experienced: After everything he'd done, he believed his college career was finished.

1. Is Antonio's college career really over? What should his next steps be if he wants to stay in college?

2. What can Antonio do in the long term to make sure he doesn't face a similar crisis down the road?

3. Is there anything Antonio could have done to have avoided this situation in the first place?

4. Do you think Antonio was right to support his brother while he was injured? Would you have done the same thing in a similar circumstance in your own life?

5. Have you ever had a moment when you thought your financial plans had been ruined? In the end, was the situation as bad as it first appeared?

A Final Word

Throughout this book you've seen how the principles of P.O.W.E.R. Learning can be applied to a variety of situations, ranging from reading and writing to coping with stress. You can use the framework in any situation where you need to organize your thinking and behavior in a systematic way. It's a tool you can call on throughout your lifetime.

College is the beginning of a journey that leads to your future. This book has been designed to help you with the demands and challenges of college, but at the same time to prepare you for life after school. It has tried to show you that it is *you* who must make things happen to fulfill your goals and aspirations.

Ultimately, however, there are some key ingredients to success that no book can teach you and that only you can provide: integrity and honesty, intellectual curiosity, and love and affection for others. I hope this book will help you as you consider what your contribution to the world will be as you work to make your impact on the world.

Glossary

Academic honesty Completing and turning in only one's own work under one's own name.

Acronym A word or phrase formed by the first letters of a series of terms.

Acrostic A sentence in which the first letters of the words correspond to material that is to be remembered.

Active listening The voluntary act of focusing on what is being said, making sense of it, and thinking about it in a way that permits it to be recalled accurately.

Advance organizers Outlines, overviews, objectives, and other clues to the meaning and organization of new material in what you are reading, which pave the way for subsequent learning.

Analogy A comparison between concepts or objects that are alike in some respects, but dissimilar in most others.

Attention span The length of time that attention is typically sustained.

Auditory/verbal learning style A style that favors listening as the best approach to learning.

Blended (or hybrid) courses Courses in which instruction is a combination of the traditional face-to-face classroom interaction and a significant amount of online learning.

Blog A web-based public diary in which a writer provides commentary, ideas, thoughts, and short essays.

Browser A program that provides a way of navigating around the information on the web.

Budget A formal plan that accounts for expenditures and income.

Call number A unique classification number assigned to every book (or other resource) in a library. Call numbers are used for ease of location.

Career portfolio A dynamic record that documents your skills, capabilities, achievements, and goals, as well as providing a place to keep notes, ideas, and research findings related to careers.

Classical conditioning A type of learning in which a neutral stimulus elicits a response after being paired with a natural stimulus.

Cognitive bias A limitation, blind spot, or mistake in thinking that leads to illogical or erroneous decisions.

Concept mapping A method of structuring written material by graphically grouping and connecting key ideas and themes.

Coping The effort to control, reduce, or learn to tolerate the threats that lead to stress.

Cramming Hurried, last-minute studying.

Critical thinking A process involving reanalysis, questioning, and challenge of underlying assumptions.

Cultural competence Knowledge and understanding about other races, ethnic groups, cultures, and minority groups.

Culture The learned behaviors, beliefs, and attitudes that are characteristic of an individual society or population, and the products that people create.

Cybersecurity Measures taken to protect computers and computer systems against unauthorized access or attack.

Daily to-do list A schedule showing the tasks, activities, and appointments due to occur during the day.

Decision making The process of deciding among various alternatives.

Distance learning The teaching of courses at another institution, with student participation via video technology or the web.

E-mail Electronic mail, a system of communication that permits users to send and receive messages via the Internet.

Educated guessing The practice of eliminating obviously false multiple-choice answers and selecting the most likely answer from the remaining choices.

Emoticons (or smileys) Symbols used in e-mail messages that provide information on the emotion that the writer is trying to convey. Emoticons usually look like faces on their side, with facial expressions related to the intended emotion or tone.

Ethnicity Shared national origins or cultural patterns.

Evaluation An assessment of the match between a product or activity and the goals it was intended to meet.

Flash cards Index cards that contain key pieces of information to be remembered.

Freewriting A technique involving continuous, nonstop writing, without self-criticism, for a fixed period of time.

Frontmatter The preface, introduction, and table of contents of a book.

Growth mindset A belief that people can increase their abilities and do better through hard work.

Hearing The involuntary act of sensing sounds.

Information competency The ability to determine what information is necessary, and then to locate, evaluate, and effectively use that information.

Interlibrary loan A system by which libraries share resources, making them available to patrons of different libraries.

"I" statements Statements that cast responses in terms of oneself and one's individual interpretation.

Learning disabilities Difficulties in processing information when listening, speaking, reading, or writing, characterized by a discrepancy between learning potential and actual academic achievement.

Learning management system (LMS) The software that delivers a distance learning course and typically provides the course content, calendars, and tests, and tracks grades.

Learning style One's preferred manner of acquiring, using, and thinking about knowledge.

Learning theory A broad explanation about how one learns.

Lecture capture technology Technology in which instructors upload in-class lectures, slides, and videos to a website, which students can later access to review the material presented in class.

Left-brain processing Information processing primarily performed by the left hemisphere of the brain, focusing on tasks requiring verbal competence, such as speaking, reading, thinking, and reasoning; information is processed sequentially, one bit at a time.

Link A means of "jumping" automatically from one web page to another.

Loneliness A subjective state in which people do not experience the level of connection with others that they desire.

Long-term goals Aims relating to major accomplishments that take some time to achieve.

Master calendar A schedule showing the weeks of a longer time period, such as a college term, with all assignments and important activities noted on it.

Meta-message The underlying main ideas that a speaker is seeking to convey; the meaning behind the overt message.

Mnemonics Formal techniques used to make material more readily remembered.

Motivation The inner power and psychological energy that directs and fuels behavior.

Online database An index in electronic form composed of an organized body of information on related topics.

Operant conditioning Learning in which behavior is modified by the presence of a reinforcer.

Overlearning Studying and rehearsing material past the point of initial mastery to the point at which recall becomes automatic.

Plagiarism Taking credit for someone else's words, thoughts, or ideas.

Podcast An audio or video recording that can be accessed on the Internet and viewed on a computer or downloaded to a mobile device.

P.O.W.E.R. Learning A system designed to help people achieve their goals, based on five steps: *Prepare, Organize, Work, Evaluate,* and *Rethink.*

Prejudice Evaluations or judgments of members of a group that are based primarily on membership in the group and not on the particular characteristics of individuals.

Priorities The tasks and activities that one needs and wants to do, rank-ordered from most important to least important.

Problem solving The process of generating alternatives to work on.

Procrastination The habit of putting off and delaying tasks that need to be accomplished.

Race Traditionally, biologically determined physical characteristics that set one group apart from others.

Read/write learning style A style that involves a preference for written material, favoring reading over hearing and touching.

Recall A way to request library materials from another person who has them.

Receptive learning style The way in which we initially receive information.

Reflective feedback A technique of verbal listening in which a listener rephrases what a speaker has said, trying to echo the speaker's meaning.

Rehearsal The process of practicing and learning material.

Reinforcer A thing that increases the probability that a behavior will occur again.

Right-brain processing Information processing primarily performed by the right hemisphere of the brain, focusing on information in nonverbal domains, such as the understanding of spatial relationships and recognition of patterns and drawings, music, and emotional expression.

Search engine A computerized index to information on the web.

Short-term goals Relatively limited steps toward the accomplishment of long-term goals.

Social support Assistance and comfort supplied by others in times of stress.

Stacks The shelves on which books and other materials are stored in a library.

Stereotypes Beliefs and expectations about members of a group that are held simply because of their membership in the group.

Stress The physical and emotional response to events that threaten or challenge us.

Study notes Notes taken for the purpose of reviewing material.

Tactile/kinesthetic learning style A style that involves learning by touching, manipulating objects, and doing things.

Test anxiety A temporary condition characterized by fears and concerns about test taking.

Text messaging (texting) This communication method permits you to send short messages from mobile phones to other phones or e-mail accounts.

Time log A record of how one spends one's time.

Video message service Video messages that are sent between smartphones.

Virtual study groups Small, informal groups of online students who connect electronically to share materials and notes in order to work together to study for a test.

Visual/graphic learning style A style that favors material presented visually in a diagram or picture.

Visualization A memory technique by which images are formed to help recall material.

Web A highly graphical interface between users and the Internet that permits users to transmit and receive not only text but also pictorial, video, and audio information.

Web page A location (or site) on the web housing information from a single source and that (typically) links to other pages.

Weekly timetable A schedule showing all regular, prescheduled activities due to occur in the week, together with one-time events and commitments.

Working backward The strategy of starting at the desired solution or goal and working toward the starting point of the problem.

Index